The Old Car Nut Book

Created and Edited by David Dickinson

Evancourt Press
Seattle, Washington

Creator/Editor: David Dickinson
Cover Design: David Dickinson
Interior Design: Susan Leonard, Rose Island Bookworks

ISBN# 978-0-9898065-0-3

Published in the United States by Evancourt Press

Dedication

This book is dedicated to Beverly Clark, my wonderful partner in life, my spouse, playmate, and M.O.M. (My Other Mother) to my young adults. Without her love, support, and encouragement this book would not have been possible.

Excerpts from
The Old Car Nut Book

My wife said, "You paid how much for what? What are you, president of the Stupid Club?" I guess I have yet to learn my lesson. Maybe my dad was right!

Excerpt from Lessons in Stupidity *by Gary M. Hughes*

She had heard me coming from a block away and watched with amusement as I tried to extract myself from the Pantera. As I clumsily attempted to exit the car, my foot caught on the seat and I almost landed on my keister in front of the whole neighborhood! Vicki chuckled and said, wryly, "Any cool factor you may have by owning that car will immediately be obliterated when they see you trying to get out of it!"

Excerpt from Pandora *by Chris Kimball*

I put my foot to the floor and unleashed its full explosive power. It kicked the car into a hard fishtail to the right, which is exactly what I wanted. I held my foot to the floor while looking out the right side of the windshield. I could kinda hear my passenger screaming something, but didn't care. I slammed it into second gear and the force caused the rubber dash pad that covered the entire length of the dash to fly off into John's lap. (Damn, I kept forgetting to replace those clips). The pad had also fallen into the steering wheel, but I was too focused to stop now. Fishtailing to the left now, the screaming was getting much louder but

I still couldn't make it out clearly. I slammed it into third, revving between gears enough to go sideways one more time before shifting to fourth and coasting.

Excerpt from A Ride To Remember *by Jim Muckenfuhs*

I'd slide behind the huge steering wheel, peer out the tiny windows, and dream that I was driving it. Of course, in my dreams it was pristine, rather than the rusting hulk sitting in the briars on two flat tires that it really was. Someday, I'm gonna have one of these, I'd tell myself.

Excerpt from Good Job Kid *by Tom Glide*

Resigning myself to saying goodbye, I bent and gave her a final kiss on the hood and walked away. I was so upset that I forgot to even take any pictures. Walking away, I didn't look back and I've never seen her again, but I keep going back to the New England Summer Nationals every year.

Excerpt from Telltale Skirts *by Domenic Tringali*

I raced with some of the biggest names in Stock Car Racing, like Ralph Earnhart, Gale Yarborough, David Pearson, and Lee Petty. I remember a young Dale Earnhart hanging around with all of us drivers at the track when he was just a little boy.

Excerpt from Go Karting in the Fast Lane
by Captain Jack McClure

When I attended junior high, all that I could think and talk about was being a racecar driver. I would draw streamlined cars, close my eyes and imagine what it would feel like to go over 200 mph.

Excerpt from Drag Racing's Good Ol' Days
by Ky Michaelson

Again, he revved his engine to demonstrate the deep throaty sound of the old glass pack mufflers as he rocked back and forth in his seat, anxiety about to get the best of him. I was sure he was going to jump the light early. I revved back.

Excerpt from The Race That Never Happened
by David Dickinson

He was awe struck, to say the least, and didn't speak for a few minutes. He was just taking it all in. This was an extremely "special" moment for us both and one I will carry for with me forever.

Excerpt from "Bonneville Bob" *by Ron Shincke*

Table of Contents

Acknowledgements

My sincere appreciation to my longtime friend, Craig Mathews, and his company DPHQ, for the insight, technical knowledge, creative support, and many favors provided over the years. Craig's better half, Belinda, also deserves my gratitude for putting up with me when I need Craig the most.

It is always my pleasure to give thanks to the members of the Steeds Car Club, my family away from home, for their belief in my book project, the many contributions they have made along the way and for the unconditional love that they show me at every turn.

A big Thank You goes out to Lance Lambert for his friendship, inspiration, and encouragement to write and see this project through.

And to Old Car Nuts everywhere...

Recognition must be given to all of you lovers of the old iron, past and present that have made an impact within the old car hobby and in your own communities. You don't have to be famous to make a difference. Your legacies will live on through those you have mentored, taken along to events and shared your garage time. Passing on your knowledge, and the true passion that goes into loving the steel, chrome, rubber, glass, and paint that sooths your souls or awakens your beasts is what keeps this hobby alive.

Foreword

by Lance Lambert
Automotive journalist and host of television's
"Vintage Vehicle Show"

Over the past 120 years, the automobile has grown from an unreliable contraption to a low maintenance marvel of technology that is necessary for everyday living. Yet, for some people, there is much more to it than that. Their rolling machines combine freedom, adventure, and beauty.

Many of these people saved hard earned dollars during teenage years to buy the car of their dreams, or something less. The accumulation of $50 to $500, depending on what generation was saving, often resulted in an old and tired car parked in the driveway or backyard. Then every penny earned from working at the local grocery store, gas station, or fast food restaurant became investment capital to repair and improve the car.

Time in high school classrooms was spent covertly drawing crude pictures of cars rather than paying attention to the teacher. After school, the drive home included a stop at the local hamburger emporium to show off the latest improvement to the car and to talk about cars with friends. Evenings were spent convincing parents that homework was being done while a young driver was actually reading copies of Hot Rod, Rod & Custom, and Sports Car Illustrated magazines.

At bedtime, these aspiring vehicle builders fell asleep while thinking about cars and the automotive adventures that lay ahead. Weekends included turning wrenches with friends while discussing the latest George Barris, Gene Winfield, or Ed Roth creation.

As time passed, the "real life" of these young charioteers began making demands. Education, military duty, marriage, family, and jobs took the majority of time, energy, and money. For most, the automobile became just another necessary appliance used to get from one place to another safely and economically. But, that was not the situation for everyone.

The lucky ones managed to find enough spare time and money to continue enjoying the world of timeless cars, be it behind the wheel of a sexy and sleek sports car or an old fat fendered and finned cruiser similar to what they drove in their youth. Others temporarily left these cars in their past and patiently fulfilled life's responsibilities until they had enough time and money to return to the world of wheels.

Nearly everyone has great memories of riding in the family car and, of course, smiles form as they think back on their own first car and what happiness it brought to their lives. Old photos, pulled from dusty albums and boxes, spark memories from "back then" and these lovers of vintage vehicles are still creating new memories today.

The Old Car Nut Book is full of stories from the distant past to current day and David Dickinson and his like-minded storytelling friends are true Old Car Nuts.

Introduction

by David Dickinson
Creator, Editor, and Contributing Writer

Old Car Nuts are a curious sort. At car shows, they wander around looking at the old iron and quite often see people talking and telling stories about their colored and varied pasts. As they do, they can't help but wonder what is being said. What are those unique tales being told, revealed to only a handful of guys in lawn chairs behind the bumper of a car or occasionally in the quiet and intimate confines of a shop or garage?

Many of the storytellers would love to share, but they don't have their own personal stage and microphone to connect with a broader audience. The Old Car Nut Book was conceived with the idea that EVERYONE in the old car hobby has a story or two to tell and provides a place to share those personal short stories as contributors and readers.

While there may be some recognizable individuals included in this book, most are the guys and gals that are living out of the spotlight. They have been involved with cars for most of their lives as a hobby, or professionally, but not in the public eye. The Old Car Nut Book has asked people to dig deep into their memories and old photos and tell their unique stories from their own perspective and in their own words. This is a unique concept, because most books or magazines feature articles written about the individuals that are in the spotlight.

The stories in this book tell about the contributor's experiences from the time that cars first caught their eye up to their latest project and reveal the people and events that made an impact on them.

If you've picked up this book to read, you're probably an old car nut. You, or someone close to you, have probably spent a lifetime of buying, selling, and admiring old cars... and if it weren't for Old Car Nuts like you, the rubber, glass, and steel wouldn't have the value that it does. You bring value to the cars and the cars bring extra value to you.

Millions of Americans are obsessed with old cars of one variety or another and feel that the newer cars have no soul. There are no memories in a car that just rolled off the showroom last week or last year and for many, the fondness for old cars has more to do with the memories of days past and fun adventures with friends than the up to date quality or reliability of a new car.

Many old car nuts are attracted to the older cars because they have class and style and don't look like they were carved out of a bar of soap with four wheels attached. The mechanically inclined appreciate that cars were basic back then and didn't require a degree in both Mechanical and Electrical Engineering to fix. For some, it's more than likely a hereditary disease.

In the end, The Old Car Nut Book is about people and it gives readers an opportunity to find out more about like-minded people that they may never hear about otherwise.

Some of the stories in this book are of people finding garages storing timeless classics, those "barn finds" that have always been sought after, or of rescuing jalopies rotting away in open fields or under overhanging trees and being used as chicken coupes. Some of those cars were restored and some only needed to be preserved. Others were discarded, once again, in favor of an easier or more desirable project. More importantly, you'll read about the emotions, decisions, and adventures that went along with them.

You'll read about the first ride in a hot rod, the first time driving, and double dates in old beater cars available to young and nearly penniless teenagers many years ago, and how some of those old beaters are now priceless classics that sell for big bucks. First car stories are a few page flips away.

Many of the storytellers reveal how dreams of building cars began at an early age, starting with models, bikes, scooters, or dune buggies. Several painted cars with their mother's vacuum cleaners in the back yard. More than once, you'll find the authors of these stories lament, "I wish I still had that car!"

Old Car Nuts come in all shapes, sizes, and varied levels of interest and involvement and for many, speed and power were the things that mattered as they moved through life. Some raced and some watched. Some wrenched and some drove. Some raced at the track and some on the street. Some went to extremes to win and some were happy just making a run whether the outcome was the thrill of victory or the necessary agony of the occasional defeat.

A few witnessed historical moments and several played a part in building iconic cars. A handful of these guy's cars made their way to private collections or museums and a lot of them wound up dismantled for the valuable parts.

Social media and the internet in general have had an incredible impact on old cars and bringing people together. Wherever you find an online forum that lends itself to cars, you'll find old car nuts huddled together, sharing stories and pictures, keeping the dream alive.

You'll find that you will enjoy reading these stories over and over again and will want to share them with friends and family, as well. For now, dig in and enjoy!

The Old Car Nut Book

Lessons in Stupidity

by Gary M. Hughes

In 1964, I was seventeen years old and working for a crop dusting outfit in Great Falls, Montana. My job was driving the chemical truck and flagging for the airplanes in the field.

One day while driving to work in my primer gray 1941 Chevy coupe, I spotted a 1940 Chevy convertible parked in a yard with a 'for sale' sign. At the time, I thought it was the ugliest car I had ever seen and pitied the person who was trying to sell it. It was painted a light pinkish red, which was actually a faded red. The paint job was done with a brush or roller and there wasn't  a straight panel on the entire car. What a mess! The second day I passed by the car, I thought it was so ugly it was kind of cute. The third day I stopped to look at it and the fourth day, I had to have it! I had never seen another one like it.

The gentleman who owned the car drove a hard bargain, unwilling to dicker on the three-hundred-dollar price tag. That was a mountain of money to me at the time, but I thought I would be able to earn that much during the summer. The gentleman agreed to accept payments until it was paid for, as long as he kept possession. Faithfully, each week, I would cash my thirty to fifty dollar paycheck, take a few dollars for expenses, and give the rest over to him. At the end of the summer when the job was done, I had paid only two hundred eighty five dollars. I was fifteen dollars short and I was devastated!

My father thought I was crazy for trying to buy a rattle-trap ugly old convertible and I should put the money away for college like sensible people my age were doing (yada yada yada). It was he, however, who came to my aid and gave me the extra fifteen bucks. I gave him a ride the day after we bought it and that was the first and only time he ever rode in that car. His advice was to have it towed to a junkyard and consider the investment a lesson in stupidity. Mom thought it was kind of cute and talked to him. She convinced him it would be a better lesson in stupidity if I had to keep it. She was successful in rescuing my car from the crusher.

My '41 coupe was a real dependable car. It had a 1953 six-cylinder motor with 235 cubic inches of raw horsepower. In fact, I had set a track record at the drag races in Lewistown, Montana by running aviation fuel. It did a quarter mile in less than one phase of the moon. However, it wasn't long until the '41 became motor-less and the convertible had a real dependable 1953 six cylinder motor. In the end, the '41 ended up going to the crusher. It might be living its life disguised as a Toyota these days.

Winter was coming and my only car had a hole in the canvas top where a cat fell through and a heater that didn't work. The winters in Great Falls can get a little chilly (like forty below zero) and my dad said I should bundle up. My mother was correct about the lesson. I was proving myself to be the stupidest person my dad knew. I simply couldn't be his son!

Over the next two years, I had many jobs and I bought and sold at least a dozen cars, but I always kept the convertible because I really loved the damn thing.

During the year of 1966, I was living in Idaho Falls, Idaho and was working for Delmonte Foods, driving a forklift… without aviation fuel. I was able to put away some money and the convertible got its first face-lift at Lloyd's body shop. Lloyd allowed me to do some of the grunt work in his shop to save some of the expenses. He taught me a lot about bodywork in the time I spent there. The project took about three months, cost about four hundred dollars and the Chev ended up with a straight body and a midnight blue metal flake paint job. Unfortunately, the primer cracked and the paint job ended up looking like a sun dried mud bog, but looking at the car from down the block wasn't too bad. Lloyd said he would repaint it, but I would have to help. About that time, Uncle Sam decided I should help him in the Viet Nam effort instead. So, I did. The convertible would have to wait.

Late in December 1968, I returned to Idaho and found the car smashed on the driver's side rear fender. Someone had run into it while it was parked and no one knew who did it or when it happened. I found an old fender, put some primer on it, bolted it on, and drove it back to Great Falls on January 2, 1969. The trip was not uneventful as the radiator blew up and the starter ate the flywheel. A trip that should have taken a few hours took about a week and I received more lessons in stupidity. That January was the coldest in the history of Great Falls. The top still had the same hole, which was a little bigger now and the heater still didn't work, but I was smart enough to have worn really warm clothes.

After a couple of months of celebrations, the convertible and I moved on to Missoula where higher education was more desirable than going to work. The State of Montana in conjunction with the University of Montana had a special program to re-train and re-introduce veterans who were having trouble adjusting to civilian life. I guess they thought I qualified because I never showed up sober for my unemployment check.

The next six or seven months in Missoula was a great time. Many of my oldest and best friends from both Butte and Great Falls were going to school there and we really had fun.

I really was getting smarter, because I finally found and replaced the blown fuse for the heater, though it was right before summer came. The only bad experience I can remember is getting evicted from an apartment because I had rebuilt the transmission for the convertible on the living room carpet. Some landlords don't have any understanding at all. It was too cold to work outside, after all, and I did get most of the grease out of the carpet!

After graduation, I decided to move to Seattle and look for legitimate work. My parents were in Seattle and said there were plenty of good paying jobs there.

The trip to Seattle ended for the convertible just west of St. Regis, Montana where the front universal joint on the drive shaft came apart. Like Humpty Dumpty, even with the help of all the King's horses, the universal joint was not going together again. Gene, from Gene's Standard Service came, got the car, and towed it back to his shop. He was very nice and said I could leave it there for a week or two and come back and get it when I could. I paid him and hitchhiked to Seattle. The following week, my dad decided he should protect his fifteen-dollar investment and help me gain possession of the car one more time. We got a tow bar, trailer hitch and away we went to St. Regis.

November, we found, is not the month to tow a car with every component in the front-end totally shot, across three mountain passes. After about two miles and ten feet, my dad reminded me of the opportunity I missed a few years earlier to haul it to the junkyard and again reiterated his doubts about being my father.

The car went back to Gene at the Standard Station. He agreed to store it until the spring of the following year and refused any compensation for his trouble. He had lots of room and liked doing favors for people. We stuck it in the corner of his shop, covered it up, and left it in hibernation for the winter. The trunk contained most of my worldly possessions, like my record collection and my hi-fi record player.

After the spring thaw, I decided it was time to get the convertible. During a phone conversation with Gene, he revealed his wife was in the hospital with cancer and was not expected to live much longer. Since the hospital was in Missoula (40 miles away), Gene's shop was temporarily closed and he asked me to wait a few weeks before I came for the car. Three or four weeks later, I called Gene and was informed by an AT&T recording that the number was disconnected. That day, I drove to St. Regis and discovered that Gene's wife had died and Gene had declared bankruptcy because of the medical bills. There was a Sheriff's auction and everything in the shop was sold, including my car!

There were no records of the auction and even though I had title to the car, it had been left for over thirty days without anything in writing and was considered an abandoned vehicle. Someone told me that they tried to contact me but could not find me because I was such a transient. I had trouble believing that one, however. At any rate, the car was gone and no one could tell me where it went. The only thing I knew was it had sold for fifty dollars.

During the next ten years, I wanted to spend most of my time trying to find the car. Instead, I got married, had a couple of kids, bought houses, started businesses, and became less and less stupid. I really would rather have spent all my time being a bum and looking for the car, but pressures from outside sources controlled my destiny. I did spend a few vacations in Montana looking for the car, but not as many as I could have.

In the summer of 1979, I had given up any hope of ever seeing my beloved convertible again. I had decided to go to Montana and see if there was another project car that I might be able to purchase at a reasonable price. Ten years away from the automotive hobby was wearing me down and for my own mental health, I needed to get involved once again.

A guy named Pete had a lot of old junk cars parked in his yard in Superior Montana. He saw my shiny new 1979 Thunderbird automobile with T-tops and Washington plates and decided his cars were a lot more valuable than I thought they were. Flaunting the appearance of possible wealth in front of Pete was another lesson in stupidity. The stupid one decided that there would be no purchase of any of Pete's cars on that day.

I told Pete the sad story of the loss of the convertible and he then astounded me by saying the convertible that was at the auction was a '41 and not a '40. That didn't make much sense to me and further conversation determined the car he witnessed being sold at auction was, in fact, my blue metal flake '40 convertible. He knew who bought it and knew that the person still had it.

The only thing I had to do to get the information was to provide Pete and his family tickets to the Baseball All Star game being played that summer in the new Seattle King Dome. I told Pete I thought the game was sold out but I would try to get him some tickets for the information. Pete then gave me directions to Fred's property where I should find a big green barn and a small mobile home.

The road to Fred's property was not much more than a glorified Jeep trail but dents and scratches on the Thunderbird was a small price to get there. Nothing was going to keep me from my visit with Fred. Stupidity converted the Thunderbird into a mountain goat and I arrived at Fred's property to find the barn door open. The convertible was sitting inside. In my excitement, I guess I forgot to introduce myself to Fred and went straight to inspect the car. It had been repainted a light blue, which was actually a faded royal blue. Again, a paint job had been done with a brush or roller and there wasn't a straight panel on the entire car. What a mess! There was a hole in the top and there was no doubt that this was the very same rattletrap ugly old convertible I loved.

There is something distinctive about the clicking sound of someone drawing back the hammer of a shotgun. Hearing the gruff voice telling me not to move reminded me of how impolite I had been. Pleading and begging, I introduced myself to Fred. That convinced him to lower the gun barrel and after my fear subsided and I told him the story and produced the title to the car. He then informed me it was his property as he had purchased it legally at an auction, had owned it for ten years, and it was rightfully his. Besides that, he was the one with the gun! I had no defense for his arguments, but I wasn't going to give up just yet.

Fred's wife, Isabel, was a lovely lady around three hundred pounds, curlers, Mumu, and sported less than five brownish colored teeth. She and Fred didn't get much company because of the road, and she was eager to share some fresh baked brownies and coffee just to be able to visit with someone other than Fred. I obliged her offer.

Getting to know Isabel and Fred was easy and we had a meaningful conversation about my youth in Montana and the history of the convertible. During the conversation,

Isabel said, "Fred, you are an old man and you only drive that car on the fourth of July. I think you should give the car back to Gary." Words cannot describe just how beautiful that woman appeared to me at that moment. Fred, like most husbands, paid little attention to his wife and again stated the car was his and he was keeping it.

Knowing the little woman was on my side, I decided to make a bold gesture. I placed ten one hundred dollar bills right there on their kitchen table and offered them to Fred for his trouble. Isabel could not stop staring at the stack of money. Fred said, "You have got to be kidding!" I assured

him that I was not kidding and started feeling stupid again because I may have been able to offer far less with the same effect. At that point, old Fred produced an Old Cars Price Guide, which listed the convertible having a value of about twenty thousand dollars. I had no idea the car was that rare and Fred obviously knew more about it than I had given him credit for. My budget was one thousand dollars and I was getting nowhere fast. After a series of negotiations, Fred finally settled for five thousand dollars. There went my budget once again!

My wife said, "You paid how much for what? What are you, president of the Stupid Club?" I guess I had yet to learn my lesson. Maybe my dad was right!

In reality, I own the car to this day and it is in show quality condition. I often take awards at car shows and people always ask me… "Where did you find this car?" It's a story I love to tell.

Modesto Speed Freak

by Ron Jacobs

Like a lot of old car guys these days, the car bug bit me early in life. As a child, I would watch the cars go by and dream of the day I could drive and have my own set of wheels. In 1955, my cousin and best friend, Frank, found a cherry 1940 Plymouth Sedan for sale with only 45,000 original miles on it and I quickly purchased it for the grand sum of $90! With such low miles, it was a very nice car that didn't need much, but even at fourteen years old I needed more power to suit my young ambitions and need for speed.

In searching for ways to make it as fast as I could, I found and made friends with a professional motor builder by the name of Charlie Bell. He raced at the San Jose race-track and was the lone wolf with a Chrysler product in a pack of Fords and Chevys. He'd consistently get put in the back of the pack because of his low qualifying times. Before long, he would be leading in each of those races and was always  a winner. Many thought he was a cheater, but he followed the rules. He was simply a magician when it came to building motors and he did some things that were way ahead of his time.

My relationship with Charlie lasted for many years and the 1940 Plymouth ended up with lots of Charlie's motors. He'd build one for himself and run it in his hardtop for a while and then, eager to try some new idea he'd have, would say, "You want to run this motor? I'm going to take it out of my car, Ron." Well, each one always had more power than the one he'd passed on to me before, so it was a no brainer. Between 1955 and 1959, when I graduated high school, my car became the grateful recipient of five of Charlie's motors.

In the end, that '40 Plymouth wound up with a Chrysler six-cylinder motor that was just shy of 300 cubic inches and produced almost 200HP. That's not bad for a flathead six in anybody's book! It also had a 1938 Imperial T-85

 Borg Warner 3 speed transmission with overdrive and ran 86 mph in 15 seconds on the 1/4 mile track.

Charlie was more than just a source for inexpensive and fast motors. He was truly a friend and someone I respected, if not idolized. I spent many hours just watching Charlie do his magic motor builds in his shop. The guy was an artist with a motor, doing innovative things that no one else considered possible at the time.

As a side note: At some point along the way, a young guy named Bobby Gaines became Charlie's partner in the shop. Charlie obviously had a great impact on Bobby, as well, because when Bobby went into business for himself years later, he left Charlie's name on his business. To this day, the business is still located in the heart of Modesto and is called Bell and Gaines. Charlie passed in 1977 of a heart attack.

In 1956, I took my '40 Plymouth and joined a car club called The Modesto Throttlers, a long time Modesto car club. The club had about 15 members, both young and old. We rented a garage with a pit and a resting room and loved to work on our cars to our hearts content and or the limit that our budgets would allow. Over the years, I've had some wonderful times and built some cherished memories with the guys in The Throttlers. I still am a member and at 72, I am one of if not the oldest member.

I attended Thomas Downey High School in Modesto. George Lucas was two grades behind me and was in the same class as Bobby Gaines. George's movie, American Graffiti, was a true chronicle of our high school days and a lot of what was depicted in the movie actually happened. In those days, when we cruised, it was called Dragging 10th. There was a loop that everyone would gather on, drive back and forth, and yell out windows, just being teens in cars. It really was just like in the movie.

That's where we would cruise and there was just cruising there, no racing.

I raced on the other side of Hwy 99 on Maze Blvd and Blue Gum Ave, but never twice in one night. If I'd been seen, I didn't want to be seen again. There was also racing on Paradise Road, which was the main road to Tracy, but I personally never raced there. All racing was done with one person in the car, just the driver, and no passengers due to the additional weight. We were serious about our racing and all of the races were done from a dead stop. I don't recall anyone getting tickets from the CHP.

If I lost a race, I was upset and needed to figure out a way to do better. This usually involved one of Charlie Gains more powerful motors and a tweak here or there to optimize performance. Charlie was all about performance.

The movie, *American Graffiti*, was pretty realistic. There

is one scene in that movie that I think stands out as one that movie goers have probably wondered about for years. Here is the real deal as I watched it happen. I was standing at Burge's Drive In, the inspiration for Mel's in the movie, looking south on 9th St. About 200 yards away, across street and to the south, two cops were sitting in their car and not doing much. One of the guys from school crawled under the car and chained the axle of the cop car to a pole. A close friend, who shall remain nameless, in a '50 Olds with a beefed up motor, went smokin' up the street. Just like in the movie, the cops fired up their motor, lit out after him, and made it as far as the end of the chain. If the movie had never been made, this still happened. Whether George Lucas was somewhere in the vicinity and saw it or heard about it later, I don't know. I do know that I saw it and knew the people involved very well. As they say, that's my story and I'm sticking to it.

After I graduated in 1959, life led to more cars and more adventures. For graduation, I got a 1959 Plymouth and went to school in San Francisco. I should have slowed down and studied, but I couldn't help myself. Going fast was in my blood, I guess. Instead of buying schoolbooks, I bought car parts. Instead of hitting the books at night, I hit the Pacific Coast Highway in my '59 Plymouth and ran the wheels off of it racing anyone that thought they could go faster than I could.

In 1962, I married my high school sweetheart, Donna, and in 1972, we moved to Cypress, CA, where we live to this day. She is still my bride and best friend and very much a part of my addiction to the old car hobby. While we don't run as fast and as hard as I did in my youth, we still play in the old iron.

Our fancy these days is old Ford trucks and we belong to the Orange County Chapter of Pickups Limited. We have made many great friends and the club is growing rapidly. We love to go with them to local shows and have tons of fun. There are members who have stock trucks and some members that have pretty expensive show trucks. Lots of the work trucks back in the day are now trophy winning show trucks.

In 1997, I came across a 1954 Ford F-100, which I purchased from a neighbor who was in the process of moving. The truck is stock with 223 cubic inch six-cylinder motor and a Ford-o-matic transmission. It has been a pleasure to work on and maintain and has won many trophies on the strength of being stock, with very minor changes. It has fifteen-inch wheels and tires, electric wipers and a header that I added so I could have dual exhaust. Other than that, the truck is original.

I have lots of fond memories of my youth and the fast times, but these days I'm enjoying life with my wonderful lady and great friends and still enjoy each moment I get behind the wheel of my favorite ride. So, what more could an old Modesto "speed freak" ask out of life?

My First Car

by Carl King

My first car was a 1930 Chevrolet four door sedan. I bought it from a man on my paper route. Like many of the first cars purchased by young guys, I found it in a backyard where this old boy had left it out in the weather behind his house for quite some time.

The '30 Chevrolets were wood framed cars and most roofs leaked at some point. This one had leaked for quite some time and that time and the elements had taken their toll. The doors were secured to the wood frame with screws and had long ceased to being anything close to secure. The doors were quite literally close to falling off and for the most part the entire vehicle lacked anything close to what might resemble integrity. I had to have it.

I paid about $15 for it, since it was in such bad condition. I think the seller realized that it was not worth even $15, and since he couldn't talk me out of buying it, he volunteered a couple of extra tires after the deal had been made. I called upon a friend to tow the car home since it had no battery.

The year was 1948 and I was sixteen years old. The home was in Lake Forest Park and I live on the same property to this day. Back then, it was still a pretty rural area and we had lots of property to spread out on. I had an area where I worked on the car, but I didn't have much in the way of tools. In those days, when something needed to be repaired we did it ourselves with the limited selection of tools available.

Once home, with the car settled comfortably in its new spot, I got a battery hooked up and finally got the engine started. It knocked pretty badly so I decided to proceed with an overhaul, which meant new rings (regardless of the condition of the cylinders and pistons), adjusting the connecting rods and main bearings (regardless of the condition of the crankshaft), and lap in the valves by hand (no matter how bad they were). If one of the rods had lost half or more of its Babbitt, a used rod from the junkyard replaced it for $1. Then, I'd reassemble everything with lots of Permatex and fill the crankcase with re-refined oil at fifteen cents per quart.

I started it up and after driving to high school just one day it was knocking worse than ever. I tore the engine down again and discovered I had installed one of the little dipper scoops on the rod cap backwards, so I had to purchase another junkyard rod for $1. The engine was improved, but it always knocked and used oil. That was the type of backyard rebuild that was common back then and I was proud to be able to do it and lucky to have a running car.

The body was another story. The wood framing was badly rotted, and unlike today, I did not have the skill or tools to rebuild a wood framed body. The rear portion was particularly bad, and the rear doors were about to fall off. In my infinite wisdom, I figured the best thing to do was to convert this sedan to a pick up. I removed all of the body behind the front seat, and manufactured a truck bed out of 2x4 and 4x4 lumber sheathed over with one-inch boards. Of course, this was all used lumber that I had on hand. The wooden truck bed extended back over the gas tank and covered the gasoline filler cap, making it impossible to fill the tank. I solved this problem by leaving one small board un-nailed so it could be slipped out come time to re-fuel.

So, now I had a pickup. However, the portion of the original body that remained (now the truck cab) was so rotten and loose that if I jerked the clutch upon starting up, the cab lurched backward, causing the radiator brace rod to pull the radiator into the fan. This made a helluva noise (clang-clang-clang), so I would then slam on the brakes, causing the cab to lurch forward with the windshield and cowl moving away from me and pushing the radiator away from the fan. Then I would release the clutch slowly and proceed on my way. It was always a tentative start followed by an even more tentative stop. The old Hudson in the movie "Grapes of Wrath" was a better vehicle than my pick up.

We moved to the property in Lake Forest Park in 1944 and our family raised chickens so we would have eggs and chickens to eat. My chore was to clean the chicken house each Saturday. If you've never had the pleasure of scooping chicken poop early on a Saturday morning, you've missed nothing. But, I started a little business whereby I would load up "the pickup" with chicken house cleanings (chicken poop and straw) and sell it to other people in the area for fertilizer. It took me about all day to load the truck, drive to the customer, and unload. It really was hard work and I'm glad I didn't have to make a life's work of it.

One Saturday, I had an order for a large load. So, after loading up the truck, I proceeded up the street when I noticed the gas gauge was on empty. The '30 Chev was equipped with an electric gas gauge, which worked! Many, even more expensive, cars of this era used a less reliable hydrostatic fuel gage. Anyway, I realized that I was about out of gas and in less than a minute, the engine starved out. Fortunately, I was on a gradual downgrade and able to coast far enough to roll into a gas station where I simply stopped at the pumps.

I had a minor problem, however. How could I fuel up? The little removable board was now under this big pile of chicken crap! There was only one thing to do and I did just that. I started shoveling the load of chicken manure and straw out onto the concrete apron. I needed to get at the tank so I could fuel up.

This gas station was quite close to my home and the man that owned the station knew me as the annoying kid who was always asking for gas on the cuff, patching tires, trying to borrow tools, making messes, and using all of his shop rags. He actually liked me, but I took advantage of his graciousness at every opportunity. Times were tough for him and making a profit in business was hard. I was oblivious.

He came running out of the office and shouted "get that @#&*^ pile of +%$&* out of here!"

"I would but I can't move. I'm out of gas!" I replied.

So, he just stood there looking disgusted as I shoveled down to the tank, throwing chicken poop on his lot. I removed the board, pumped in three gallons at 25 cents per gallon, and then shoveled as much of the chicken crap as I could, with my inadequate shovel, back into the truck. Then I was on my way. He was never very happy with the fertilizer I left or the weeds it helped to grow through the cracks of his asphalt.

The next year I obtained a La Salle, which was a much better vehicle, and I promptly quit the chicken poop business. These days, my stable of cars include a 1932 Auburn V12, a 1930 Packard big 8 roadster and a 1921 Ford Model T; all very nice cars and quite a step up from my first car.

Purple Haze

by David Dally

I have been around and interested in cars all my life. Some of my earliest memories are going to Soldier Field in Chicago to watch the stock car races on the cinder track that ringed the field. They actually did figure eight races across the Bears' hallowed football field. It was a family affair with my older brother, Ned, my sister, Edie, and I piled in the back of my Dad's '52 Plymouth wagon. We were about a half hours drive away. I can also remember many fender benders on the way home as some of the crowd seemed to be hopped up on the races.

Ned was a budding teenager, very interested in cars, and fed his car habit by working part time in the local gas station. His first vehicle was a '34 Ford Pickup with a four-inch chop and a beautiful black finish. He bought it with no engine or transmission and quickly found a LaSalle transmission and a '53 Rocket Olds engine to put in it. That thing flew! Street racing was the norm in those days and I can remember him saying he blew the doors off Corvettes and most other cars on the road. Being 7 years his junior, I worshiped him.

My Dad had been a bit of a Hot Rodder in the late '20s. He talked about a Model A with a boat-tail speedster body on it and a souped up four banger under the hood. He and one of his buddies started a filling station and car repair business, which succumbed to the Great Depression. I remember every Memorial Day, as he was outside working on projects or enjoying the day bar-b-qing, he would have the Indy race on the radio. Later on, we would be treated to watching it on TV.

When I was six or seven, I had a tether car that was a model of an Indy car and I'd lie down on my back in the street and swing it around in front of my home. I jumped the curb between two driveways with that car and swung it around so much I wore the wheels right off of it.

A neighbor kid, Billy Sparks, whose family was rather well to do, got a brand new Raleigh English three-speed bike for his eighth birthday. I was green with envy. Raleigh's were not in our family budget, but Ned came to my rescue by fixing up a bike for me. It was an old balloon tire Schwinn twenty-inch frame with no fenders and he put a sprocket from a 26 inch Schwinn on it. It did not have much off the line, but once I got rolling, I blew off the doors of that Raleigh. That was my first taste of drag racing.

Ned ended up going to college and sold the Ford for a beautiful navy blue '52 Olds Coupe. Later, he sold that because of the lack of fuel economy and bought a '55 Chevy 150 sedan with a six cylinder motor. He continued to work at the filling station on the weekends and helped his buddies work on their hot rods. I remember the driveway being filled with lowered '50 Mercs and Read Sinclair's '47 Ford. One guy, named Eddie, bought a Green '38 Cadillac four door sedan, and put a new Cadillac motor in it. It seemed like there was nothing they couldn't or wouldn't do with a car.

When I was twelve, Ned bought me a Cushman Motor Scooter. It was barely running and the brakes were marginal, but it had a motor and it was mine. My buddy Al and I wrestled it down the basement stairs and in the cold Illinois winter proceeded to take it completely apart. We cleaned it up, took the head off and lapped the valves by hand, had the head shaved, painted it lavender, and put it all back together. Getting it up those stairs proved more of a struggle than we expected, but we persevered and got it back into the sunshine. We took it out on the still icy roads and loved riding with the wind in our hair. I went all over on that Scooter; even to the local junk yards when I was working on my first car.

At fifteen, my Dad helped me buy that first car; a '35 Chevy 3-window coupe that had been chopped. It didn't have an engine, but it did have a '39 Ford top loader tranny. The brakes were converted to hydraulics and the floors

and firewall had been replaced with aluminum. I proceeded to wrench on it. A friend, Guy Held, helped me channel it in our driveway with nothing but hand tools to get it lowered. Ned's friend Read Sinclair, who went on to have a very successful sprint car engine building business, took me under his wing, and helped me put together a motor. We bought a couple of 265 Chevy engine blocks and selected the best one for the base. We bored it out to 283, got some domed and notched fuelie pistons, reworked the heads, and found a dual quad intake and carbs. It was balanced and blue printed and purred like a kitten. A mechanical dual point distributor supplied fire. We put that motor together and got it running in my '35 Chevy Coupe, only to have it rear-ended on a local highway late one evening while we were tuning it. I cried.

I salvaged the motor, and found a '55 Chevy 150 two-door sedan with no motor and a tired three-speed transmission, which was quickly removed. We put a 270 motor in it along with a Corvette close ratio three speed transmission and that was my daily driver in high school.

I remember my Dad asking me to take him for a ride in that car one day. I was on my best behavior cruising slowly around the neighborhood. When he asked me how it went, I answered by standing on it and breaking the rear end loose. I never shifted into second. His only comment was "Feels like you have a pack of wildcats under the hood."

That car took me to school every day and to work every evening in the local grocery store. I was working thirty-five hours a week all through high school to feed my hot rod habit. Weekends were spent street racing and hanging with my girlfriend and buddies. That Chevy was never beat on the street and I was very proud of her.

At one time, I counted over twenty cars I had owned by the time I was twenty-one years old. Four of those cars were '55 Chevys, including one purple customized convertible. It was shaved and decked, had '57 Olds side trim, and '54 Packard taillights.

Another one that I remember fondly was a red and white 1955 Chevy Sport Coupe. I found it in a gas station with no motor (sense a theme here?) and two Powerglide transmissions in the trunk. I paid $65 for it and towed it home. After selling the Powerglides, and reclaiming the change from under the seats, I was into the car for $7. It was a rust bucket, as were all five year old cars in Illinois. I had just wrecked a '58 Impala, so I pulled the 348 four speed and dropped, or should I say wedged it, into the '55. It ran OK, but my buddy Tom's 327 powered '55 Chev 150 would always beat me.

As luck would have it, I spun a bearing in that 348. So, I saved my nickels, bought a 409, 425 HP short block, and made the 348 heads and tri-power work on it. It ran better, but once I scored a set of heads and dual quad carbs off a 409, she really started to fly. Tom could no longer keep up with me; nor could anyone else.

We used to street race for $20 and I never had to buy gas on the weekends. It wasn't much to look at with the bumpers pulled off and sporting a rattle can black primer paint job, but man was it fast!

My posse consisted of four other guys who all drove '55 Chevys, except Willy who had a fuelie '57 red convert. We all wrenched on our own cars and each other's as often as we could.

Marriage and children put a cramp in my hot rodding, but I never lost my love for cars. As my kids were growing up, we worked on their cars together, which has been very rewarding. Fortunately, I went on in my career to be involved with computers and eventually started my own consulting company. It has treated me well.

About two years ago, I started dreaming about having a '55 Chevy again. The internet has brought the whole world to our desktops and I found myself surfing eBay and other forums and the burning desire became too much to resist. I was torn between finding a basket case or one that was complete. While I have a lot of pride in doing a job well, I have learned that I do not have the patience to build a car that looks as good as it runs. I have never been one much for body and paintwork, and interiors were another area where I did not have many skills. I'm a wrench.

So, I started looking for a car that had a nice body and interior, figuring that I could do whatever mechanical work was needed. Magically, eBay delivered. I found a car that looked really good, except it was Lavender, (sense another theme here?). I watched it on eBay and it did not meet the reserve price.

A few weeks later, it was back on eBay and the bidding went higher, but it still did not reach the reserve price. I waited a couple of weeks and it was back again. This time the same thing happened, it did not reach the reserve. I called the seller to learn more about the car and to see if there was some room for negotiation. He was firm on his price, but I decided to go look at it anyway.

After my Illinois experiences, I wanted to make sure it was not a repaired rust bucket. I was assured it was not, so I hopped a jet to Oakland, CA, rented a car, and drove out to Sacramento to see the car. It was more beautiful than the many pictures and once up on the rack, the undercarriage proved to be solid. It was manufactured in Oakland and had always been licensed in Sacramento. We went for a test drive and didn't have to get towed back, so we began negotiations.

One the purchase was complete, I named her "Purple Haze" and since she's come to live at our home, my kids and I have done a lot of suspension and mechanical work on her. We've added rack and pinion power steering, headers and exhaust, sway bars front and rear, Bilstein shocks, new wheels and tires, carpeting, a Tremec 5 speed, an updated radio and sound system, new windshield, electric fuel pump, aluminum radiator, replaced the door poppers and others things to really make it mine. So, we are slowly working the kinks out of her.

My wife, Linda, and I have become involved with the Yesteryear Car Club, the NW Classic Chevy Club, Good Guys, and have attended many shows. We are tickled to be a part of our local hot rodding community, which is alive and well.

When I climb into "Purple Haze," it takes me back to my high school years and the days of tooling around in my first '55 Chevy with not a care in the world. I literally get shivers up and down my spine. After all of the cars I've owned in my life, this may be the last one. But, I wouldn't guarantee it!

Sun Valley Adventures

by Herb Bender

One late spring day in the late '50's my best friend, Buddy, and I were told to sit down in the living room of his house. Something of a challenge and an ultimatum was laid out to us. His Dad flatly stated, "You guys are screwing up by not making much effort in school and I want you both to get more serious!" I was treated like a second son and practically lived at their house. My folks had divorced four years earlier, so I had a stand-in Dad. A year ahead of me in school, Buddy would start his senior year that fall.

After the usual words of advice about performance and diligence came a huge, but wonderful, surprise. Buddy's Dad said, "Son, you bring your grades up to a low 'B' and graduate with your class next year and (to me) you bring yours up to a 'C+' and Buddy can have an older car of his choice, at my expense, just as soon as the diploma is in hand."

We both thought this promise was bogus, but after repeatedly having the offer reaffirmed that summer, we bought into it. We were lower middle class economically, so car dollars were not easily found. This was indeed a "BIG DEAL"!

We made good. Both of us got our acts together and buckled down; nose to the grindstone, studied hard, did every homework assignment, and worked with and for each other toward the goal of getting the car! Buddy graduated right on time the next spring, and I got my G.P.A. up to the required mark. We struggled at first, but it got easier through doing and we got as close as two brothers could be through the process.

Buddy and his Dad, and yes I was included, started car hunting on his Dad's next day off. Of course, we two boys had been hunting all the used car lots for about a month, so we had a good idea what and where the "cool" rides were. After looking at enough car lots to satisfy his Dad's need to feel he got the best car for the price, we settled on a used five year old Mercury Monterey Sun Valley hard top with the glass roof in a beautiful two tone green. It had all the bells and whistles that a teen could want with the OHV V-8, three speed, radio, and fender skirts. We were in Seventh Heaven and riding on Cloud Nine!

The deal was made on a Saturday, so we picked up the car and took it home on the following Monday. We washed, waxed, and shined until we had it absolutely sparkling. Our summer of a lifetime had started, though we didn't realize the significance of that moment in time right then. What kid thinks past today or at best tomorrow?

Buddy's Dad covered the cost of the car and three months of insurance, but left it to us to figure out money for gas, oil, and other expenses. We scouted out a half dozen lawn mowing jobs and used an old reel style, muscle powered mower to accomplish the work. We did a lot of pushing! We also had a morning paper route and along our path picked up beer and soda bottles for deposit returns. We made it work and two happier guys never existed.

We cruised all over the Greater Puget Sound area from our home base in North Seattle. This was all before Interstate 5 so it took hours to get to Silverlake or Norm's Resort in Woodinville. A trip out what is now Interstate 90 across the floating bridge to Lake Sammamish or Carnation was a real day trip back then. We had the freedom to be goofy kids, just laughing and fooling around. It was glorious.

The end of summer came all too soon and now the word was "get a job" for Buddy and "back to school" for me. All car insurance and expenses became ours, plus board and room! We were systematically being led into adulthood by our guardian and mentor.

Buddy decided to enlist in the Army. This was still a time when every red-blooded kid was patriotic and believed that America, right or wrong, was worth serving. He came home from Boot Camp in late December and we experienced what turned out to be the last days we would have together. We spent cold nights sitting in that old Merc with the radio on, listening to Al Cummings on KJR 95 AM, of course.

A couple of months later, I just grew tired of trying to go to high school and work a thirty hour a week part time job to pay for room and board, so I dropped out of it all and joined the Navy. This was back when high enough entry scores got you in without a diploma. Buddy and I stayed in touch through letters, though not as often as we should have. He was in a unit on Okinawa and I was on an old fleet oiler out of Long Beach, CA.

That following spring, I got a letter from Buddy's Mom. She had delayed writing the letter, knowing how hard I would take her news. It told me that Buddy would not be coming home. I still have the short note with its tearstains, both hers and mine.

As the years passed, I exchanged letters with Buddy's Mom. His Dad had passed away in his sleep and his Mom went to live with a sister, and the old "Memory Maker Merc" was sold. I raised a family, had a career, and finally had the funds to get serious about finding a car like the one in which we shared so much living, laughing, and loving. Yes, girls had been a major part of our summer. I spent months searching the web, digging through magazine ads in Hemming's and contacting the International Mercury Owners Association without luck.

Then, about six years ago, the perfect car magically appeared right here in Everett, WA at the Spring Car Show.

 To my wonder and amazement, it was for sale. Needless to say, I struck a deal and made this '54 Sun Valley my baby. It is nearly identically equipped. My Sun Valley has overdrive and is yellow and green instead of two-tone green. But now, over fifty years later, Buddy is gone he is not forgotten and never will be. Buddy not only lives on in my heart and mind; he rides with me every time out.

But it Was My Car

by Jim Ballard

In the spring of 1955, I was beginning to get highly interested in the idea of owning my own car. Of course, I didn't want any just any old car. I wanted a Street Rod. Though I was still more than a year away from obtaining my first driver's license, it seemed like all the automotive forces in the universe were attacking me from every direction.

I was growing up in Maywood, California, which at that time was a hotbed of hot rod and custom car activity that would affect me for the rest of my life. Just short bicycle rides from home were Bell Auto (Racing) Parts, soon to be the birthplace of Cragar Wheels; Keith Black Racing Engines; Bill Gaylord's Custom Upholstery; Eddie Martinez Custom Upholstery; Ed Roth; and Bud "The Baron" Crozier, as well as the Holy Grail, George Barris' Kustom shop in Lynwood.

I can't count how many times George Barris kicked this 14 to 15 year old boy out of his shop, always saying it was too dangerous for me to be in there, but I didn't care. I wanted to soak up any knowledge about customizing and modifying cars that I could possibly get.

My biggest inspiration at this time was Jim Eubanks, an older boy, who lived two houses away from me. He belonged to the Drag Wagons car club of Maywood. Some of the members were really into hot rods and street racing, but it seemed to me that most of them were more into custom cars and girls. While still in high school, Jim displayed a work ethic and determination to go after what he wanted that still guides me today. I believe that he was in the 11th grade when he got a factory job where he worked six hours or more each night after school in order to buy his first car, a 1950 Ford Tudor, which he promptly started to customize.

What he completed in about six months would today be considered the epitome of a shoebox custom. It was nosed and decked with "frenched" headlights and taillights, featuring a '54 Pontiac grill. Jim lowered the car to the ground and painted it in a beautiful teal color, accented by an all-white, leather tuck and roll interior. The final touch was pin striping by a local boy, Kenny Howard, who was becoming better known professionally as Von Dutch! All this was accomplished while Jim was still in high school. He quickly followed this car up about a year later with an equally nice custom '54 Chevy Bel Air, which I got to drive once while I was still fifteen.

My point in telling you about Jim Eubanks is that he made this heady atmosphere of custom cars and hot rods that I was growing up around become real close and personal. The closer I got to my fifteenth birthday, the more I wanted to show up at school at age sixteen with a finished car that would be worthy of the Drag Wagons car club, even though I would probably be too young to join the club. It was about two weeks before my fifteenth birthday that I approached my parents with the idea that I should have my own car to drive to school when I turned sixteen. What a surprise when they said that this was a good idea, on one condition; it would be one hundred percent my own money. That very night, I started looking in the local newspaper want ads for a suitable car.

What was going to be a suitable car? I knew I didn't

want anything that remotely looked like a "family" car or just any old car because it might be cheap to buy. Most of the older guys that I considered "cool" were into customized Ford, Chevy or Oldsmobile two door sedans or convertibles; the newer the better.

How does a fifteen year old compete with this when he has less than $100 to play with? Since I plainly didn't have enough money for a later model car, I decided to temporarily drop the custom car idea and go with an older hot rod type car.

From my perspective at that time, a hot rod was usually an older Ford coupe or roadster and, of the two, the coupe was usually cheaper and easier to find. So, I narrowed my search to a 1948 or older Ford coupe. It didn't take long for me to realize that whenever anything is more popular or desirable to a particular group of people, it becomes scarcer or more valuable and I wasn't finding any Fords in running condition for under seventy-five dollars that were worth bringing home. I couldn't spend all of the $100 or I would have little or no money for any needed repairs.

It was about a week after I started looking for just the right car when a particular ad caught my eye.

1938 Chevrolet coupe. $50. LUdlow X-XXXX.

It was a very simple ad. It was a coupe. It was cheap. But, it was a Chevy.

I didn't know one single hot-rodder that drove a Chevy. I didn't even know what a '38 Chevy looked like, but I have always been a little different from the larger crowd and something deep down inside told me to call the listed phone number; like right now! An older man answered the phone and informed me that I was the first person to call and therefore, that put me first in line. A short time later, my dad got home from work and agreed to take me over to look at the car. After having looked at a number of rusted-out, half-wrecked old Fords, this Chevy turned out to be a very pleasant surprise.

When we arrived to check out the '38 Chevy, I was amazed to see what good condition it appeared to be in. It had the original factory light green paint in slightly oxidized condition. The body, fenders, bumpers, and grill were absolutely perfect except for a dent in the left rear fender about the size of a small pancake and less than quarter of an inch deep. The upholstery was original and in very good condition with the seat protected by a seat cover. It even had an original factory installed AM push-button radio that still worked! The styling wasn't half-bad either and there was no visible rust. Wow, pinch me!

Alas, everything has a downside. The car did run quite well, but it had over 300,000 miles on it. My heart sank, but then he explained the high mileage of the car. He went on to explain that he had taken good care of it with regular maintenance and oil changes.

The old guy told me that he had just retired from a job that was sixty-five miles from home and he had driven the Chevy to work for many years, but the engine had been rebuilt three times. He explained that it could use a new set of rings, but it didn't actually need them for a while. I quickly counted out the $50 in cash to pay for the car, as there was no point in haggling on the price for something this nice. Maybe I would have the first old Chevy hot rod in my town.

I spent most of the first week or two getting acquainted with the car, which was mostly accomplished by sitting in it and starting it a couple dozen times a day. There was a small amount of blue smoke coming out of the tailpipe, which indicated that the engine probably did need new rings and maybe a valve job, as well. I told my dad of my conclusion that the engine needed a rebuild before I drove it to school next year and that the sooner it happened, the better. This was when I received a second surprise from my parents. I already knew that all costs of buying the car were all on me, but now I was informed that the costs and labor of all maintenance and repair was mine alone, also. My dad handed me his copy of the big blue Motor auto repair manual and told me that I was free to use any of his tools in the garage. If I needed any help or assistance, I was on my own. If I needed any advice, he would be in the house! At this point, I had only seen the inside of an engine once and had absolutely no experience in working on one.

My dad did offer me one bit of advice as I was contemplating how to reach the engine to take it apart or get the oil pan off. It seems that if you remove the bolts fastening the front fenders to the running boards, remove two bolts from under the radiator, and disconnect the headlight wires, you can lift the entire front fenders and grill off as an assembly. What a time and labor saver that was. Thanks Dad!

Using the Motor manual as a reference, I slowly disassembled the engine while learning what each part was and what it did. My dad agreed to drive me and the cylinder head down to a local machine shop to have the valves ground. Other than the cylinder head, I was on my own including riding my bicycle to the auto parts store for gaskets, piston rings, and other parts. I figured out, with the help of the manual, how to inspect and adjust the Babbitt bearings, hone the cylinders, install the piston rings, and how to do whatever else was needed. That Motor manual was as valuable as gold to me.

After about five months, I finally got everything back together and was ready to start the engine for the first time. After following each step in the Motor manual exactly, I was quite confident that I knew what I was doing. I double-checked everything one more time; the spark plug wires for the correct firing order, the engine oil and radiator water levels, and added several gallons of fresh gasoline that I'd brought home on my bicycle. The battery was freshly charged.

Per the Motor manual instructions, I cranked the engine over for about a minute, with the key off, to assure oil was distributed everywhere it was supposed to be. Everything was ready, so I poured a small amount of gas into the carburetor to prime it, sat down in the driver's seat, turned the ignition key and stepped on the floor-mounted starter switch next to the gas pedal. I wanted to whoop for joy when the engine instantly roared to life and immediately settled down to a slightly rough idle. With a screwdriver, I did a slight adjustment to the idle screw in the carburetor body and the engine purred more smoothly than it ever had.

Then, I made what was probably the biggest mistake of my life up to that day. I was so proud of how well that engine ran that I bolted into the house to get my dad and show him. As usual, I found him at the kitchen table reading the newspaper. He reluctantly put his paper down and followed me out to the car. When we got there, I immediately started the engine and as soon as it settled down to a smooth idle, I reached into my pocket and took out a fifty-cent piece and balanced the coin, upright on its edge, on the valve cover of that still idling engine. My dad just stared at that coin for what seemed forever then looked over at his 1941 Studebaker, then looked again at the coin, then looked again at his Studebaker, then took one more look at the coin still balanced on that idling engine. Without a word, he simply reached into the car, turned the engine off, removed the key and placed it in his pocket!

He had casually appropriated my car and then drove it to work for the next six months; right up until I received my driver's license. As a result, I wound up driving my car to school the next semester, unfinished, with primer spots. I was so bitter and disappointed that I sold the car, still unfinished, about six months later.

Since my dad had placed total responsibility on me for the purchase, repair, and maintenance of this car, I felt it was only fair that he should have asked me for permission to drive the car to work now that it ran better than his own car. I would not have been thrilled with the idea, but I would have understood and I am quite sure I would have allowed him to do it.

Time has a way of softening us and sometimes I can now think about my first car without feeling angry. In later years, there were a few times I needed (and asked) to borrow his car for an errand and he never refused me.

Obsessive Motorhead

by Tom Smith

How did I become an old car nut? Well, at 46, I'm not that old, but I am definitely an old car nut! It probably started when I was a baby. My dad used to take me out to the garage and rev up the motor in his hot rod so I could get used to it and not cry when he took us to the drag strip. Dad was the quintessential motorhead. He had a '66 Plymouth with a 426 Hemi, a '39 Plymouth with a 348 Pontiac motor and a '48 Chevy truck with a 327 Vette motor. Having been fully indoctrinated at that infancy, I would either watch events closely or sleep right through the drags, but I certainly wasn't frightened.

As I got older, I got Hot Wheels and Tonka trucks and spend hours looking at dad's Hot Rod Magazines. By the

time I was five, I could name all the parts on an engine. By age 6, dad had me washing parts with a pan of gas or lacquer thinner and a wire brush and scraper. When he got into VWs, I started learning about them. By the time I was 11, I could pull the engine and transmission out of a Bug in about 45 minutes.

I had already started building my own bicycles and working on other kids bikes. A young entrepreneur, I started learning about buying and selling and trading and had my own little bike junkyard. In the winter, when it was cold or snowy, I took to building model cars and never ever made them like the box, sometimes buying two or three kits to make one. I'd take a blown Hemi from one, body from another, slicks and Centerlines from another, and I would chop tops, shorten, section, build flares, and anything else my young, creative mind could imagine.

At 13, I got a riding mower from my grandpa and stripped as much stuff as I could off of it to make it faster. I bypassed the governor, fooled with the carb and more. About 6 months later, I took all the money I made shoveling snow and bought a 3 HP mini bike for 50 bucks. I think it was a Montgomery Wards or Sears. It was great! I had freedom, speed, and envious or jealous friends. Then, one of my friends got a real motorcycle. I wasn't so fast or cool anymore. So, I saved up snow shoveling and yard work money, sold the mini bike, and bought a Yamaha 250cc dirt bike. I was the king again! I weighed about ninety-five pounds and had a 400 pound rocket! I learned how to work on my motorcycle and even painted it.

At fourteen, I got caught stealing moms VW. I had taken it and my dad's Dodge Power Wagon several times before and not been caught. But, this time I hit a tree stump with mom's Bug and didn't get the bodywork done before they got home. I tried, but didn't pull it off. Surprisingly, I didn't catch much grief over it and about a year later, when I was 15-1/2, mom gave me the bug. It was my first car. The only downside was that it had no motor. I started saving for that and in the meantime, I put a 3" body lift on it, twisted up the torsion bars, cut and turned the front end, and put big tires and wheels and off road lights on it. I found a used motor for it and I was unstoppable. I would go where 4x4s couldn't. I had a typical teenage problem though. I couldn't afford gas and insurance.

I got a job at Superior Auto Electric, not far from my home. The boss, Carl, was a great old motorhead and he taught me how to rebuild starters, alternators, and water pumps. He did a lot of side stuff, too, like buying and selling cars. So, I got to work on those with him. I'd pull motors, transmissions, and other things most guys my age had no idea how to do. It was an invaluable experience.

A guy came in one day that had a beat up '66 Buick Special that he wanted to part with. He didn't have a clear title, but he only wanted $150 for it. Bam! My first V8! On the way home, I pegged it at 125 mph! In my mind, it really flew! I whipped it around the woods for a month or two, learning the way to drift corners and jump it. I cut off the roof with a torch, then thrashed it around some more, and even knocked down trees with it.

Finally, one extreme jump broke both motor mounts and the transmission mount, allowing the motor fly into the radiator. So, I ended up selling the transmission for $50 and the engine for $300. I had all that fun and still made a profit!

Another guy came into the shop and wanted to sell the boss a '70 Olds Cutlass Supreme for $400. I really wanted that car, but all I had was $200. The boss talked the guy down to $300 and then loaned me $100. It was mine! Mom was less than enthusiastic, but I couldn't take it back, of course, so she conceded that it wasn't the end of the world after all.

Business got slow and Carl laid me off. I missed the money, but I missed hanging with him at the shop, learning all I could even more. After that, I started buying old bugs and parting them out. My parents had separated and I filled mom's yard up with dismantled cars and spare parts.

I was in my second year of auto shop at school and was learning even more about how to do alignments, heads, rebuild blocks, and more. Happily, I got another car related job. I started working at Minute Lube and was changing oil on 30 to 75 cars a day. Doing that, I got to drive some really cool rides, like a new Vette, a cop car and a beer truck of all things. It wasn't a bad gig for a motorhead kid, like me.

I loved my Olds. It would do long burnouts effortlessly. It ran, looked, and sounded really cool with its Edlebrock intake and carb, Turbo Sonic mufflers and big fat tires. To me, as a young guy, it was scary fast. I took it up to 120 on the speedo and a half inch past that. God only knew how fast I was really going.

I ran out of gas in it constantly and, of course, lost my license in it. One say I saw a bunch of cute girls by the high school and did what any red blooded seventeen year old would do with a hot rod; a block long burnout! I thought I was pretty cool, but Officer Angry, at the end of the block was less than impressed. He wrote out a big stack of tickets for everything he could think of. Well, the girls weren't impressed and neither was my mom. Before I went to court, I ran out of gas as usual and walked the rest of the way to see the judge. He wasn't very amused with me, either. By the end of the day, I had no license, a pile of fines, and someone had broken the windows out of my car. I sold it a few days later for a couple hundred dollars.

When I finished paying my fines off and got my license back, I bought a '67 Ford van from a guy at work. How much trouble could I get into driving a van? Well, I had it about a week and a drunk pulled out in front of me during my first trip to town in it. The guy's insurance company totaled it and gave me $900 for it. I bought it back from them for $200 with a salvaged title.

I needed a new driver, so I bought a 64 El Camino from the next door neighbor for $500 and started driving it while fixing the van. I got a door, radiator and windshield for the van for $150 and after a couple of weeks with the hammer, torch, and some bondo, the van was on the road again.

Once I turned eighteen, I was ready to move to the big city. I sold off all my VWs except a '62 Karmann Ghia that my roommate gave me when he moved to Oregon. It was awesome to be in Phoenix in the 80s, cruising on Central every Friday and Saturday, two drag strips, illegal street racing, junkyards, car shows, speed shops, mud bogs, sand drags, and even boat racing. It was motorhead nirvana!

Once settled in, I got a job and I sold the van. I could tell a lot of stories about the things that went on in that van, but most of it isn't car related. At this point, I really started working on the El Camino. It got a new motor and a good friend put a really cool Firemist Red metallic paint job on it with gold pearl on top. It was a beautiful chick magnet and I hit the cruise scene for about three weeks before a lady made an illegal left turn in front of me. I hit her doing about 45 mph. The insurance totaled it and only gave me $1,000 for it. Apparently, they didn't care how much the girls liked it.

When my sister got married and moved to Canada, she sold me her '74 Datsun truck. It was the only "rice grinder" I've ever owned but naturally, I had to modify it and make it as cool as I could. I put a header and a side draft Weber carb on it, which probably doubled its power. I drove it while rebuilding the El Camino. It seemed like I was always rebuilding wrecks!

I actually had two El Caminos. As I got into it, I decided to make one really nice one, so I did a frame and front clip swap, sandblasted the frame and installed all new bushings, new motor, transmission and resprayed the Firemist Red metallic paint; this time with violet pearl. It turned out spectacular and it was the first paint job that I actually did on my own! To me, it looked like a show car and I couldn't have been prouder of it. I drove it about a month and a half before a guy ran a stop sign and hit me in the driver's side. I start to spin and the passenger door hit a fire hydrant. I rolled three times and landed on the roof, totaling, yet again, another car. There was no saving her this time. The insurance company only offered to give me $3,000 before I showed them $5,000 in receipts. In the end, they paid me $6,000 and gave me back the car with another salvaged title. While I still wasn't satisfied, they wouldn't go a dime more.

For my 21st birthday, my dad gave me his '39 Plymouth. I needed to get something drivable right away though, and the coupe hadn't run since the '60s. The neighbor had a '66 Biscayne in his backyard with no motor or trans-mission. It had been his uncle's car before he had passed away and I gave him $50 for it. After re-trieving it from the trees and other old cars that surrounded it, I did the  brakes and put the motor and transmission from the El Camino in it and started driving it. Today, the Biscayne is show worthy and I race it, as well!

The rest of the insurance money went into Dad's old Plymouth coupe. It got a narrowed rear end, big block mo-tor, Mustang II front suspension, and a bunch of other rac-ing goodies. I wanted to be in the pro street scene, which was huge in the late '80s and early '90s, but I fell for a girl and the coupe went on the back burner. I still own it to this day and it's just about time to dig it out and make it every-thing I always wanted it to be. Yep, I'm an old car nut, for sure!

Road Runner

by Jim Lykken

It's possible that I had more cars in my early years than the average teenager. I certainly changed cars more than any that I knew. My first cars were all six-cylinder cars. Mostly, because they were cheap and cheap was all I could afford. I preferred the older Chevys and while I had some that were from '50-'54, the majority of them were the more stylish '55-'57 Chevys. I had two doors, wagons, convertibles; pretty much any model would do. I strayed occasionally, but not much.

One time that I did go astray involved the purchase of a beautiful '64 Plymouth Savoy at a state auction. It was 1968 and, although it was a lot more than I was used to spending on a car, I couldn't pass up this four year old beauty at $500. I bought a lot of cars at the auction and a lot of them were only $25-50, but running and driving cars. I drove the Plymouth for a while, but my brother had a '64 Gran Prix that was gorgeous and a gas hog. He needed something with better mileage to drive to work. He offered to trade me for the six cylinder Plymouth I was driving and I couldn't pass up that kind of deal. I thought I was a pimp. I drove the wheels off of that car for a while.

I had a pretty good job at the Boeing plant in Renton, making decent money as a mechanic. Actually, "mechanic" was a pretty lofty title for what I really did. I drilled holes… lots of holes. But, I decided I could afford the car of my dreams, so I traded the Gran Prix in on a brand new 1969 Plymouth Road Runner with a 383 V8 and a four speed. That was the year that Motor Trend Magazine named the Roadrunner "Car of the Year" in its class and it was my first V8. Wow! What a day that was. It was Blue Fire with a blue bench seat interior and that big V8 that put out 335 horses.

In all of the six bangers, I had to go around a corner and nail it to get the tires to burn rubber. With all this new-found power in the Road Runner, I wound up spinning it around 360 degrees. Now, I had a hot rod. It was going to take a little getting used to and I ended up getting in a little trouble with this car. For some reason I couldn't keep tires on it. I had all four original tires burned off in the first month. Then there were the speeding tickets.

The State of Washington sent me a letter saying if I got one more violation, after the three I had already received, I would lose my driver's license. So, to prove a point, I got two more. I should have known better, but didn't. The state was good to their word and I lost my driver's license for 6 months. It seemed like there was a cop waiting for me around every corner. In fact, all of the last three tickets were from the same cop in Kent. I don't think he was really on the lookout for me, but I didn't make myself very hard to find, either. Dad was really proud!

We all went to what was called the "Renton Loop" in Renton, WA to go cruising and street racing almost every Saturday night. I won quite a few of the races on those exhilarating nights. One night, I was racing a Corvette in front of the high school. We lit them off from the red light and in no time, I was pulling away from the Corvette as I passed a cop on the shoulder. I knew I was dead meat and simply pulled over and had all the necessary paper-work out before the cop even got to me. He must have been amused that I was sitting there with all my paperwork ready. He didn't give me a ticket, but did mention less than calmly that I should "GET THE HELL OUT OF TOWN!"

I was known for shifting gears without using the clutch pedal and I wore a hole in the front dash from hitting third gear so hard. Yee Ha! I had a buddy that bought a new '70 Road Runner and we would always race each other. He couldn't beat me. So, he put in a new cam, high-rise intake, and bigger carb and I still beat him. It was all because I had learned how to shift the four-speed. The Road Runner speedometer went to 120mph, but I had to find out if it would do it. It sailed right past that mark and then kept going. I would say it went at least 130mph. The power was intoxicating.

I had a neighbor that hated the Road Runner and wasn't very fond of me and I suppose I gave him ample cause. I'd come haulin' butt down the street too fast, I admit, and rack off the pipes. He'd come running out, yelling at me to slow down and I'd speed up. If I wasn't in a hurry, I'd go slower, but I'd pass him and really crank up the RPMs just to annoy him with the loud exhaust I ran. Man, he would get pissed and run after me until I was out of site. This went on for the whole time I owned that Road Runner.

Sadly, I had to get rid of it when Boeing went through layoffs in the '70s. I loved that car, but with car payments, gas, and my huge insurance premiums, I just couldn't afford to keep it. So, I traded a guy for a little MG1100 sedan. I got the MG and the other guy got the payments on the Road Runner. My gas bill and insurance premiums went way down and I didn't have car payments. I know I wasn't the only one who lost their dream cars this way, but at the time, it broke my heart. I still miss that car. There have been lots of other cars since, of course; mostly more '55-'57 Chevs. I just love old cars and can't stay away.

I spent most of the years after Boeing working in body and paint shops and I've done tons of body and paint in my own shop on the side for friends, friends of friends and anyone else that wanted to pay for my work.

My recent claim to fame comes from a short stint working at Divers Hot Rods on Ferrambo, winner of the 2008 Ridler Award at the Detroit Autorama. It is a gorgeous 1960 Rambler station wagon with a 2002 Ferrari 360 Modena drive-train, featuring a 405hp, 3.6L, V-8 engine and a 6-speed manual transmission with the classic Ferrari shift-gate. An absolutely awesome car, it was recently donated to LeMay – America's Car Museum by Mike Warn. I was part of the team that installed the car at the museum and my son-in-law and I can proudly say that we contributed a lot to the body and paintwork that went into making Ferrambo the outstanding show winner that it is.

My last special ride was a '36 Chev with a 383cid stroker motor. It was a very nice hot rod. While we are resettling into a new home, the old cars are on hold for a bit and I'm not sure what is next in my long string of automotive history. Something fun and fast, I would think.

Cousin Gary Saves the Day

by Dale Moreau

1957 was an eventful year for me. I say this because I was an excitable sophomore in high school during that unforgettable year. One cold clear evening during that winter stands out in particular and I can recall it in my mind's eye as if it happened just last night.

The streets were damp and looked as if they were made out of shiny black coal. I remember the dampness boring right through me as it came off nearby Lake Ontario and into the country town of Newfane, New York. Eighteen miles from Niagara Falls, the area often got the brunt of the lake effect.

Newfane High School's basketball team was playing Starpoint High at Newfane on that Friday night just before Christmas. Newfane's hot shot star player, Jim Gow, lived up to his reputation of twenty plus points a game and Starpoint's hopes of winning the Western New York championship were frozen out.

Jim was from a long line of farm families and his relatives owned half of the places between Lockport and Olcott Beach. The small farm community had a Ford dealership and most guys had Fords. Some of them worked after school at a local grocery store and could buy a nearly new car. Interestingly enough, that grocery store is now a Ford dealership. I was only a sophomore, and too young for a driver's license, but I had a nineteen year old '38 Ford coupe in the back yard that I could drive around a 400 acre farm next to my home. I could go quite a ways further if I closed the gates behind me on the neighboring place. I thought I was quite the hot shot!

After the game, there was a dance in the school gym, where the lights were low and the girls were attentive, if you played it cool and kept out of sight of the Vice Principal. One such lovely had been going with an older guy of seventeen. She'd finally had enough of his over inflated ego and dumped him. She was a slim, local Italian girl of about five foot whatever with shoulder length black hair; a real class act.

Having gone steady with this other guy for quite some time, she was used to slow dancing very close. We had some classes together and had spoken on occasion, but I was surprised when she came up and asked me to dance. Of course, I said yes. Girls in my own class in high school always went with older guys, so this was a real surprise to me.

We danced and chatted together for quite a bit of the evening and I was certainly enjoying the attention she was showing me. Dancing with a beautiful girl like her was definitely a new experience for me and I was beginning to hope the night would never end.

At one point, I decided that the Cokes were wanting out, so I excused myself and headed for the boys room. I was just about done when her former boyfriend strolls in, with several of his buddies for back up, looking for me. He was ticked off that she was dancing so close to me, even though she had given him the heave ho some time before.

They were about to let me know just how much displeasure my dancing with her had caused him when the scene changed. In walked my cousin Gary and his best buddy, Norm. They were seniors and the two toughest guys in school. Everyone liked them, as they were good natured and funny, but you didn't want to cross either one of them if you liked living with all your limbs attached. Gary quickly sized up the situation and all hell broke loose.

Mr. Smart Ass Tough Guy's buddies suddenly disappeared. He, on the other hand, was quenching his thirst from one of the long porcelain "drinking fountains" found along the wall in boy's high school bathrooms across the nation. Of course, he had a little help in the form of a flush from my cousin Gary. I had to pay for this help by enduring a punch on the arm that I was supposed to pretend I didn't feel; even though I thought I was going to die on the spot. I never saw the guy again. He kept a wide birth, not wanting to have another drink with Cousin Gary. I went back out to the dance and my newfound love. Thank you, Cousin Gary!

Norm and Gary dated some very nice looking girls. Norm's girl had been my secret heartthrob... prior to the night of the dance. She was one of my young sophomore classmates, naturally. He squired her around in his '55 Chevy ragtop, she enjoying the attention of an older guy with a cool car. He could get away with a Chevy because he was Norm Fitz Hans and was one-half of the two toughest guys in school. No one was going to challenge him. Gary, on the other hand, was the laid-back type of guy who wisely spent his money on beer and girls, wasted the rest, and drove anything that would run.

Jim Gow and his girl, a knock out blond, stayed for the last dance of the year and he basked in the glow of being Mr. Wonderful on the basketball court. Jim was one of those guys who worked a lot and always had a nice set of wheels. He was driving an eight month old '57 Ford hardtop with a three on the tree standard transmission and factory special T-Bird V-8 with dual four barrel carbs.

About the time they left the dance, the temperature had dropped several more degrees and black ice had started to appear in patches on the road. He dropped off his date at her place and then, retracing his steps past the school, was almost to Gary's girlfriend's house when he hit one of those patches of black ice.

The car slid for what Jim thought was forever and now out of control, hit a passing fire hydrant. The point of impact was between the hood ornament and the right front

fender, pushing the engine and the transmission back into the passenger compartment far enough that if his girlfriend had been with him it would have been curtains for her. The fuel lines had snapped and the car erupted into flames. Jim, now cut from head to toe down his right side, was trapped in the car. His short white jacket, white pants, and white bucks (shoes) were turning red. The driver's door was jammed and the fire was getting worse.

Gary and his date had already left the dance and made their way to her house. The sound of the impact when the car hit the hydrant interrupted my Cousin Gary's pursuit of his girlfriend's newest purchase from the lingerie department of the AM&A store in Lockport. He ran across the street and seeing Jim inside the '57 and the car on fire, Gary grabbed the door handle, according to Jim, ripped the door off its hinges, and dragged him out. The car was destroyed, but Jim was saved and Gary wound up being the real hero of the night.

The last time I saw Jim Gow was in 1963 and he had a Hemi powered '57 T-Bird. He spent his career selling cars in western New York State. Gary and Norm joined the

Navy, and after that, Gary started a lifelong career with one of the railroads. He is now semi-retired and is doing very well and living in Wisconsin.

I am a professional photographer and still in love with cars.

I Got Off Easy

by Jim Muckenfuhs

In 1980, I worked for Busam Datsun in Cincinnati, Ohio. Starting in 1979, the 280ZX was all-new and they were selling like hot cakes. We sold every one we could get.

The higher ups decided to have what they called a "Sell-A-Thon," a new concept at the time, where the dealer would stay open for 24 hours each day from Friday through Sunday. I personally thought they were nuts, but I was just a bottom rung mechanic at the time.

The U.A.W. took it pretty seriously though, because they called Joe Busam, the owner, and threatened to kill him if he went through with it. They told him he would never make it home again. There were even bomb threats. You see, in 1980 the popularity of the Japanese auto makers pissed off a lot of people. But, I digress...

The dealer had Datsun send us truckloads of leftover 280ZX's from the 1979 model year for the big sale. Keep in mind, southern Ohio is damn cold in January. There was a foot of snow on the ground with the temperature below zero and all of the cars they were sending had been sitting in a port in California for a year. By the time they arrived, all fifty of the cars we received had dead batteries and all fifty cars needed to be jump started before being moved off the carriers. Unfortunately, I was the chosen one elected to freeze his nuggets off and jump all of those damn cars.

Here's a fun fact about 1980 Datsun technology. The 280ZX's were fuel injected, starting in 1975, and took a minimum of 9.6 base volts in the battery before the injection would operate. In other terms, you couldn't just hook jumper cables up and go. You had to leave the cables on each battery to charge for at least 20 minutes. It wasn't going to be a fun day.

The first load of car carriers arrived and I started on its bottom row. I would hook up the cables and go stand by the running engine on the parts truck to try and keep warm. This worked well for the four cars on the bottom row. There were three levels so I started on the middle row next. There were three cars in the middle row and the first one came off without a hitch.

When I got to the middle car in that middle row, my life was about to change. As you can imagine, I had to climb up a bit to get to the car. Keep in mind the hoods opened backwards on these cars, so it was an extremely tight fit. The hood only had about a five-inch space to open so just getting the cables hooked up properly was quite difficult. Once secured, I hopped back down to stand by the warm running motor.

I was on the right side of the car carrier and the driver was on the left side where we couldn't see each other. I didn't even give it a thought when the front of the car I was jumping started to rise in the front. I mean surely, the man knew what he was doing, right? But, the ramp kept rising up in the front until it starting squeezing the hood closed. I was getting concerned as it kept going up and started crushing both front fenders. I yelled "HEY ASSHOLE, YOUR SQUISHING THIS CAR OVER HERE."

I heard him say, "Oh shit," and watched as he started running around the front of the truck right when the windshield exploded. Then, just for good measure, the back of the car started to rise. All I could do is stand there with my mouth gaping wide open as the rear quarter panels started to crush.

Out of the corner of my eye, I see this 6'5" 400 lb. truck driver slip on the ice and I swear his feet went clean over his big ass head as he crashed hard on the back of his neck. That's when the second explosion happened. Yep, the rear hatch and both rear quarter glasses blew out at the same time.

I'll give this big man credit. He got up so fast I couldn't believe it. It was as if he never even slowed down. I couldn't believe he didn't knock himself out cold as hard as he had hit the ground on his five gallon pickle bucket sized head. He flew to a stop two feet in front of me, grabbed the lever for the controls, and stopped the carnage with one flick of his wrist.

It only took mere seconds to realize what I had done and I immediately bent over the fender of the truck and puked all over the ground. Suddenly, I wasn't freezing any more, but was sweating from every pore in my body. Apparently, when I jumped down from the truck, my coattail got snagged on that lever.

I instantly feared for my life, knowing that either he or the boss was going to kill me. What he said next almost made me love him. He actually chuckled and said, "You know, I've been driving these car haulers for twenty years and this is my very first load without one single scratch of freight damage." With that, we both busted out laughing. I said, "Well, I just blew the hell outta that!"

Once we stopped laughing, we assessed the damage. The hood, front fenders, the windshield, rear hatch, both rear quarter panels, both rear quarter glasses, rear hatch glass, , and, of course, the entire roof were demolished. In the span of a few minutes, a '79 280ZX was destroyed and turned into a pile of rubble. At least that car didn't have the glass T-tops that 90 percent of them did.

What was my punishment you might ask?

Well, I had to drive the destroyed sports car eight miles down I-75 in a snowstorm with no windshield and eight inches of roof clearance to our body shop. In the end, the car was repaired and sold and while it was hard to believe... I got off easy.

You Can't Do That!

by Larry Montana

O ne hot summer night in 1969, in a small B.C. town, we neighborhood boys were cruising on our bicycles when we heard the sound of Rock and Roll guitars and drums screaming from car radios. As C.C.R. rang through the streets, our hearts pumped. We continued riding until we saw three longhaired dudes and a bunch of other people just hanging around the source of the music; an assembly of what we knew to be some pretty fast cars. My sister was five years older, and known well by all the guys in the group. They had sort of accepted me, so I had no problem rolling right into the crowd.

These were the dudes that had quit school and started working in the local sawmills. They would walk across the street from their work into the car dealerships with their paychecks and roll out with factory Hemi's, Shelby's, and various G.M. performance rides. I bragged to these guys, standing around drinking beer and laughing, that my dad had a '65 Chevelle. I didn't mention it was a four door.

Sitting off to the side, having just been fired off, my eyes and ears caught a lime green Datsun pickup. It was gloriously loud and had big fat tires on the back. My only thought was "WOW!" The hood was opened and there sat a Mustang 289ci V8 engine with a four speed. I noticed a semi rough cutting of the inner fenders and wondered to myself what is going on here? You can't do that!

Obviously, the truck had come with a much quieter, smaller motor, and certainly not those big smooth tires. I shouted over the lumpy exhaust "You can't do that! You'll crash!" The dude sitting inside said, "You can do anything you want and if you want something, dream it up and then build it." That was the start to my fabricator mind-set... those golden words "You can't do that!"

Well, I wasn't old enough to build a real car, but I found myself gluing tires together and melting them smooth with a hot butter knife to make big fat sets for my model cars. The model instruction sheets were all in the garbage. I didn't need instructions. I needed parts. After many tubes of glue and all my models cut up and patched together, some with three motors glued together and some with weird paint jobs, I decided that was enough dreaming. I took all of them downstairs into our cement basement, poured glue on them, lit them on fire, and shot them up with my 22-caliber rifle.

The hippy age was here. The Beatles were singing "Come Together." Flower power, drugs, fast cars, and bikers were in. It was a time that I didn't even mind getting kissed by my sister's friends, because I was so cute. My first dates with young girls were spent ice skating and going to the local movie theater. "Easy Rider" was the movie playing the Friday night that the "DREAM" was born. Bright eyed and bushy tailed on Saturday morning, a chopper design was put in motion. With hacksaw in hand, eye balling my Mustang banana seat bike, I was ready to create. My best friend Duane yelled, "You can't do that!"

With those inspirational words, I began by cutting the front forks off my bike and then I cut the forks off a donor bike. With a few relief cuts and a couple hose clamps, a Chopper was born. As I rode my custom-forked front-end chopper bicycle, grownups and other kids looked at me as if I was either a famous movie star or just plain weird. After the forks started falling off, and with me incurring the many scars that such mishaps caused, I needed bigger dreams.

One day, as I walked with my sister up town, Peter Wolka drove by and waved at us or I should say her. He locked up his brakes and a loud screech filled the air. Peter backed up his '70 'Cuda that sported a thundering 426 Hemi, shaker hood and a pistol grip shifter. A ride was offered, but my sis politely declined. Undaunted and still wearing a big smile, Peter revved up the Hemi and the dropped the clutch. The car, still in reverse, burned the tires backward until he shoved it into first gear and dropped the clutch. The Posi-Trac rear end laid down a big, black, dual fishhook pattern on the road! WOW! Thus, another dream was born. I needed a fast car!

By this point, a paper route led to a farm job, while working after school at the tire store, too. I also scored a weekend cleanup job at the local sawmill. I was making some money. With resources starting to become available, it was time to consider a vehicle of my own. My father was a Chev man and I decided I wanted a Chev, too. So, I borrowed some money from my Grandma and bought my first project car. It was a 1937 Chevrolet Tudor sedan with no motor or transmission. Everyone back in those days had 283 motors lying around, pulled out of cars to be replaced with big blocks, and I scored one. Next, I bought a four speed Muncie. I lived out in Lister on a farm and after school and finishing chores, I went over to an old man that lived next door. He was a smart old farmer that could make something out of nothing.

He laughed at my dreams, but was willing to help me build. We cut old machinery apart to fabricate motor and tranny mounting brackets and he tacked them together, armed only with a set of jumper cables hooked to the tractor with a piece of carbon in one cable and the other connected to ground. He used a coat hanger as a filler rod. All put together it became an impromptu arc welder. I took my fabricated mounts to school and finished welding them together in the metal shop. Once the motor was in, we made the drive shaft work by putting the fan real close to the radiator. Now, I needed exhaust.

Because I was living right on the Canada-U.S.A. Border, it was easy to go to the States and find an auto parts store specializing in speed equipment. I walked into a speed shop and asked for a set of small block headers. They asked me "For what?" I said I just wanted a set of small block headers for a Chev. They again said "For what and what year?" I said "I'll take them; those hanging on the wall." He replied, "They won't fit! You can't do that!" They had said the Golden words that always inspired me and I completed the purchase.

Back in Canada, the old farmer was still smiling, but shook his head. He thought I should just settle for the stock exhaust manifolds. I had no torches, just a 7/16 wrench and a hammer. A week later, I had actually beaten those headers into place, clamped on two cherry bombs, and let it roar. The loud exhaust was music to my ears, but the horses and other livestock were less than thrilled.

I filled the radiator with water, got some purple farm gas, and then turned the key and fired it off. After the smoke cleared, I shifted the car into reverse and in my excitement just about backed into the pit on my way out of the shop. I had the biggest smile of anyone in the world. I finished off the interior with bucket seats, an 8-track stereo, and a wrap-around back seat out of a T-bird. That was another head shaker, but I did it anyways.

On my sixteenth birthday, I got my driver's license and was legally on the road. A week later, school was back in session and I drove my flat black '37 Chev to school. What a proud moment!

In reality, I was driv-  ing a car that had a worn out old steering box and a dangerous front suspension. It got up to 70 mph real fast, but drove like a fishing lure. Fat tires just magnified each movement. Other friends had newer cars and criticized mine, suggesting it wasn't practical. With the ribbing that got from my classmates, I decided that I needed to make it look better.

My grandmother looked puzzled when I walked out of her house with her Electrolux vacuum cleaner. I masked off the windows with newspaper and stuck the nozzle line in the back of the vacuum cleaner, thus creating my first air compressor. Adding the glass jar attachment, I blew on some satin black enamel paint. I am sure I would have heard those golden words "You can't do that!" from someone, but no one was around. All things considered, like what I had to work with, it turned out pretty good for being my first paint job.

I drove the car all winter until spring. By then, I was ready to create my first custom paint job. I laid down a white base coat, a blue outline of the panels, and another outline with a bright orange spray bomb with a brown spit finish. Then, I put a set of Mickey Thompson fat tires on it and called it my first hot rod!

Even though I was still just a sixteen-year-old kid, people started thinking of me as a car builder. From that moment on, I knew what I wanted to do most in life... Build hot rods!

I'm still building cars and nothing stops my imagination. To this day, I run into small town car guys that still tell me "You can't do that!" Now I just stay quiet, build my dreams, and in the end, I know I can do it until the day I die! My motto is "Dream it... Build it."

The Story of the '40

by Clark Jackson Jr.

My appreciation for old cars started at an early age. Growing up in Mississippi during the '60s and '70s, I would hear my dad tell stories of the hot rods he and his friends had once had. One of his first cars was a 1940 Chevy two door Sedan with a 283ci V8 motor. When I was growing up, he would always say, "I wish I still had my '40," any time we would see an old car. So, I obviously got the old car bug from my dad.

Like most high school boys, I wanted a cool car that was fast and an attention getter. I'd eyeball some of the cars my friends had, like the Corvettes, Trans Ams, and Z 28s and remember hoping that I'd have an eye catching hot rod of my own one day.

One evening, I was passing by a local car lot in town, there sat a 1957 Chevy truck, and I just had to have it. I had a little truck that my mom and dad bought from me so my little brothers would have a vehicle to drive and with that money, I was able to buy my first "old" vehicle; that old '57 Chevy that had caught my eye. I worked on fixing it up for a couple years and had it looking pretty good. It was good enough that people were always trying to buy it or swap me for something else. I wouldn't ever bite, until one day a buddy of mine offered to swap it for his '55 two-door Chevy 210 and the deal was done.

Twenty-three years had passed since my dad sold his '40 Chevy and at 25 years old, I started thinking about that old car more and more. So, I decided to call the gentleman my dad had sold it to. He told me he had sold the car, but gave me the name and number of the man who bought it from him. After calling a string of several men who had since owned it, I got in contact with the man who now owned the car and asked him if it was okay to come and look at it. He agreed and when I arrived at his house, he took me to a field behind his house.

In the field, I saw a '41 Chevy Coupe in pretty bad condition, a '66 Corvette Stingray, and the '40 Chevy two door sedan my dad had told me so many stories about over the years. It was exactly how he had described it, right down to the decals on the windows. To my surprise, it was in pretty good shape after all those years, although it had no motor or rear end. With $1,000 cash in my pocket, I asked the big question; would he sell it?

He said no and I asked him what it would take for me to buy it. Then he spoke those eight dreadful words so many of us have heard… "I'm going to fix it up one day." A year or so later I sent a friend of mine to try to buy it and the old boy still wouldn't cut loose of it. So, I continued working on the '55 Chevy and came to terms with the fact that I wouldn't be fixing up my dad's old '40 Chevy as I had hoped.

I sold the '55 Chevy, because a new beauty entered my life; a '70 Ford Mustang convertible. I didn't keep it long because a '68 Barracuda came along. After the Barracuda, there were a string of different cars and trucks over the years and I ended up buying back my '57 Chevy truck. There were lots of other cars and trucks along the way, as well, and like a lot of car guys, I would change rides at the drop of a hat if it suited me. Luckily, I married a woman that understood (Thank God) that I had an old car addiction.

One day I came home with a '65 Cadillac Hearse and my wife thought I had lost my mind. Needless to say, I got rid of the Hearse not long after buying it and bought a '66 Chevy Truck. I drove the '66 Chevy for a while, but slowly got out of the old car hob-by. Well, kind of.

My dad had bought a new Jeep in 1985 and then passed it on to my brother. In 2006, I bought the Jeep from my brother, with the idea of keeping it in the family. It had a 350 Chevy  motor in it. I started fixing up the old Jeep so my wife and I would have a ride to cruise around in, but even after 20 years had passed since I tried to buy back my dad's '40 Chevy, I still couldn't get it out of my mind. My wife and I took the Jeep for a ride one afternoon and I noticed she had a strange look on her face. I asked her what was wrong and she told me, "This thing rides too rough." That's when I knew my Jeep was not something she and I could just enjoy cruising.

I had the 283 Chevy motor that my dad had put in the Jeep years before my brother replaced it with the 350. It was still bagged in my shop at home. I decided I wanted an old car to put it in, so I started watching EBay, looking at a lot of different old cars and one day I spotted a '40 Chevy two door sedan that had a three inch chopped top, with shaved doors and trunk.

The seller had a reserve on it, so I added it to my watch list and followed it as the bids came in. The listing ended with the reserve not met, but on the sellers information about the car it said, "Willing to trade," with an email ad-dress listed.

I contacted the gentleman and told him I had a Jeep CJ 7 if he was interested. He emailed me back a phone number. When I called, he said he might go for a trade if the Jeep was in reasonable condition. I sent him pictures of it and the deal was made. With me living in Natchez, MS and him in Stillwater, OK, we agreed to meet up in Shreveport, LA to make the trade.

Now came the fun part. I went to see my dad to ask about getting rid of the Jeep, which was like a part of the family. I said, "Pop, I need to ask you something," and he  asked what it was. I told him I wanted to get rid of the Jeep and he said, "That's your Jeep now, do with it what you want." I told him that I wanted to trade it for an old car and he responded with, "Great! What kind of old car?" I smiled and told him about the '40 Chevy two-door sedan with the three inch chopped top and shaved door handles. He looked at me for a minute and said, "Are you joking with me?" I told him "No sir! We are going to meet and trade this Saturday in Shreveport. I want you to go with me to get it." With a smile on his face, he happily agreed with a "Yes indeed!"

We made the trip to Shreveport and got to where we were supposed to meet the man before he arrived. When my dad saw that old car on that trailer coming off the exit ramp, tears came to his eyes and he looked at me and said, "Damn! That brings back a lot of good old memories." We brought the old '40 Chevy back home with us to get her running and looking like new again.

The story behind the '40 Chevy started back in 1965 in Natchez, MS when my dad first bought his straight out of the Navy. I was born a year later in 1966 and in 1970, with my parents second son on the way, he couldn't afford to keep a hobby car.

I found dad's original old '40 when I was twenty-five, but couldn't get my hands on it. I'm now forty-five and he's sixty-nine, and while this '40 may not be his original '40, we are just as happy and I have a '40 Chevy two door Sedan for the old 283 Chevy motor. It's just like my pops had back in the good old days.

The Race That Never Happened

by David Dickinson

I had just finished stuffing a 327 V8 into a 1955 Chevrolet two door sedan body that my brother had turned me on to. The guy that had the car just didn't want it anymore and I was able to pick it up for a pretty good price.

This was in about 1974, so prices were still low for a piece like it. It wasn't perfect, but it had a decent burgundy paint job and a black interior that featured some pretty cool bucket seats. Even all of the glass was good. All I had to do was install some running gear and new brakes.

I found a used engine at one of the local junkyards that is long gone now. It had good compression and a four-barrel carburetor on it. With a little cleanup and some fresh gaskets, it was just like new. Well, kind of. I was hoping it

would work well enough to have some fun.

I went down to NAPA and got a brand new clutch and throw out bearing to install with a flywheel and bell housing I'd gotten from a neighbor, a serious old car buff. Jack had a Chevy that he had wrecked and parted out. He had already sold most of the parts off it, but still had the exact pieces I needed and it couldn't have worked out better.

"Here," he says, "I never sold it for what I wanted for it and now I guess I have to give it away!" I didn't expect it for free, but he wouldn't have any part of my money. "If you can't give something you like to someone you like, then you probably don't like anything!" he quipped. I laughed at his odd joke with an appreciation of the sentiment behind it. I'd given lots of car parts away over the years, too.

"Thanks, Jack," I replied. "It will be put to good use."

I had a four-speed transmission that was lying in the garage from a car I'd had back in high school and after a quick inspection, I determined that it was in as good of shape as I remembered. I had taken it out of a '56 Chev and it still had the shifter and linkage attached to it. A little cleanup and a shiny new shift ball and I was in business. In the end, it shifted smooth and held up just fine. It was another few bucks I was grateful that I didn't have to spend. This project was turning out to be pretty inexpensive and was fitting into my limited budget pretty well.

After a couple of days of wrench turning, more than a few beers and some harsh language one weekend, the old Chevy came to life and rolled out of the garage just as planned. I was anxious to get it out onto 6th Ave for some fun. It wasn't all that pretty and it wasn't going to be all that fast, but it was a V8 and a 4 speed. It was going to be fun!

Cruising 6th Ave in Tacoma, WA wasn't the same in the mid '70s as it was in the late 60s, but there were still a few of the old guys out there and my beater Chevy attracted some attention right away. It had an exhaust that made it sound way badder than it was and I hadn't made it half way up 6th Ave before a guy in a rattier looking car than mine pulled up beside me and started stabbing his gas pedal. I looked over and smiled, having no clue whether the old Chev would scoot or poop.

I didn't know what gears were in the rear end or how the carburetor was jetted. Those were just two of the elements that would play a role in any attempt to show off. I really had no intention of racing this jammed together toy, but I had gotten in trouble more than once for not being able to control myself under the pressure of competition. Let's just say I wasn't chicken.

So, I stabbed my pedal a couple of times, too. I didn't have a thing to lose, except my driver's license and I had already been there when I was a teenager. There were too many lights for it to be a very long race, anyway.

My challenger, in an old Studebaker Hawk, was anxious. He kept revving the motor in the old low slung, yet to be classic, two door coupe. Paint was nonexistent. The black primer had spots of smeared grease on the fenders and wheel wells. This guy was not into looks. I suspect he was a real life back yard mechanic by the greasy knuckles of the hands firmly gripping the cracked and greasy steering wheel. His hair was greasy and his forehead had smears of grease.

He revved his motor a couple more times while straining his neck to see the light turn yellow for the traffic coming from his right. He was going to get the jump on me at all costs! I revved back.

Vanity plates were not yet available, but if they had been, this guy's plate would probably have said something like GRSBALL. I was hoping to meet a girl or two, dressed in my clean jeans and T-shirt. The Hawk guy's shirt looked as if it was woven from a mixture of cotton and grease.

Again, he revved his engine to demonstrate the deep throaty sound of the old glass pack mufflers as he rocked back and forth in his seat, anxiety about to get the best of him. I was sure he was going to jump the light early. I revved back.

Moments before the light change, I spotted the police car turn onto the avenue a block behind us and pull up behind the Studebaker. Studebaker guy revved his motor again. I was about to split a gut; ready to laugh aloud. I could see what was about to happen. He didn't see the light adorned city issue Ford behind him. I revved back.

As the light changed, the guy in the Studebaker stomped on the gas and slid his foot off the clutch, breaking loose the tires, smoke building up in the wheel wells as he made his escape from the motion-inhibiting red light. As soon as he had gotten through the intersection and was about to forget one red light, another one came on behind him.

I slowly released my clutch and gently pushed the gas pedal, departing from the green light as if I was 80 years old. Studebaker man was just pulling over to the side of the road as I passed by. I turned my head, shrugging my shoulders at him as I rolled past his driver's window. He was not as excited as he had been a moment ago.

I thought I had seen the last of him for a while, yet a little later, as I was telling an old high school buddy the tale of the race that never happened, I saw Studebaker man drive past with the officer a few car lengths behind him. He turned into the bowling alley and the police car continued down the street.

I considered going over to the bowling alley and finding the guy with the intention of offering to buy him a beer. But, in the end, I thought better of it. I guess it was best to leave it be, satisfied with the fact that I came away from the whole thing without a ticket and only a story to tell.

I Wish I Still Had That Car

by Gary M. Hughes

When attending car functions, visiting with fellow enthusiasts is always one of the greatest pleasures of the event. Almost everyone has a story about their favorite teenage ride and each story usually ends with "I wish I still had that car." So, naturally, I have a story about a car I should have kept.

During the summer of 1962 in Butte, Montana, my best friend Jay and I were dating the Christovich twins. Being twins, they were very competitive with each other and any double date proved an action packed delightful experience. Another advantage dating twins is if one of them got mad at either of us, they simply switched us as boyfriends. Jay and I didn't mind, because most of the time we couldn't tell which one we were sitting next to anyway. The problem was Jay was driving a '33 Chevrolet Coupe and my ride was a '39 Studebaker pickup. Neither vehicle was acceptable for double dating, especially for two first class ladies like the Christovich twins. Occasionally, my mom would loan me her '47 Buick Roadmaster. Rarely, was I allowed to use my dad's '61 Chevy Bubble Top.

One day, Jay and I were working at the Conoco station and a man came in with a '47 Chrysler that was stuck in second gear. He said he was on his way to Knieval Imports to trade it in on an Austin Healey and was late for his appointment. While we were trying to figure out what was wrong with the transmission, the man continued his journey on foot and left the car with us. The Chrysler had a straight eight motor and fluid drive transmission. A large screwdriver used as a crow bar was all we needed to free the linkage and we got the fluid drive shifter sort of working.

Two hours later the man drove in with his brand new Austin Healey 3000. What a sweet ride! He said they wouldn't have given him much for the Chrysler on trade anyway and he was looking to sell it. We asked him how much he wanted and he replied, "How much you got?" Since we had just cashed our paychecks we were temporarily wealthy and offered him thirty-five dollars. To our amazement, he accepted our offer and signed the title over. Wow! Jay and I now had our double date mobile.

The Chrysler proved itself not very dependable and almost every double date required work under the hood at one time or another. Among other things, the shift linkage just kept jamming up. The girls weren't too impressed, especially when our hands got greasy and everyone could tell where we were touching them. That was especially problematic when Judy wore her favorite white shorts.

Very soon, good fortune came my way when my mother got a good deal on a '53 Lincoln Capri and I became the proud owner of a hand me down '47 Buick Roadmaster. The Chrysler no longer had a purpose in my life and so, it had to go.

Watching a hot rod movie at the drive in with the Jay and the Christovich twins in my Buick, there was a scene where a car flew off a cliff, exploded halfway down, and landed at the bottom in a ball of fire. The four of us decided it would be great fun to recreate that scene with the Chrysler. On the road up to Marvin Gardens Theme Park, there were plenty of cliffs and private places where we could have our fun.

We took the Chrysler up to one of these areas and poured kerosene all over the car. We then lit it on fire and pushed it off the cliff. To our disappointment, it did not fly off the cliff. In fact, it got high centered and we had to help it a little to get it to go. It did not blow up half way down, or at all, but just kind of landed with a crunch and we watched it slowly burn up. It wasn't fun at all and it's too bad we were so short sighted.

In 1947, Chrysler produced 2,651 Town and Country convertible models. It is one of the rarest and most desirable collector cars today. They routinely sell at auction anywhere from one to two hundred thousand dollars.

Man, I wish I still had that car!

Nicknames and Car Games

by Bob "Fudd" Elms

I was known as "Fudd" from about age 13. It came from my last name, Elms. A guy from our neighborhood had a knack for giving out nicknames for everybody and mine was no exception. His name was Al Turner and we started calling him "Harv" because his middle name was Harvey. At first the neighborhood gang called me Elmer Fudd, the cartoon character. I didn't care for that much and had no qualms about letting my young peers know, so over time, I morphed it into "Fudd," and to this day it remains my nickname. Many in Tacoma, WA don't know me by any other name other than just "Fudd."

In the spring of 1967, at the urging of a friend I bought a 1953 Chevy Tudor post with a screaming 283 with three speed tranny and Hurst synchro-lock shifter. After about three weeks, my Mother forced me to sell it because it was too fast and too loud. I can't fault her. It was too fast and it was awfully loud. It could have quieted the exhaust, but I couldn't keep my foot out of it.

The consolation prize was that she and my dad co-signed a loan so I could buy a '59 Impala. It was all original, including the stock 283 V8 with much less power than the '53 hot rod, and it had a factory three speed "three on the tree" with overdrive. While many of the cars of the day were jacked up and had straight axles, my '59 was laying on the deck. The factory color was called Gothic Gold but, to me it looked like coral and so I quietly called her "Coral." I mean, just like me, she had to have a nickname, right? She had an off-white top and trunk lid with a distinctive, narrow white trim panel down the side. These were the days when Detroit was putting out custom designed cars that changed each year and in my mind, "Coral" was already a classic.

Soon after I bought "Coral," I realized that her motor was pretty tired. So, I did what a lot of young car guys did back in those years and had been doing for years before that. I rebuilt the motor in my driveway. That's back when you could rebuild a small block Chevy for $150-200 bucks.

We loved cruising around Point Defiance Park and Sixth Avenue (simply known as 6th Ave.) between Frisco Freeze and the Tacoma Narrows Bridge, which crosses  over Puget Sound. Frisco Freeze was the ultimate hang out for young cruisers and remains the topic of fun times in the stories of many old car guys still. As we cruised down 6th Ave we would drive right by the Auto View Drive-In Theater (commonly known as the "finger bowl), where you could see what was playing for a few brief moments.

Like many "gut" in America, 6th Ave was no different; a several mile stretch of small businesses, running east to west with plenty of pizza joints and burger stands. My girlfriend, Deanna, worked at the Goofy Goose, a hamburger joint on 6th Ave. We were high school sweethearts at Wilson High School and then married in 1971 and had two kids. We divorced in 1974.

On Friday night, November 3rd 1967, I had just taken Deanna home after a typical night of cruising 6th Ave. This became a night that I will always remember.

It was 11:30 pm and I decided to drive 6th Ave one more time before heading home myself. I pulled onto the Ave westbound and a buddy, Bob Grennon, pulled up alongside. We shot the breeze while driving along chiding each other to a race. Bob owned his car jointly with another guy named Al. Their car was also a '59 Chevy, although it was a blue two-door post sedan. We never raced, but I think I would have beaten him if we had.

The light had just turned green and together we "racked off the pipes" as we accelerated away together. As we cruised on, I didn't notice the two motorcycle cops sitting at their usual perch next door to Busch's Drive-In restaurant, another popular hangout back in those days. For whatever reason, Bob had somehow disappeared. Maybe he had spotted the cops and bailed on me. I continued up the Ave and as I passed K-Mart, Officer R. Otis was hot on my tail. He was the nemesis of every young guy with a car. He lived and loved to be hated.

Within seconds, there were lights and sirens behind me, causing me that sickening feeling that you get when you know you're the object of too much attention by the long arm of the law. In a panic, I immediately pulled over and stopped at Bucks A&W Drive-In at the curb… in the right turn only lane.

"Young man, do you know what you did?" Otis snapped.

"No sir, I don't." I replied.

"Well as long as you kids are going to continue racking off your pipes, we'll just keep writing tickets. Wallet please." he ordered.

As he ran a check on me, I could feel the back bumper drop what seemed to be about a foot with the weight of his motorcycle boot as he used his knee for a writing desk. I was, of course, scared and embarrassed as everyone in the drive-in was getting a free laugh at my expense. Because I had received a ticket a few months prior, I was worried to death that another ticket meant traffic school for sure.

Dressed in his leathers, Officer Otis seemed to be about 10 feet tall. He gave me back my wallet and firmly stated he was busting me for defective equipment. I replied, with a wimpish "Yes sir." I told him of my prior ticket, which he already knew about, and asked if I would have to go to traffic court as well as traffic school.

"Yes son, I'm afraid so." was his stoic reply.

I knew my folks would be mad as hell. I next asked Officer Otis if I would have to go through court and the boring school if I were eighteen years old.

"NO." he retorted. So, I asked him what time it was. He looked a bit puzzled and said "Well son, it's four minutes after midnight."

"Well then Officer Otis, that means it's November 4th correct?"

"Yes son, that's correct."

"Well sir, as you can see from looking at my license, that would make me eighteen years and four minutes old and therefore I would just need to pay the ticket, right?"

He asked for the ticket back and scrawled a corrected date on it and as he handed it back to me with a wink in his eye, he said "Happy birthday kid. Now get your butt home." I realized at that moment that he was a decent guy after all.

Sadly, my days with "Coral" were short lived. In the spring of 1968, I was forced to sell her as I had a car payment and an insurance payment due at the same time and not enough money to pay them both. My folks had co-signed the loan and they weren't going to let me put a dent in their credit or drive without insurance, so "Coral" had to go.

Of course, there are always more cars in the life of a true lover of old iron. Aside from "Coral," one of my very favorites was a '30 Model A Ford pick-up that my Dad had bought in 1954. He painted it for me in our dusty alley and little by little, it became my everyday driver. I eventually converted it to a full street rod and won many car show trophies with it.

These days, I've slowed down a bit and my interests have gone to creating smaller vehicles. I build motorized bars stools that only go about 25 miles per hour.

Who's the Boss?

by Tom Glide

It was just another nice summer day in the sleepy little town I lived in. My friend Bob and I were at the local tavern having a burger and a beer for lunch, when an older man dressed in farm clothes walked up to us and asked "Are either of you Bob Dawson?"

That depends on why you're askin'." Bob said, motioning him to sit next to us at the bar.

He slid up on a stool next to Bob, ordered a draft beer, and said, "They tell me you like old Mustangs."

That was quite an understatement. Both of us had an eye for old cars, but Mustangs were Bob's first love. He had owned a whole corral of nice Mustangs over the years and currently owned a beautiful burgundy '69 Mach I, which was sitting out in the parking lot.

"That I do… Why?" Bob asked.

"I have one I want to get rid of, if you're interested." He had our attention.

"I might be. Is it a fastback or convertible?" Bob asked. He never cared for the coupe versions.

The old guy took a sip of his beer. "Yeah, it's a fastback… I think; some special model, too. I don't know that much about it. My son had it and told me it was okay to sell it. I just want it gone."

Now he had our undivided attention. We got directions to where it was and told the guy we'd come look at it when we finished our lunch. Oddly enough, the car was behind a barn just a few miles out of town and right under our noses for years. Why hadn't we heard of it or seen it before?

After he left, we started to wonder about what "special model" it could be. And, was it really a fastback? The guy did say he "thought" it was.

"How much ya wanna bet it's a rusted out six cylinder coupe that someone tacked some ugly tape stripes on?" Bob asked me. I nodded in agreement. Both of us enjoyed buying old cars and flipping them. However, if either of us had a nickel for every time someone called a pile of crap "special" just to try and get a ton of money for it, we'd be doing well. But, as promised, we drove out to see it.

We were both pleasantly surprised to see that it not only was a fastback, but a '70 Boss 302! We both stood there, slack jawed, looking at it. It looked very straight and solid and still wore the original orange paint and black day glow stripes. It had Magnum 500's all the way around, and what looked to be the original, albeit bald and dry rotted, Goodyear Polyglas tires. The telltale front, sitting high with an open hole in the hood where the shaker scoop once resided, suggested the engine was gone. It still was a very desirable car. Upon further inspection, we noticed it had a perfect black interior and the shaker scoop was in the back seat.

The top loader four-speed was found in the trunk, complete with a Hurst shifter. Closer inspection of the body revealed it was relatively rust and dent free and 100% complete. It had never been butchered in any way and all of the hard to find parts like original style battery cables, hose clamps, etc. that normally are long gone were still there. Even the smog pump was in the trunk.

"This thing is worth a fortune." I told Bob. He agreed. We didn't know what the price was, but we began to think it was something we'd have to pool our money together to buy. Just then, the old guy came around the barn and joined us.

"I see ya found it," he told us. "Look like something you'd be interested in?"

"I'm definitely interested." Bob told him as he walked around the car.

"Then make me an offer."

"I can't be both the buyer and seller." Bob replied.

"Tell me what you'd like to get for it… and keep in mind, the engine is gone, which is a big part of what makes this car special."

"No, it's not. The engine is in my machine shed. My son was gonna soup it up." he said.

We couldn't believe it! He took us to the shed and showed us the complete, but dusty, engine sitting on a crusty old engine stand. We wondered if we were going to have to find a third investor.

"Well, it's definitely all there." Bob said. "So, how much are you asking?"

The old guy took off his dirty John Deere cap and rubbed his balding head. "I dunno… $300 sound fair?"

I almost fell down. He had asked Bob about buying it, so I had to let him have first dibs, but I had the words "I'll take it" firmly pressed against the inside of my lips, just in case Bob would pass on the deal; like that was going to happen!

"Would you take $250?" Bob asked. I wondered if he'd lost his mind. The louvers on the back window were worth the asking price.

"Yeah, I'd probably take that." the guy responded. "But, I ain't storin' this damn thing for God knows how long! If you buy it, I want it out of here ASAP."

We only touched the high spots on the road getting

back to Bobs home to borrow his dad's truck and trailer to retrieve it. The car was the deal of a lifetime, but sadly, neither of us got the chance to see it completed. Shortly into the project, Bob was involved in a car accident that left him paralyzed from the waist down. In order for him to drive it, it would have to be converted to an automatic transmission, which he couldn't bear to do, but he really didn't want to sell it either.

I kept on him for years to give me a price to buy it, and eventually he told me I could have it if I found him a side-car for his beloved Harley.

Before I could locate one, a car collector came along and gave him $9500 for it, which was very good money for what was then little more than a twelve year old Mustang with special options.

I wonder what it would be worth now.

Dune Buggy in the Bronx

by Mike Trinagel

In the early spring of 1971, Hone Avenue in the Bronx was as busy as ever and school was winding down for the summer. My fascination with cars and motors started very young and I was about 12 years old when I decided I wanted to make a Dune Buggy. There was a gentleman willing to sell me his Volkswagen Beetle for between $50 and $150, if I recall correctly. Of course, I grabbed it. The Beetle ran great. The body wasn't in very good condition, but the car was perfect for building the Dune Buggy I dreamed of.

I always had to work on the sly, since my family didn't really understand my visions when it came to cars. My messes weren't very popular and it wasn't very easy to hide a VW bug in my father's garage, even though I had it all the way to the side, so his Cadillac always had its space. My father was so proud of his Cadillac! It was sky blue and his first Cadillac since moving to this country. I was so proud to go with him when he bought it! Of course, that didn't change the fact that I was now trying to conceal a Volkswagen in his garage!

I had my excuses ready and I was waiting for the infamous question, "Why is there a Volkswagen Beetle in my garage?" I don't recall verbatim what I told him but I think by this time he had given up on arguing with me about my projects.

At this point, I was getting very good at working with my hands and wrenches and it was time to start taking this Beetle apart so my Dune Buggy could come to life.

I never realized how easy it was to dismantle a Volkswagen Beetle! I unbolted the car from its floor and unhooked the wires, being very careful to remember what I had done with them since I was not experienced with wiring at all. I unbolted the steering column from the steering box, which was secured with only two bolts. The simplicity was so funny to me! I now had the body of the car completely disconnected from its chassis, but I had to wait for my friend, Neal Izzo, may he rest in peace, to get home from school to help me get the body off the car. We physically lifted the body off the chassis from the driver's side, lifting and tilting until it physically came off the drive train.

The body of the car rolled over onto its roof because it was so round and the body was so light. We sat there and watched, laughing hysterically as it spun like a top. It was slow but it was spinning, rocking and spinning… it was a sight to be seen. The only problem was we didn't want to be seen. I only wish I knew what a video camera was back then!

My father used to build cabinets and showcases for stores that he used to renovate and would use wooden dollies to transport them, so we used the biggest dolly we could find and as I pushed the car over a bit my buddy shoved the dolly underneath the roof of the car. We had the body on the dolly and were ready to start our venture to the vacant lot across the street. Mind you, a Volkswagen Beetle body on its roof, balanced on a dolly, was not easy to handle! We shoved things between the body and dolly to try to help get some stability and then we were off!

The cracks in the sidewalk were our biggest hurdle, because we needed momentum to get the body across the street into the lot. We finally got down the driveway to the street and quickly checked for people and cars. Our game plan was to get enough momentum to run the dolly across the street, have the dolly hit the curb, stopping it dead in its tracks while the body of the car kept going and slid off continuing into the lot. Murphy's Law prevailed and we got stuck in one of the crevices on the sidewalk and the body slid off the dolly and into the street.

It was almost time for my father to come home from work, so we needed to hurry. We quickly got the body back on the dolly, checked our surroundings, and made a run for it! The plan worked almost perfectly...the dolly stopped...the car slid off into the lot... but it wasn't far enough in. We had to roll the car from the roof to the base until we got far enough into the lot that it didn't stick out too much. All I knew was if I was ever asked about it... I KNEW NOTHING!

I rushed back to my yard and quickly built up the steering column, put the driver's seat back in, rigged the gas tank and hooked up the vital wires so I could drive the chassis back into the garage. This was high pressure to avoid getting caught. I didn't want anyone to figure out where the body came from. I got into the garage and shut myself in.

I began designing the roll bar I needed and had to figure out how to weld the pieces for the Baja frame. I had in my mind what I want to do, but I had no welding materials and no experience. However, I did know Skee who lived up the block. He worked at the Shell station when he wasn't out driving his tractor-trailer. I didn't know him well, but I admired him. He was a big guy who seemed cool. After all, anyone with a motorcycle was cool to me back then. As if I knew what cool was at age twelve! He came across gruff, but always acknowledged me as I was growing up. I hadn't really spoken to him much in the past, but that was soon to change.

About a week later, I couldn't resist any more. I had to drive the chassis at least. So, I got it out of the garage and drove it up my block. It was too cool to put away! I hit the end of the block, made a right onto Allerton Ave., a four lane street, then went down to Waring Avenue and made another right. Waring Avenue was the block behind my house. I cruised down to Mace Avenue, made another right, and continued to sneak down to Hone Avenue, making the final right turn into the homestretch.

It really wasn't a long drive, but I knew how much trouble I'd be in if I got caught, so it was pretty exciting! As I was making the right onto my block, I noticed a police car coming up Mace from the opposite direction. I wasn't sure where he was going, so I floored it once I got around the corner. Flying past my house, I went all the way up the block and slid into Skee's driveway, jumped out and headed home. I couldn't have the chassis be affiliated with my house.

As I casually started walking back towards my house, I saw the cop cruising up the block. I was about four houses from where I ditched it and the cop was looking everywhere for the elusive chassis he saw on the main road. He noticed me, which wasn't difficult with my big bushy hair. He pulled up slowly, rolled down his window and called out "Hey you!"

I innocently walked over as if nothing was up and innocently responded "Yes?" upon which he proceeded to interrogate me. "Where is it?" I couldn't look him in the eye and I guess turning cherry red didn't help me so he asked again.... "Where is it?" My twelve year old naivety stepped in as I looked at him and said, "Where is what?" I already knew he knew but I had to give it a shot. His stern look let me know that he knew that I knew that he knew.

I asked if I was in big trouble. He tells me if I don't tell him the truth, I may be! I don't say a word, but turn and point up the street to where it was. He says, "Let's go see it." It wasn't very noticeable, since there really wasn't much to it. He followed me over to it and got out of his car. I noticed Skee watching from his upstairs porch. They exchanged nods and the officer continued with me. "Is it yours?" I had to admit that it was and he reminded me that I knew I wasn't allowed to be driving the disassembled POS on the streets.

He seemed to understand as I expressed how I just couldn't resist! I said I knew I shouldn't have done it and apologized and just looked at the ground as he debated with his partner for a bit on what to do. Then, surprisingly, he told me to take it home and said, "Don't ever let me catch you on the street with it again!" He promised that would be the only warning I ever got before he took it away and took me with it. I was speechless that he let me go.

I had to verify that I wasn't in trouble and he was really just sending me home. I couldn't believe I wasn't in trouble. I was shaking so much that my right leg seemed to take on a life of its own. I got home, parked the chassis, and went inside to regroup. I was so thankful I wasn't busted.

When I got back into it and was ready to start building the roll bars, I went to Mike's Pipe Yard; which still exists in the neighborhood to this day. He had everything you could imagine back in the scrap yard of his plumbing shop. I have to assume it was because I was so young and taking on such a large endeavor, but he let me take all the used black threaded pipe and threaded elbows I needed. I rode my bike holding onto a wagon filled with all my pieces of pipe down the road to get started on my roll bar.

This is where Skee came back into the picture. He worked on weekends at the Shell station on the corner of Allerton Avenue and would often do welding. I went to him, explained what I was doing, and asked how much a job like this would cost to have done. I had only designed the roll bars and had no way to connect everything and attach it to the chassis. He listened carefully then told me to bring everything to him. Of course, I did exactly that. I still didn't know what it was going to cost but, he told me not to worry about it so I didn't.

When he was ready, I took the chassis up to him, sneaking across so I would avoid being seen by any police. I had a group of friend's keeping an eye out on every corner between my house and the Shell station to make sure I didn't get caught again. I told him my vision and he just took it all in. He told me to check back the next day. I made my way home and waited to hear something. I anxiously ran over the next day as soon as I was able. I walked in and was in awe. Everything I envisioned was done!

Because of my age, Skee was very impressed with my plans and expressed how surprised he was at the general layout and that I was able to figure out where the crossbars needed to be. I was so proud that I impressed this big tough guy! I had some big 15" snow tires that I took from my father's garage that Skee put on the rear rims for  me; and the skinny little VW tires stayed on the front. I was also able to bolt the wheels on backwards so they looked like deep-dish rims, which gave the buggy even more width. I bought a Volkswagen tow bar from the JC Whitney catalog, so now I not only had my dune buggy, but a way to tow it and was on my way to creating some new and exciting personal adventures. Once again, my friends regrouped and kept lookout so I could get the dune buggy back home.

It was almost summer and my father, who would not get me a mini bike at twelve years old, was willing to tow this buggy upstate to the Catskills where my family had always gone to the bungalow colonies every year since before I was born. This bungalow colony was adjacent to a ski resort that was closed during the summer and I had an amazing time, cutting my way through the woods to get over to the hotel parking lots and the mountains.

As soon as I would wake up, I was out the door to the ski chalet to ride my dune buggy and find those new and exciting adventures. This was the most incredible summer of my young life! It was a thrill, discovering the trails and mountains, roads, woods, and sandy areas. Everywhere I could get that buggy to go… I went!

It is so incredible to think back on how much trust and respect my father had developed for me. At twelve years old, I could not have asked for more than to be able to express my thoughts and convert them into actual realities. Uncle Chaim, may he rest in peace, was still my biggest fan with his hugs and kisses and that bite on the cheek that I hated so much!

The dune buggy never made it back to the Bronx at the end of summer, but a seed that was planted then has grown and I continue to create at an aggressive non-stop rate to this day.

I Didn't Mean To

by David Dickinson

When I was in high school, I usually had a job. Some jobs I liked and some I didn't care for, but I was always looking for a better job. One of the best jobs, at least in the area of things that truly interested me, lasted the least amount of time.

That short-lived position found me as a lot attendant on a used car lot. But, this was in about 1968 and all of the used cars were destined to become classics. I loved being around cars then as much as today. There were Corvettes, Impalas and Corvairs, Thunderbirds and Mustangs, Ambassadors, GTOs and Bonnevilles; many of the cars that are considered orphans today, the manufacturers having gone out of business.

Having to meet the needs of a cross section of buyers, the mix of vehicles included muscle cars, family cars, sports cars, and the occasional pickup. Most were in great condition and had low miles. I was in, what would be considered today, old car heaven. I loved washing the not yet classic cars, making sure they were standing tall and ready for new owners.

Once finished, I would pause on the front porch of the office and admire my work, looking down over the long narrow lot that ran out to the post and chain barrier that separated the inventory from South Tacoma Way. South Tacoma Way was Tacoma, Washington's "Auto Row" back then and still is pretty much today, although it is hard to consider today's late model cars as possible classics, where-as the cars back then were already timeless in my mind.

However, it wasn't really my domain to survey, being just the "wash boy." It was Dave Grassi's domain and there was never any doubt left to the imagination. When I was there, I was paid to do as I was told. On one particular occasion, doing exactly what I was told cost me my job.

Dave was not only a used car salesman; he was a drag racer, as well. Dave Grassi had become a household name

locally, had an exquisite looking dragster with a really elaborate paint job and was a competitor at the Puyallup drags on most weekends. His car was much nicer before I got next to it.

I was not raised in a garage and some of the products and tools and their uses that many took as common knowledge was not in my knowledge base. Solvent, at that time, was not something I had ever used. As a result, it turned out to be a mistake for Dave to send me up to the shop to degrease the painted panels of his dragster with solvent. Yes, you can see this coming, can't you? Well, it happened just like you are probably envisioning it.

"Hey, Dickinson!" Dave called from high atop his perch one Friday afternoon. Always wanting to please, I ran up and made myself ready to do his bidding. "Go up to the shop and clean the panels of the dragster." Well, that should have been child's play, right?

"What should I use?" I replied.

"Just wipe down the painted panels with solvent. It's

in the silver can under the bench up there," he instructed.

Those were simple enough instructions and off I went, eager to do a good job. The lot rose from the street to the shop at a pretty good angle and it was a bit of a hike to get up there. Upon entering the shop, I paused to catch my breath and stood still, in awe of the fire breathing mechanical beast before me. I went to the drags almost weekly, knew just what this thing would do, and was truly impressed with the guys that would strap themselves into such a powerful pavement pounding missile.

I headed over to the bench, where I found a rag and the silver can under the bench. The panels were removable and had been laid out flat on a table next to the car. Not thinking a thing of it or suspecting that what I was about to do would be so wrong, I tipped the can and poured a small amount of its contents onto one of the panels. The liquid that poured slowly from the can onto the custom painted panel wasn't solvent.

Much to my chagrin, the grease was not the only thing that was going to come off. The paint began bubbling and curdling, literally lifting off the panel. It had happened so quickly that there wasn't anything I could do. I was sunk. Telling Dave was not going to be pretty and I was mortified.

I dropped the rag on the floor where I stood and turned, not sure whether to run and never return or go face the barrage of emotions that I knew would be displayed by the proud owner of a once meticulously painted car. I chose the latter, knowing that there was no way to avoid the truth of what happened.

When I went into the office, the boss was on the phone, laughing and sharing a story with one of his buddies. I sure hated the prospect of ruining his mood. However, once he hung up the phone, there was no turning back, and looking at me quizzically, he asked "You done already?"

Well, quite certain that I was, in fact, "done," I had to spit out the truth. "You'd better come up and take a look," I said. I wasn't sure I wanted to be around when he saw my handy work, but I wasn't going to be a coward. It was a longer walk back up to the shop than it was before. Each step seemed to be drawn out and moment by moment, as I drew closer, I was certain of my fate.

Once he walked through the door of the shop and saw the obliterated panel, its paint lifted and wrinkled like a rotting orange, he stood motionless, not uttering a word. The anger was mounting on his face, however, and the redder it got, the more uneasy I became. "I'm sorry," I muttered.

"Sorry? Sorry?!! Do you know how much this paint job cost? Do you realize that this whole panel is destroyed and there's not time to repaint it before tomorrow? Sorry?" He calmed himself for a moment and simply said, "Let's go back down to the office. I can't look at this right now."

I quietly followed him back down the hill, the walk longer than I thought possible, keeping several paces behind him in case he turned and took a swing at me. Of course, he didn't and wouldn't do that, but I kept my distance, just the same.

In the office, he sat down in his big chair behind the neat and orderly desk where he spent so much time on the phone and doing paperwork. He was quiet. I dared not say a thing and just waited for him to break the silence, convinced that he didn't want to hear my proclamations of regret or misgivings.

"This really isn't your fault" he surprised me by saying. "You did exactly what I told you, but I'm madder than hell and I don't even want to look at you. I'm afraid I have to let you go. Come by tomorrow and I'll have a check for you, but I need you to leave right now."

It was an unfortunate event for him and his car, of course, but I was going to miss being around all of the cool old cars. I would miss watching the customers as they wandered around, closely inspecting each possible purchase and finally settling on just the right one.

Over the years, I have continued to appreciate those old cars and the older they get, the more that appreciation has grown. The mental image of those someday classics, in their youth so to speak, in such pristine condition has caused me to treasure those cars today that are original and unmolested survivors all the more.

That short experience on the small used car lot on South Tacoma Way cemented my belief that cars are at the center of many people's worlds. Those cars I was so enamored with back then are the same cars that I value and that constantly grab my attention to this day.

I don't know what became of Dave Grassi, but if you're reading this, Dave, let me say just one more time… "I'm really sorry! I didn't mean to!"

NOTE: In preparing this story for the book, I tracked down Mr. Grassi and he was as gracious as a person could be. We laughed together as he related to me that he had told the story to a couple of friends just a week before I called. It's a small world and reconnecting with Dave Grassi is a great example of how the old cars and the stories that go with them bind us all together.

Messin' With Leroy

by Paul Kelly

When I was 18 years old, in El Cajon, California, my best friend was a guy named Leroy. Leroy was black but I never thought a thing of it. He was just my best friend and I was colorblind.

One day we went out in my 500 horsepower Mustang and I got a wild hair up my "you know where" and so, I whistled at a California Highway Patrol car and I lit the tires up so I could get him to chase me. My buddy, Leroy, looked over at me as if I was crazy and said, "Paul, this is NOT a good position for a young black man to be in!" I didn't really get it until that moment that things weren't really kosher for guys like him back in the early '70s.

The whole thing started about two weeks before that. A group of us was all sitting in the parking lot at the super-market with our hot rods. We could see across the parking lot into the Laundromat and watched two guys run in and grab a woman's purse from her. When these guys came running out, I got in my car and chased them across the parking lot. I got out of my car and left it there, chasing down the one with the purse. I got in a fight with him and wound up dragging him back along with the lady's purse. So, when I got back to my car the police were there and they thought my car was "the getaway car!" That notion got straightened out once they realized what had happened.

So, this was where I met Officer Reece. He thanked me for doing my civic duty while the crook complains to him that I hit his head on the bumper of a car when we were fighting. Officer Reece told him to shut and proceeded to throw him into the back of the car. He took the crook away and the lady came over and got her purse. Everything was cool.

Two weeks later, I did this thing with the Highway Patrol were I was burning my tires to get them to chase me with Leroy in the car. Well, they got me pulled over, but by the time they did, the Highway Patrol was out of their jurisdiction. So, having restrained us in case we tried to escape, they wait for the city police to show up.

Well, who showed up but Officer Reece! He took the Highway Patrol handcuffs off both of us and gave them back so the CHP could leave. Reece came over to me and said "Kelly, I don't owe you a damned thing. Get out of here!"

Leroy was scared to death. He's a young black guy in the early '70s and has a very strict Christian mother, who I called Mom. He told me quite emphatically, "Mom can NEVER know that we did this!"

Move forward about 22 years. We're at Leroy's 40th birthday bash and we're roasting Leroy. I get up there and decide it's time to let the cat out of the bag. I said, "Mom, there's something I've kept from you for over 20 years and I've got to tell you." Leroy looks over at me, wide eyed, and says "P.K., don't go there!" I ignored him and laughed out loud, 'cause I'm in this room full of black people and I go on to explain that night long ago and how I'm running from the police with Leroy in the car and how he explained what a bad situation it was for a young black man to be in. The whole room was full of people about fall out of their chairs, cracking up. So, I go on to tell Mom about that and some of the other things we did as teens. She was crying, she was laughing so hard. So, it was a twenty-two yearlong secret that finally came out.

Shaker Do II vs. The Big Dog

by Tom Glide

It was Detroit, The Motor City, 1967 and I had already developed a love of fast, noisy, and visually striking cars. A '57 Chevy that belonged to a friend of my big brother still fills my mind's eye as if it was yesterday. Imagine the Fonz or Vinnie Barbarino in a badass street machine… cool is cool.

I couldn't tell you what it had for an engine, but my little eight year old ears could hear it coming from three blocks away. When it was outside our home, it rattled our windows. A two-door 150 sedan, painted a sinister looking dark green, it had big cheater slicks on black steel rims out back and skinny tires on mags up front. The front sat up a bit and white painted headers poked out of the fender wells behind the front tires. It had a roll bar, two bucket seats, and a Hurst white ball shifter. I vividly remember the cartoon version, painted on the trunk lid, depicting it doing a wheelie and smoking the tires with a Rat Fink behind the wheel. The words "Shaker Do" were emblazoned above it. This car was all business; a badass street machine that won a lot of trophies in the gas classes at both Detroit and Motor City Dragways.

The look and sounds of that car haunted me for years, so when I found an incredible deal on a two-door '57 Bel Air in 1983, there was no doubt in my mind what I wanted to do with it. It was also an old drag car at one time; mothballed when the engine and rear axle simultaneously blew. I painted it dark green metallic and went to work on the broken drivetrain.

I hand built a destroked 327c.i. V8 with 12.5:1 compression, a full roller cam valve train, and many more carefully  chosen parts that all worked in perfect unison. The M-22 close ratio Muncie "Rock Crusher" transmission that came with the car was now set up as a crash box, having the synchros removed for speed in shifting during racing. Power transferred to the rear wheels through a beefed up '57 Olds rear axle with 4:11 gears.

Small, subtle lettering on the corner of the trunk lid read "Shaker Do II." It sounded, ran, and even looked a lot like its namesake.

It was, weather permitting, my daily driver for years and while it saw a lot of street racing, once in a while I'd take it to the local drag strip in Ubly, Michigan. The old gas classes that the original "Shaker Do" used to run in were long gone, so I had to settle for bracket racing.

On one such occasion, the prize was $5000 to win, which was hard to resist for a lot of people. On most weekends, the track saw the usual local racers, along with a few that would venture up from Detroit now and then. With that kind of money at stake, the place was packed.

The money was attractive, but I was also there to test out a warmed over Holley carb a friend was trying to sell me. He used to run it on a similar '56 Chevy years ago, and the timers were proving it to be good for a couple of tenths of a second faster. Life was good. My car was running better than it ever had and I had the opportunity (albeit slim) to win a pile of money.

As I looked around, I noticed everyone's attention was focused on a custom painted and chromed out Chevy dually towing a matching three axle enclosed trailer as it rolled through the gates. A crowd formed around it when the crew of five, in matching uniforms, rolled a brand new, state of the art IHRA legal Pro Stock Camaro out of the trailer. The owner/driver quickly began to show the crowd how big of an ass wipe he was, bragging up himself and his car. There was even a complete spare "Mountain Motor," transmission, tires and other expensive parts in the front compartment of the trailer. He already knew that the $5,000 prize money was his. Racing for it was just a formality.

He made a few time trial runs, shutting it off at the 1000-foot mark, before writing a dial in on his window that was FAR below what his car should run. It was the oldest trick in the book. Catch 'em fast, then let off just enough to stay ahead and stomp the brakes at the end to prevent a breakout.

None of us played that game. We raced for fun. We all ran the best we could and the best car won. Often that came with help from the guy (or parts from his car) that you just beat in the last round. But, the big money had brought out the big dogs and their big bags of fancy tricks. Were this guy and his car really that good to succeed at brake light racing?

When it came time to race, I learned that I had drawn him as my opponent in the first round. Lucky me!

After writing an 11.65 dial in on my window, which was about the best my car had run, I told myself to tune "Chuckles" out, focus on the tree, stage deep and try for the best reaction time I could. I simply had to race the track and myself. "Pay no attention to the man behind the curtain!" I thought to myself.

Still, his ridiculous 10:16 dial in, for a car capable of at least 9:90, was pretty intimidating. I would only have roughly a second and a half head start. Plus, I'd be going through the lights doing almost 120 mph with this jackass standing on his brake pedal right next to me. Anything could happen.

When the second yellow went out, I sidestepped the clutch, the green lit up, and the electronic board at the finish line posted a .012 reaction time. Friends later told me that I lifted the front wheels three inches off the ground. The car was pulling like a freight train, but when I yanked the shifter to second, the engine died instantly. The front came down with a thump and I rolled along in total silence other than the sound of the electric fuel pump running.

Then, I heard what sounded like a Top Fueler taking off in the left lane and noticed his reaction time was .002! I was sickened to see that cat puke yellow Camaro blow past me as if I was backing up. He kicked it neutral, and then shut it off. He was going to show me how good he was by coasting to a win. I mentally pictured him back in the pits, gloating on about how easy it was to kick my ass.

Then, a funny thing happened.

I realized that I had instinctively pushed the clutch in when the engine died. It stopped so fast I kind of wondered if it blew up. Or did it just stall out? Either way, I thought my day was over, but I didn't see my crankshaft laying on the tarmac in the rear view mirror. The M-22 was still in second, so I let the clutch back out to see if my car would start. Hopefully, I could at least drive it off the track under its own power.

It fired right up and seemed to be running fine!

I shoved the gas to the floor and took off. When the

tach hit the 7500 redline, I cranked it into third. As I caught up to the Camaro, the driver was fiddling with the ignition switch and start button with one hand, while frantically trying to get his finicky Lenco transmission back in gear with the other.

I passed him just as the tach reached the redline again and I grabbed fourth. My foot was on the floor. That's all there is and there ain't no more. I held on and hoped as I heard his car roar to life.

The howl of his engine approaching sounded like it was going to suck up my car and spit it out this time. He passed me again just as I streaked through the lights with a miserable 13:57. The finish was so close I couldn't tell who crossed the line first. Then, the timing lights on his side lit up. He had run a time of 10:14.

He didn't have time to brake light race me, because he had to stay on it the whole way to catch me. As a result, he broke out of his bracket by two tenths of a second. The win light came on in my lane and that's bracket racing for you!

Unfortunately, I didn't go on to win the event, but I did become the hero of the day for taking out the stoutest car there in the first round. Everyone enjoyed watching the Camaro owner and crew silently load everything back up and leave before the second round started. I was happy to see a local racer eventually take home the prize money to his wife and kids. He even bought me a beer after the races.

Through trial and error, we found that the new carb made my car leave so hard, anything less than ¾ of a tank would slosh away from the fuel pickup in the front of the tank and starve the engine. Once we moved the fuel pick-up to the back of the tank, the problem went away.

A couple of years later I met a girl and started a family. As the old story goes, the toys were the first thing to go, including my beloved Chevy, but I have no regrets. The engine was sold to a local racer, who continued to pound on it for years. It just wouldn't die! The body went to a friend's son who was going to bring it back to its former glory, but he moved to Kalamazoo, got married, and sold it before he got the chance to do anything with it. I often wonder if anyone ever got it running again and had as much fun as I did. I sure hope so!

I do know that, in the event I fall into a large sum of money, one of the first things I will do is find another '57 body and start Shaker Do III. Maybe I'll start my search in Kalamazoo!

Go Karting in the Fast Lane

by Jack "Captain Jack" McClure

I've been racing most of my life and it all started because of a guy I knew in Mooresville, North Carolina that sold moonshine. He was one of those good old boy bootleggers that sold some of the best moonshine that money could buy. The funny thing was that he lived less than a block from the police department. One day, he asked me if I would start running moonshine for him. The guy that made the stuff lived about 20 miles out in the country. I would drive out to his place, park, and go inside while he loaded the car; not much (about 3 or 4 gallons in pint and quart Mason fruit jars). I would drive back to his place, park the car in his garage, and he would unload it. I got into a few police chases in those days, but I never did get caught. I would out run them every time they came after me. I was real good at it and I loved to go fast. Still do!

You know, they still make moonshine down south and it's still a thriving business. I never did touch the stuff, but those hillbillies would treat me really good every time I delivered a new batch of moonshine. They would always ask me if I was hungry and if I said I was, they would go out and kill a chicken just so I would get a fresh home cooked meal. "Them's my kind of people."

At the time, there were a lot of guys that ran moonshine for a living that turned into racecar drivers. When I moved to Columbia, South Carolina, I started racing my 1939 Ford in what NASCAR called the Modified Sportsman Division. William Tuthill, Bill France's partner and Secretary of NASCAR, signed my license. I raced with some of the biggest names in Stock Car Racing, like Ralph Earnhart, Gale Yarborough, David Pearson, and Lee Petty. I remember a young Dale Earnhart hanging around with all of us drivers at the track when he was just a little boy. NASCAR was a big part of my life from 1953 to 1958, but every year racing kept on getting more expensive and I eventually walked away from it.

In 1959, I started racing Go Karts with West Bend motors on them and won four Championships. Once my name got out there as a leader in the sport, I opened up a store called Jack McClure Racing Products where we sold Go Karts and other racing equipment.

I decided to put two West Bend racing motors on my Go Kart and took it out to the Orangeburg Drag Strip. That thing would go 100mph in the Quarter mile and the promoter said he would give me twenty-five bucks and a trophy if I would race a Super Stock, and if I beat the Super Stock, he would give me a hundred dollars. That was the first time I was paid to race another vehicle. Later on, I built a Kart with four West Bend engines that was really fast and would easily go 125 mph in the quarter mile.

I was a little crazy back then. After I made the quarter mile run, I would go down the return road at 80 to a 100 mph; and then, to entertain the crowd, I would do a 360-degree spin and keep on going. The crowd would go nuts!

If four engines was good, I thought I'd add some more. I decided to put six West Bend engines on my Kart, thinking it would gain another 10 or 15 mph. But, the thing was so darn heavy that it wouldn't go much faster than with four engines. It just handled terrible, so I went back to running the four engine Kart.

On the side of my trailer, I had a sign that said "Fastest Damn Kart in town!" That slogan got a lot of attention and one day a guy came up to me and said, "What town are you talking about?" I re-plied, "What town is this?"

One time, I was racing in Danville, Virginia, at the Danville Enduro Regional race. It was an International Kart Federation sponsored event, but the Civil Air Patrol had control of the raceway. Pete Berlt from Huntington, West Virginia, and his father were on my pit crew. Pete said, "I'll give you the seconds you are ahead or behind on the blackboard as you past the pits." After we lined up for the start and got the green flag, I took the lead on the first corner. The first time past the pits, I knew I was in the lead. On the second lap' Pete flashed the sign "10 seconds," the fourth "29 seconds," and so on until I had built up a lead of 148 seconds. Then, I ran over a spark plug on the track and blew a tire.

After making one lap on a flat tire, I came into the pits. Pete was standing in front, signaling me where to stop, and Garner was getting ready to change the tire while Pete re-fueled the Kart. As Garner got ready to make the switch, he discovered that the wheel was stuck on the axle. It took him 108 seconds to knock it off and put another one on. I was losing ground. While Garner was changing the wheel, he inhaled so much of the alcohol and oil fumes from the exhaust that he passed out before he could get the axle nut tight. I thought that when he quit he was done, so off I roared with the nut still loose. I guess my lucky stars were shining, because the wheel stayed on and I won the race by a lap and a half.

One day, I was reading a magazine and saw an advertisement for a company called Turbonique that sold rocket  and turbine engines. I sent for an 8 mm film showing various applications of the rocket motors and it really sparked my interest, so I called Gene Middlebrooks, the owner of Turbonique. I told him I had the fastest Go Kart around, but I wanted to go faster. Gene said if I put a rocket on my Kart, it would go faster. He also said that I would be the very first person to put one of his rocket engines on a Go Kart. So, in March of 1963, I took my Dart Grand Prix Kart down to Orlando, Florida. Gene installed a T-16 Rocket motor with 300 lbs. of thrust. It took him about three days to finish it.

I immediately took the Kart to a racetrack up in Georgia. It hadn't been tested, so this was a new experience for both me and the Kart. There was a dimmer switch on the floor to start the rocket engine, and I didn't know what to expect when I pressed that foot switch for the first time. There was a lot of fire and noise, but the Kart would only do about a 100 mph during the first run, so the track promoter wasn't too happy. He said, "I hired you to go 125 mph!" He wasn't going to pay me, so I took my four-engine, West Bend powered, Go Kart out of the trailer and ran 125mph. The crowd went nuts and the track promoter decided to pay me.

I needed the Rocket Go Kart to go faster if I wanted to make money with it, so that following February I went down to Florida to meet Gene again. He said I should try two Rocket Engines. We added another T-16 Rocket Engine to the Kart and took it out to an old metal shack behind Gene's place that had equipment set up to measure the thrust and fuel flow. When we first test fired it, Gene told me to go stand outside with a fire extinguisher in case there was a fire. As I was standing out there, I noticed there was a concrete and brick wall in front of the steel building and I started to wonder how safe these rockets were if you had to stand behind a brick wall.

This was the first time that two Turbonique T-16 engines were fired at the same time and there was a small fire after the engines shut down. I went back into the metal shack, looking for Gene. He wasn't there, so I went outside and found him behind a railroad car. I asked him "Why are you hiding behind the railroad car?" A little shaken, he replied, "Because I have a wife and two kids!"

I enjoyed many years of racing and defying the odds and eventually got a Kart to go over 225 mph in the quarter mile. I gave it up years ago to go charter fishing, but now, at 88 years old, I am back to racing my Kart again with the help of my good friend Ky Michaelson and others.

I have decided, however, to keep my speed down to 200 mph in the quarter mile. I'm still fearless, but it scares everyone around me if I go too fast!

My First Ride in a Hot Rod

by Jim Ballard

It was summertime in Southern California. I believe the year was 1955 and I was still a few months away from getting my first driver's license. I was out for a walk in the neighborhood and enjoying the sunshine. As I passed a house about a block from mine, I heard some banging noises coming from the garage at the back of the property. I stopped to look and see who was making all this strange noise.

In retrospect, I should have just kept walking and ignored the noises coming from the garage, but little did I know that this day was going to give me an experience and a lesson that I will never forget.

As I walked down the long driveway, I could now see that the noise was being made by a teen-age boy, about a year older than I was who lived at that house. I didn't really know this boy very well and up until now, I wasn't aware that he knew anything about cars and especially anything about building a hot rod. But, there he was in the final stages of installing an old, greasy, and well-used Oldsmobile V-8 engine into the most stripped-down, fenderless and rusty Model A Ford roadster I had ever seen.

I was totally fascinated by what he was doing. After I stood there watching him for a while, he asked me to help him push the car out of the garage. When we got the car outside, he excitedly told me that he had not heard the engine run since that day it was removed from a wrecked donor car at a local wrecking yard. As I watched, he proceeded to pour a small amount of gasoline from a tin can into the carburetor and then he reached into the car to turn the key of an ignition switch that was hanging by some wires under the dashboard. To my surprise, the engine started instantly and actually sounded quite good in spite of some minor exhaust leaks.

He turned to look at me and, with a huge grin, said, "Let's try it out!" I wondered how we were going to do that. This car really was stripped! It literally had NO seats, NO lights, NO fenders, NO windshield, NO front floorboards, and NO license plates! I did insist that he check the brakes while in the driveway and they did appear to work, though I didn't see anything resembling an emergency brake handle to fall back on. We looked around for something to sit on and found two old wooden milk crates in the garage.

We eased the old roadster out onto the narrow residential street and drove slowly at about 15 or 20 mph for a couple of blocks. This felt good! The breeze in our hair, the noise, and heat of the engine, and the many rattles of loose body parts. We were hot-rodders! Along about the third block he was gaining more confidence and decided to punch it and so he stomped his foot on the gas pedal. What a feeling! I had never experienced acceleration like this. We were at, what I would guess now, about 60 or 70 mph and still accelerating when suddenly the whole car started vibrating and shaking violently! He immediately got off the gas pedal and when the car had slowed to about 40 mph, the shaking stopped to our great relief. We returned to his house at about 15 mph with no further serious problems. Fortunately, we also had no encounters with the local police.

As we turned into his driveway, I noticed for the first

time a distinct "wobble" in both front tires. We got out and decided to check the tires and wheels first. I will never forget the look on his face when he looked at the left front wheel. His face turned pale and he started to shake! At that moment he remembered, that in his excitement in getting the car out of the garage for the first time, that he had only installed two or at most three lug nuts on each wheel as a temporary measure to make a "roller" out of the car and had only tightened each of them finger tight! Now, as we examined each wheel, none of the lug nuts was still seated and several of them were at the end of their threads on the studs and were ready to fall off.

He did eventually finish the car in what would be considered a rat rod style today, but I never rode with him again. Ever.

Uncle Chaim's Grace

by Michael Trinagel

I was only 11 years old in the summer of 1970, yet I already had a following in the neighborhood. My "customers" were mostly people trusting me to wash their cars. Surprisingly, I was even doing small bodywork for some of them. Of course, I wanted more. I wanted to add things to the cars and make them stand out, but I couldn't do that to a car that belonged to someone else. This desire had been building in me when my father's tenant "Elliot" shared with me that he was looking to buy a new car. The light came on for me... it was my chance to be the proud owner of his 1965 Dodge Polara convertible!

Mind you, Elliot had driven that car into the ground. You could hear it crying as he drove up; bald tires, creaking suspension, no stuffing left in the seats, duct tape holding the windows closed and the paint just worn off the car itself. The trunk looked like he lived out of it and I think every part he ever replaced on the car was in that trunk, as well. It wasn't pretty, but at eleven years old, I had to work with what was in front of me. I knew getting him to sell it to me was going to be a challenge, but even then, I was a determined young man.

By the following spring, Elliot had made his big purchase and was driving his "new to him" 1966 Volvo Sedan, which meant it was time to figure out how to get the Polaris for my own. I could buy the car, but where would I put it? Dad had already said no to his garage since his

Cadillac barely fit with all of my tools taking up room. He emphatically stated that he wasn't going to lose any more of his garage!

Mom was always there if I needed financial support and dad loved me, I have no doubt about that, but they had very old European ways of parenting that didn't seem to connect with me. I also had an older brother, thirteen years my senior. We had nothing in common and he was always telling mom and dad to stop "spoiling" me. His hatefulness toward me has to this day caused great pain.

In walks Uncle Chaim. He was my biggest supporter, and nothing stopped him from helping and encouraging me and in any way that he could. Uncle Chaim would always come to the back yard to check out my latest projects and bond with me, embracing the visions I had for whatever I was working on. He was my mentor on how to live my life. I believe my self-confidence and willingness to be "out there" comes from his encouragement and belief in me.

He would always greet me with a big kiss and bite on the cheek. He KNEW I hated that! (Just like I know how much my twin daughter's hate it today.) It was his special signature of his unconditional love and now mine.

As I shared my predicament of being able to buy the car "IF" I had somewhere to put it, Uncle Chaim wheels

began turning. His garage housed his Checkered Cab, which was his livelihood, so it had to have a home and the other side was rented out to his tenant. He couldn't kick him out and still have a good relationship, so he asked if I was ok with putting the car in his back yard. Of course, I was, but I replied, "I wish we could." I thought he was kidding because his backyard was fully fenced and there was no way to get the car in.

When I didn't respond, wondering to myself what I was actually going to do, he asked again. "Do you want this car in my backyard?" I tepidly asked if he was kidding and he replied, "No, if you want it in the backyard we will get it there" With tears in my eyes, I said, "Yes, I do!"

He told me to go buy the car. So, off I went to see Elliot, who struck a deal with me, and the Polara was MINE! It was the end of the week by the time everything was said and done. I didn't know what to do with the car once I got it, so I went to Uncle Chaim. He wasn't working that day, so he set about cutting a hole in his fence, ripping the poles out, cement and all! A space large enough for the Polara was left open. Once we got the car in, he simply rebuilt his fence!

I was in awe of how far this man was willing to go to help me with my dream! Mind you, Aunt Toby didn't speak to Uncle Chaim for quite some time, but that never stopped him. Don't get me wrong, Aunt Toby loved me… just not THAT much!

People would walk by just looking, trying to figure out how this car got inside a fence with no evident gate! Those that did ask went unanswered. I just chuckled and continued working. This was my little secret with Uncle Chaim.

I set about working on my Polara. I would rivet shaped tin, cut with shears and made into a spoiler, onto the car even though the Polaris didn't exactly have the right lines for my youthful and creative visions. It wasn't perfect, but it was mine to create with as I pleased. I cleared the old headlight and grill area.

Then, I made a new layout, creating ground effects out of tin and riveting them onto the sides of the car; downward not outward, because of the way the wheels were set up under the car. I didn't know how to weld at this early age, so riveting was the method I used. I molded a pro-stock hood scoop, riveted it into place, and used Gorilla Hair Bondo, since I didn't know how to work fiberglass at that point, either.

I even removed all the chrome trim, wherever there was any, and filled in all of the holes. It was my early efforts in shaved chrome and was all pretty crude by my standards today.

Sometimes, I would just hang out with the car, listening to the stereo. I loved this piece of machinery and I dreamed that I would complete it and it would still be mine when I got my license at sixteen. Uncle Chaim sons, Abe and Paul, would come out and watch me as they played catch beside the car.

I loved taking the top up and down and used that as an excuse to start the car, since one of our agreements was that I would not run the car unless necessary. One day, Abe was in the passenger seat when I got out of the car. I had left it running, so I could listen to the motor as I worked on the custom grille. That was a big mistake!

Abe had decided to get in the driver's seat and then knocked the car into reverse as he played with the shift lever on the column. I saw the car moving and yelled for Abe to "step on the brake!" This did no good, since he didn't know what the brake was. The terrible reality hit me in the form of gravel and dirt as he stepped on the gas! The fence was soon a torn ribbon of metal, strung across the sidewalk, including the posts and chunks of concrete. It was a mess!

By the grace of God, there were no cars parked in the direct path of this beast as it flew out of the yard and across the street to a vacant lot. Abe was in shock when I reached him. I was scared out of my mind and couldn't speak. I put the car in park and just looked in awe at the chain link fence, bent poles, and dirt tracks on the sidewalk where the wheels had spun. I didn't know what to say or do.

Uncle Chaim wasn't home. Nobody was around. At least nobody came out. I got the car back in the yard, closed up the windows, raised the top, and headed home. I told my mother what had happened and she called Aunt Toby... who called Uncle Chaim.

I sat on the stoop of my parent's home for what seemed like an eternity. When Uncle Chaim came home, I was so scared of how angry he was going to be and what he was going to do that I sat silently, expecting my world to coming crashing in around me. I had never done anything like this before and I expected the full wrath of his anger.

Finally, he came walking up and greeted me with one of his big kisses and bites on the cheek. As I was wiping the saliva from my cheek, he whispered, "It's alright. As long as nobody was hurt, it's nothing. You, Abe and Paul are OK. So, I'll take care of it." I was in shock, as I had never seen anyone so cool under pressure. This was an important lesson in my life!

Uncle Chaim taught me much about life before Alzheimer's took him, but this memory stands out. His grace under pressure and unconditional love superseded his fears and the possible what ifs. One of my goals in life was always to be a man that Uncle Chiam would always be proud of!

The 1965 Dodge Polara Convertible soon found a new home in the junkyard. Aunt Toby won the battle of the car in the backyard after "the incident," but I carry the lessons taught by Uncle Chaim to this day and I will always miss him.

Drag Racing's Good Ol' Days

by Ky Michaelson

W hen I was a young boy, I lived right next to the air-port in South Minneapolis, which is where they trained the fighter pilots during WWII. I would gaze up into the sky and watch the planes accelerate as they took off from the airport and was amazed at how fast the planes could accelerate. That is when I discovered I had a need for speed!

When I attended junior high, all that I could think and talk about was being a racecar driver. I would draw stream-lined cars, close my eyes and imagine what it would feel like to go over 200 mph. A favorite pastime was building small cars, installing homemade rockets into them, which I made from my Gilbert chemistry set, and then shoot them down the alley where I lived to see how fast they would go.

In 1953, I turned fifteen, took the money I had earned and saved from my paper route, mowing lawns, and paint-ing houses, and bought a '33 Ford three-window coupe for eight dollars from a friend of mine. I thought I was in heaven when I tore the fenders off and installed a Ford truck motor with three Stromberg carburetors on it. It had high compression alu-minum finned heads and a nifty dark gray primer paint job. Now all that I needed was a place to race. The closest track was thirty miles away, but I had no trailer or truck with which to pull it. My other problem was that I had no driver's license, so one sunny Sunday morning I decided to forget about the minor details and take side roads, hoping my loud exhaust pipes would not attract the attention of the local police.

On the way to the track, I stopped at a stop sign that was next to a fire station. There was a fireman out washing the sidewalk with his fire hose and my first thought was to ask if he would turn his hose on my car and give it a quick wash job... and so I asked him if he would. That was a mistake. The water pressure was so high that it blasted the car inside and out and the engine started to sputter. I hollered, "Stop!" as loud as I could and drove away on about five cylinders.

It took me over an hour to get to the track. When I heard the roar of a dragster going down the track my heart started to beat faster. I thought to myself, at last, my dreams were coming true. Then, I momentarily had a new problem. Don Voge, the owner of the track, asked me how old I was. I told him I was sixteen. He wrinkled up one side of his face, shook his head, and replied, "No you're not! You're eighteen." He handed me a piece of paper and a pencil and told me to write a letter from my mother saying it was all right to race. Suddenly, no problem!

I drove the car up to the starting line and have to admit I was very nervous, but when the flagman dropped the flag, my competitive juices started to flow. I had my first taste of speed, even if my speed was less than 100 mph; and reached my goal of racing a car.

While at the track, I noticed that the motorcycles were almost as fast as the dragsters and eventually decided to go with the flow and build a drag bike. My first bike was a

'54 Harley Davidson KHK. I ran my first 100 mph with this motorcycle at Twin City Speedway; raced it for a year and won a few first place trophies.

I went to work at Paul's Cycle, a BSA dealership in St. Paul, MN. The owner, Paul, didn't like the fact that I was  racing a Harley, so he gave me a deal on new 1959 BSA 650cc Spitfire Motorcycle. This bike came from the factory with straight pipes and a high compression engine. It was a beautiful red and chrome beauty that I began racing in 1960 at Minnesota Dragways and at Twin City Speedway for 2 years, winning over 35 trophies.

During the off-season, I decided to stretch my BSA and add another 650cc bike engine. This was the first dual engine motorcycle in the Midwest. Because of its extended length, I decided to call it the Centipede and it was the fastest motorcycle that had I raced up to that point.

Then, one night at Twin City Speedway I let a good friend of mine, Clem Larson, ride the Centipede. As he shifted into fourth gear, he accidentally stuck his foot into the rear wheel. He immediately came off the bike and ended up with a little road rash that only required a couple of stitches. The Centipede, on the other hand, was completely destroyed.

Because of my interest in drag racing, I had joined a racing club called Gopher State Timing Association in 1956. This was the governing body of a number of hot rod clubs in Minnesota. The club saved enough money from holding car shows to buy a top gas dragster from Jack Moss.

If you worked on the car you could drive it, so in 1963 I decided to stop racing motorcycles and jumped into the seat of the GSTA dragster. It had a short 101 inch wheelbase and we named it "The Little One." It was powered by a 362 cubic inch small block blown Chevy motor. My first run on the car was 160 mph in nine seconds. I drove that car for the season and then decided to build my own.

I had a full time job working at Melo-Glaze Bakery and a part-time job at a motorcycle shop when I started a company called KM Specialties, selling aftermarket motorcycle parts and building motorcycle-racing motors. Needless to say, I was a busy guy. I lived in a large old farmhouse with no garage and with the cold winters in Minnesota, I had no choice but to build my dragster in the basement of my house.

I felt like I was working around the clock with all of my jobs so that I could pay my bills and complete the dragster. I finished the basic car, but I had no engine. So, my friend Ted Smith teamed up with me, supplying a 301cubic inch injected Chevy that ran on alcohol. I named the car "The Miser" because of what I had to do to finance  it. We ran it for a short time, but it wasn't fast enough for me and I decided to just drive the GSTA car for another year until I could afford a competitive blown racing engine.

We had five drivers for the GTSA car. It was kind like playing musical chairs and we would flip a coin to see who would drive first. The other drivers would make fun of me because I wouldn't get in it unless I could use the steering wheel out my own racecar. They didn't understand the reason why I would go out of my way to change the steering wheel. It was simply because I wanted to have the feel of the wheel from my own car so I could pretend I was driving it.

That next season, I bought a new dragster chassis from California Chassis Engineering. This was a super lite car with a super charged 327 Chevy motor and I competed in the top-gas dragster class. This car proved to be very competitive and the only other car that could constantly beat me was the GSTA club car. Personally, I didn't think it was fair that I had to race against my own club car, because GSTA could afford much better equipment than I could. I needed more money to support my racing hobby, so I started to go out of the State and race. I also competed in the NHRA division five point's races.

The next year I built an all-new car with a 427 blown Chevrolet. This car had plenty of power and I could light up the tires like a top fuel dragster. Halfway through the season, at about the thousand foot mark, I felt a hard vibration. I looked down towards the clutch can and just then, the clutch exploded. I pulled both of my feet back as far as I could, but not soon enough. A three quarter inch piece of cast iron from the bell housing hit my foot. It cut right through my shoe, penetrating my foot and cutting the tendons. It felt like someone hit my foot with a large sledgehammer. That was the end of my driving for the summer.

I recruited Bill Bisonett to drive the car. He also had a good friend that was a top-notch mechanic by the name of Byron Nelson. We finished the season with a number of wins and for the first time I didn't have so much pressure on me. It wasn't easy to drive the car and do most of the mechanical work, too. I finally had a chance to sit back and enjoy drag racing. The only time I got nervous was when Bill drove the car. He was a good driver, but I always worried that if something happened, he could get hurt. We had become very close friends.

For the next season, I bought a top fuel dragster chassis from Jerry Boldennow. Frank Hauser of RCS had originally built it. It was a super light car and equipped with the best that money could buy. We built a new 436 cubic inch Chevrolet top gas motor with a new Hampton blower and hauled it around in a brand new enclosed trailer. Kenny Winters painted the car with a really flashy purple and black psychedelic paint job. After all, it was the 60's. We were loaded for bear and ready to go racing!

When we were not following the NHRA division five circuit, we raced the rest of the season at Minnesota Dragways and North Star Raceway. One of the more memorable moments I had with this car was when we were racing up in Winnipeg, Canada.

Waiting in the staging lines, getting ready to race, there were four other cars sitting in front of us. A fellow racer by the name of Dave Babler made a qualifying run in his California Woody top fuel car. The car had a huge explosion, which cut the frame rails and damaged it severely.

I was told that when Dave was working on the car, he accidentally dropped a socket in the clutch can and could not get it out. So, he left it in and made the run, which was the cause of the engine explosion.

On that same day, one of my mechanics adjusted the clutch on my car and dropped an Allen socket in my clutch cam. We tried desperately to get the socket out, but we couldn't get to it. I really needed the money and was upset that we had come all of that way and couldn't even race the car. I sat in the car, all bummed out, and then it struck me like a bolt of lightning. Why not roll the car upside down on the roll cage and shake it until the socket fell out!

I jumped out of the car and started shouting orders like a drill sergeant. Everyone thought I was crazy when we rolled the car over onto the roll cage and started shaking it.

One of the race officials said that it was too late to run the car, but I pleaded with him to give us another minute. At that moment, the socket fell out of the clutch cam and we rolled the car back onto its wheels. Bill jumped back into the car and signaled me to push the car to start it.

Bill waited for the oil pressure to come up and then he hit the ignition switch. The motor started to sputter. Oil, gas and a lot of smoke were coming out of the exhaust pipes. He kept revving the motor up and it started to fire on all eight cylinders. Once staged, the engine was running fine and when the green light came on Bill had a great run and qualified the car. I don't think anyone has ever made this radical of a decision before, but it worked for us.

Every time we traveled out of state I would always say to Bill, "I sure wish I could catch a rattle snake" and Bill would say, "Michaelson, what are you going to do when you catch that rattle snake?" I would joke around and say, "I'm going to take that old snake and twirl it above my head and snap its head right off." Bill would always laugh and say, "I sure would like to get a picture of that!"

When we raced down in Bowling Green, Kentucky, there was a carnival right next to the racetrack, so I decided to check it out. When I was walking through the carni-  val, I saw a real big, authentic looking rubber snake. I thought to myself, I'm going to buy that snake and get even with Bill because of all the jokes he played on me through the years.

We had decided to drive back home from the race instead of staying overnight and at about 3:00am we stopped to get gas in Wisconsin. Bill was sleeping with his contact lens out in the back of the station wagon. Tom Ferrin was driving the station wagon and as we pulled out of the gas station, I noticed thousands of fireflies alongside the service road.

I told Tom to pull over because I wanted to try to catch some fireflies and, of course, I took my big rubber snake with me. I was running through the weeds pretending to catch fireflies. I dropped my rubber snake on the ground and starred screaming, "Snake! Snake! Snake!" Bill sat up in the station wagon and started hollering, "Ky, watch out it could be a Water moccasin!" I pretended to chase it and Bill became more and more upset so, I drug it out for about five minutes total.

I finally picked up the snake, ran over to the car, and threw it into the back of the station wagon where Bill was. He started screaming and almost went into hysterics. Let's just say I sure got his attention. Tom and I had to jump on top of him so he wouldn't kick out the windows. His heart was beating about ninety miles an hour, but after we got him settled down he said, "Ky, this is the best joke you have ever played on me."

Bill reminded me of the time that we were driving up to Canada to race at Bison Raceway. It was late at night and he was driving the pickup with a camper on it. We exited off the freeway and headed down a gravel road, all very tired, where we pulled over and parked for the night.

The next morning, I woke up and looked out the window. Bill had parked us right on a railroad track. Thank God, no train came down the track at night. At the time this happened, I thought Bill had done it on purpose, so I told Bill that I would get even with him some day. Bill thought scaring him with the snake the next season was my way of getting back at him.

In 1970, I had Bob Myers build me a new 215-inch wheel base car. We chromed and polished everything that we could on the car. Dave Dewars built the 465 cubic inch Hemi engine, with a Lenco two speed transmission. The car was painted with a beautiful combination of yellow, orange and candy apple red paint. We entered it in the GSTA Rod and Custom Show and won 'Best Dragster' and 'Best Engine' trophies. This was a great way to start out the season!

Unfortunately, the rest of the season was not as successful. Halfway through that season, we were heading back home from a race in Wisconsin and Tom Ferrin was driving the tow vehicle. We were driving down a long hill when disaster struck. A semi-truck drove very close past us at high speed, causing our trailer to whip violently from side to side. Tom tried everything possible to straighten out the trailer, but we eventually went into the median sideways, flipping the trailer where it tore away from the tow vehicle and burst into flames.

Luckily, a wrecker came by and hooked a cable around the roll cage, and pulled the twisted dragster out of the trailer. The only thing saved was the engine and drivers compartment. The trailer and all of its contents were a total loss. Needless to say, the racing season came to an abrupt end.

For the 1971 season, we had Bob Myers build a new car using the old driver's compartment from the burned car on

an extended frame. It had 219 inch wheelbase, making it the world's longest wheel base top gas car. We painted it black with white lettering that read 'Michaelson Bissonet Nelson'. I also bought a new rear engine car from Larry Simpson, which I planned to use the following season. Unfortunately, 1971 was also the year NHRA dropped top gas from the professional category to make room for pro-stock. Personally, I think if it has doors, it's not a racecar.

About eighteen owners of top gas cars teamed up and formed up a group called the Midwest All Stars. We circuit raced throughout the Midwest for two years and wound up losing interest and decided to go exhibition racing, where I was guaranteed to make money. I also had plans to set the world's fastest and quickest quarter mile record.

At 74, I'm still going strong and playing with cars, bikes, jets, and every other big boy toy you could imagine!

I Was There

by Martin DeGrazia

B ack in the mid 1970's, and earlier I'm sure, Seattle had its own illegal racetrack along the waterfront at the entrance to Golden Gardens Park. The immediate surroundings consisted of a public beach, a couple of nice restaurants and lots of moored sailboats. On the other side of the road were railroad tracks. They're still there to this day. Racers had room to run, because there was about a mile of straightaway without intersections and just a few parking lots to contend with.

It was ideal for the purposes of a group of young people out for an exciting time. The water, the beach with its bonfires and lots of other people looking for fun made for a good mix on a Friday or Saturday night. Sadly, I am just old enough to have caught the tail end of this era. I must've been 15, maybe 16 years old and was looking forward to hanging with hot rodders and racers. There was, of course, a lot of posing going on, too.

The area was relatively quiet at night until the cars would start gathering, some intending to race and some intent on just watching. This crowd ultimately included all of us teenagers that showed up in our wannabe hot rods.

The standard wardrobe of guys back then consisted of bell bottom pants, t-shirt or floral print tops, very wide belts, and a lot of us wore platform heal shoes. You weren't cool unless your hair was long and your ears were completely covered.

When you first arrived you could drive around "the loop," careful to look just right. The posturing is no different from today, just different players in different cars and clothes.

When they were ready to start racing, there would be cars in both the north and southbound lanes with both cars heading south. The race would start at the entrance of the park. There was, of course, the prerequisite pretty girl who stood between the two cars and dropped her arms for the start. It was just like you see in the race scenes of nostalgic movies that have been made ever since the baby boomers came on the scene.

I'm really not sure how long these races lasted because I was always watching them from the sidelines at the beginning of the race. The driver in the left hand lane would get the choice of who he was going to race. The driver on the right either would be given thumbs up or thumbs down. It was understood that you didn't get to race unless you were deemed worthy enough. If the other driver didn't want to race you, then you had to go the back of the line again. Each line usually had about fifteen cars in it.

One hot summer evening while "cruisin' the Gardens," my friend Larry, in his $300 dollar '55 Chevy, decided that he needed to race another '55 Chevy that was there. Even back then, you didn't get much for $300 dollars, but Larry was a pretty good back yard mechanic. So, it was a lot better than some of the cars, but not as fast as many of them. It had a stock V8 and a three speed. Today the patina on Larry's car would be desirable, back then it was just another beater with expiring paint, breeding corrosion.

Larry watched the '55 Chev that he intended to challenge go into the left hand lane and swing over to the right. The other '55 got to the front and started waving off cars to the right. This was getting exciting. Larry looked over at me and forcefully said "Marty, get out of the car!" I said, "What? Why?" I wanted to be a part of this and didn't understand why he was suddenly kicking me out. "Get out of the car" he repeated. "I need my car to be as light as it can be when I race!"

Boy was I bummed. I got out and stood with about 30 to 40 other people. The '55 on the left continued brushing off the other cars until Larry had slowly made his way to the front, where he got the thumbs up. I was over my feelings of dejection and was back in the spirit, anxious to see how Larry would do.

The dueling '55's began revving their engines, each ready to peel out as soon as the pretty girl dropped her arms. Off in the distance, a couple of cars approach from the south. As soon as they were out of the way, the race would be on. Suddenly, their blue lights came on. It was the cops!

Larry and the other '55 quickly exited to the left and up the hill into Ballard. All the other bystanders scrambled hastily to their cars and took off. I found myself standing alone. About 10 minutes after the cops left, I realized that my friend Larry was not coming back. I started making the trek up the long winding road he had gone up. It felt like about a mile or more. It's a very steep hill. About the time that I finally got to the top, Larry pulled up. He said he took so long because he wanted to be sure that the cops were gone.

That night was the closest I ever got to racing at Golden Gardens and it wasn't long after that night that it was pretty much on lock down as far as racing. I had always heard about the racing at school and had just wanted to be a part of it; and I got to be, if only for a short time.

These days, the Golden Garden stories are legendary and I am glad to say, "I was there."

Respect for Tradition

by Tom Glide

Take me to any car show, and I will naturally gravitate to the "traditional cars."

They are the cars built using parts and modifications that honor the early days of hot rodding. I think they have a lot of soul and character, which is why I gravitated to the black primered and customized 1949 Ford Coupe at the 2010 Maritime Festival car show in Harbor Beach, MI.

Having done work similar to what had been done to this car, I could see and appreciate all that had gone into it much more than the average person might. I took two

trips around the car, admiring the work, knowing the countless hours and dollars it took to make the modifications. They were all done correctly, very detailed, and in time honored fashion. This was the real thing. The primered finish, which might look unfinished to some, was even a tribute to the old days when the builders often couldn't afford paint right away once the custom work was done.

"Is this your car?" I asked the tattooed, well-traveled looking man with the long silver haired pony tail and ZZ top style beard sitting at a picnic table behind it.

"Yep," he replied.

"Nice car." I said. He thanked me, and showed my lady friend and I pictures of the small fleet of similar cars he had back home. I joked with him about how tough it must be to decide which car to drive. (Wouldn't you love to be in that position?) We were having a nice conversation when he suddenly stopped talking. He stood up and peered over his dark glasses toward the front of his car.

"Lady!" he shouted at a middle-aged woman leaning her full weight on the front fender of his car, laughing and talking to some other people.

"Hey! Lady!" he repeated much louder, startling her from her conversation, causing her and everyone within earshot, to direct their attention to him. She gave him a look of contempt, staring at his tattoos, long hair and cigar clamped in the side of his mouth.

"I ain't done paintin' that yet… 'preciate it if ya didn't sit on it!" he told her.

She gasped. "These are one hundred percent cotton!" she huffed, tapping the seat of her pants and returning to leaning against the car. It wasn't the cotton he was concerned about at this point. It was her considerable weight that she was applying to a very old fender with countless hours of work done to it, not to mention the very easy to scuff primer finish.

"Yeah well, I still don't want ya sittin' on my car," he replied. I wouldn't have either and had it been my car she'd have gotten the same request, verbatim.

She gasped again. "Don't sit on your car?" she shrieked. "Fine! Here's what I think of your car!" She stood up and slammed her butt into his front fender. The car bounced, coming back up and tapping her in the behind. She then wiped the back of her pants down half the length of the fender.

"Aw, that ain't right…" the owner said.

She took a digital camera from her purse and began to take pictures of the car and the owner.

"Don't sit on this car?" She screamed, snapping more pictures. "I work for the NEWSPAPER... I'll show you... I'll be damned... This is going in the paper... don't sit on this car..." She was babbling incomplete sentences, snapping pictures as if she was Federico Fellini.

The gentleman that she was with was giving an amen to each of her sound bites, confirming that she was in fact employed in some manner by an undisclosed newspaper. The car owner was in BIG trouble now.

I won't tell you the expletive the car owner gave her. Let's just say that when they parted ways, it wasn't on the best of terms.

I felt bad for the car owner, mostly because I knew the amount of work he had invested in his car. Her big ass did leave scuff marks in the fragile primered surface, too.

I don't know why, but I felt compelled to talk to her about it. I knew she didn't understand the amount of work that went into the car and hoped I could put it in terms she could understand. Maybe give her a hypothetical situation of someone showing little regard for something she put a lot of effort into, like a well-tended flower garden that someone else trampled through perhaps. How would she feel? I even thought of asking if he were clean-shaven and tattoo free like me, would she have reacted the same way. I hoped to get her to go back and look at the damage she had done.

I saw her a while later and approached her. "Ma'am, I'm not condoning his language, or his approach," I said, "but you have to realize the amount of work tha..."

"I know how much work goes into these!" she interrupted. She leaned against a beautiful red Corvette and began to preach, "It was how he tried to humiliate me in front of… what? Forty people? Unbelievable!"

"But ma'am, I…"

"No! I will not put up with this!" she shouted, pounding on the front fender of the gleaming red Corvette. "He could have asked nicely… ma'am could you please move away… please don't touch. But, no! This is going in the paper!" she shouted, continuing to hammer on the shiny 'Vette she was using for a pulpit.

It was becoming more and more apparent she hadn't seen the entry signs on every car that, along with car and owner information, read "Look, Reminisce and Admire, but PLEASE DON'T TOUCH!" in bold three inch high letters.

"Ma'am, as someone familiar this sort of work, I'm just saying…" I tried once more while trying to figure a way to stop her from assaulting the Vette before she cracked it.

"I'm tired of these Goddamn tourists! Do you know he is the second one that has yelled at me for doing that?"

No kiddin', I thought to myself.

"I will not be talked down to in my own town! If these tourists don't like it, they can go back down to the damn city where they belong!" she said, pointing to the owner of the '49 Ford. Had she read the sign in his car window, she would have seen he was from Sebewaing, a similar small town some thirty miles away… not the city.

Now she had made me angry. I have very little respect for those with that sort of backwards, Klan-ish thinking. It's way up there on my list of things I won't tolerate. I walked away from her, knowing I wasn't going to get a word in edge-wise.

"You should have saved your breath," my lady friend told me. "She just doesn't get it."

I agreed. She not only didn't appreciate the amount of work in the cars, but the amount of dollars brought into the area by the tourists she holds so much contempt for. The car owner was part of a club that brought four cars to the show, all paying the entry fee. They all spent the day in town. So, I'm sure they and their families patronized at least one business. I hope they all had a great time and left with some good memories of Harbor Beach to offset the bad one.

As a resident, I apologized to the car owner and expressed hope to see him again to talk cars at another show... hopefully, in Harbor Beach someday.

My advice to the lady from Harbor Beach would be to show a little respect for people and their property and they'll do the same. Also, if she happens to go to another car show this summer, I hope she looks, reminisce, and admire. But, just like the sign says... PLEASE DON'T TOUCH!

Especially, if it's a blue '42 Pontiac. I might not be so kind.

Is a Corvette Worth Waiting 26 Years For?

by Larry D. Brooks

I bought my first Corvette in May of 1971 at the tender age of 18. My father co-signed a loan for me, but I paid for that car. It was a '66 Nassau Blue coupe. But, at that time the newer body style of the '68-'71 models was the Corvette to have. I loved them just like everyone else, but could not afford such a car.

I was in college and working part time. Against my parents' wishes, I quit college in late May of 1971 and took a full-time job. Now, I was suddenly making enough money to buy the more desirable model year. I traded the '66 coupe for a '69 convertible with the monster 435 HP 427 CI engine... and it snowballed from there.

I went through a series of other Corvettes after that one. But, they all had one thing in common. They were used cars when I bought them. I desperately wanted my first new Corvette; one ordered exactly as I wanted it, including the interior and exterior colors, which had become increasingly important to me by that time.

So, I sold the two Corvettes, which I owned at that point. They were a Mille Miglia Red '74 L-82 coupe and a Riverside Red '63 Fuel Injected Split-Window coupe. I went to the local Chevrolet dealer and ordered what would be my first new Corvette! I was thrilled. As we went down the option list, I had the dealer check off every single option. I wanted a fully loaded car and when it came to the color choices, it had to be Classic White with bright red leather interior. By then, I had realized how much I loved cars with this particular combination of colors. It had to be this or nothing.

It was October of 1977 and I had just ordered a new '78 Corvette coupe. I was told that the time required to take delivery of my car would be about

three months. The demand for Corvettes at that time was higher than the supply. I was willing to wait, though I knew it would seem like an eternity to me.

My father, being a levelheaded, money-conscious man who cared nothing about cars, began working on me regarding this situation. I worked a split-shift job then and was still living with my parents. On my days off, my dad and I would go lots of places together.

One day as we were heading back home, he pointed out a new housing development in our area and told me to drive through it just to see what it looked like. As we drove, we were enjoying looking at all the new homes for sale and he said if he had as much money as I currently had when he was that age, he would not have wasted it on a new car. He would have used it as a down payment on a house. Suddenly, I realized his true motive for riding through that neighborhood.

As time went on and I was getting so anxious about getting my new Corvette, Dad kept on mentioning I should be using that money for a house instead of a car. He said the car would be worth nothing in a few years but the house would escalate in value. I knew he was right. I never questioned his wisdom. But, I was a car guy and the ultimate purchase for a car guy in the '70s was a new Corvette. I was this close and I was not going to be denied. But, in the back of my mind, his idea was really working on me. I began to see that maybe a new house was the better plan. I could not believe I was even thinking this way, but I was.

After a lot of gut-wrenching and agonizing days pondering this dilemma, I came to the decision I never dreamed I would have just two months earlier. I decided to cancel the order on my new Corvette and buy a house.

It was one of the most difficult days of my life as I walked into that dealership and informed my salesman I had changed my mind. He seemed as shocked as I was that I had made that decision, knowing how badly I wanted that car.

He informed me that it was too late to cancel the order since the car was in the system already. He said he would refund my deposit but the order stood. I was as dejected as a person could be. I knew I would end up seeing that car after it arrived, which would make the pain even that much more excruciating.

When I got home, I sat down and cried thinking about what I had just done. My dad came in to console me. Then he told me something I always remembered. This was not the right time to buy a new Corvette for me. The day would come when the time would be right and I would know that it was OK to do so.

I did begin building a new house after that. A friend of mine that worked at the dealership called me one day and made sure to let me know the Corvette I had ordered had arrived. I told him I had better not come to look at it, but curiosity got the best of me and I drove over to take a peek.

I opened the door and took in that new-car smell and the aroma of the leather seats. It was purely overwhelming. I walked away with tears in my eyes again and began questioning my decision to build a house then. This was tearing me apart, but as more time went by the longing for that car began to fade away, especially as my house neared completion.

The years moved along and I got another Corvette, but it was another used one and that still did not satisfy my intense desire for a new one. Other used cars that followed, too, but the desire for a new kept eating away at me.

My father passed on in 1992. I missed him terribly but I never forgot those words of wisdom he passed on to me. My mother and I talked many times, about how he gave me the perfect advice about purchasing a house.

In 2003, my mother passed on and I was the executor of her estate. As I went through the will and her other papers, I found a note from my dad telling me that now was the right time to buy a new Corvette. There was enough money in the account they had for me to do just that.

That was truly overwhelming, but I never questioned his wisdom. So, I went back to the same Chevrolet dealer I had been to in October of 1977 and placed an order for a brand-new '04 Corvette convertible. As the salesman went down the options list, I had him check off every one of  them. I still wanted a loaded car and when it came time to pick the color combination, I emphatically stated I wanted Arctic White exterior with Torch Red leather interior.

Finally, after 26 years my dream was going to come true. It took four tortuously long months for the car to arrive and when it did, I could not believe I was living this dream. It just could not be happening... but it was, because the time was finally right to do it. Thank you, Dad.

The Buggy

by Roger Patton

I met Roger Hackworth the day before I turned thirteen in Stockbridge, Michigan. The year was 1969. We became good friends and still stay in contact with one another to this day. Together, we shared many adventures and still talk about them between us and share them with close friends.

When I was about fifteen, we had moved to a town in the western part of Michigan called Burr Oak. Roger's much older brother, Joe, lived there and he began dating my mother, so we were all just that much closer. Therefore, Roger and I were always doing one thing or another together and there was always an adventure waiting.

Joe worked for a man named Dickey who had an auto body and paint business and Roger would occasionally go over and help Joe get the cars ready for paint.

One day Roger came to me and said Dickey had a friend named Larry, a thirty-some year old hippie with more creative bent than tools or skill, that had taken a 1956 Chevy pickup truck and chopped the body off it. In fact, he had actually cut up the frame and shortened it. Because he didn't have a welder, or much else in the way of tools, he drilled holes in the frame and bolted it back together. It had a seat bolted to the frame and the cowl, dash, and steering wheel remained intact to a certain degree, anyway. It had no windshield and it was an odd-looking vehicle. He called it "the buggy."

It had a six-cylinder engine with a three-speed transmission and when the front end was torn off of the truck, the rusted out radiator wasn't replaced. So, there was no radiator. Larry just poured water in the radiator hoses and then attached them back together using a pipe and clamps. It actually worked OK and would travel five or six miles before it needed more water. The wind across the open engine kept it semi cool. Sort of.

Because the frame was not welded solid, "the buggy" would bend in the center where it was bolted together. There was about three to four inches of travel up and down and when it took off from a stop, the seat and its occupants would be looking at the sky, until "the buggy" came back down.

Roger went on to mention that the guy wanted to sell it for fifteen dollars, thought I could get it for less, and talked me into buying it. So, the plan was to go to Larry's house to look it over and buy it. I actually bought it for ten dollars. Then, the issue was how to get it to my home. Obviously, if the cops saw it we were going to be in trouble. They would be wondering who the fool was driving that thing down public roads. The plan was to wait until about two or three in the morning. Well, around eleven pm, we had had enough of the boredom waiting. So, with Larry driving, and with Roger and I as passengers, we set out to get the thing home in a stealthy manner. We would take the first gravel road and slyly work our way to where I lived, which was about fifteen miles away.

We would stop and give the engine a drink every so often to keep it cool. Larry always had jugs of water with "the buggy." We got almost onto the first gravel road when we saw a police car. Roger said, "Maybe they didn't see us." Larry wasn't buying this and told us about a field up ahead.

He thought that if we could make it to the field, park "the buggy" in the drive on private land, that maybe the police wouldn't impound it. Roger looked back and said, "Yep, they saw us." Larry stopped the buggy in the driveway and we jumped out, ran into the field, and lay down in the grass. Well, the police car light came on and although he looked around for us, we had evaded capture. They never got out of the car and just looked "the buggy" over with their spotlight.

The cops left and we decided to wait for a while before continuing our journey to get "the buggy" back to my house. That wait only lasted for a few moments after they left. We figured they were gone either for good or lying in wait.

We decided that the worst they could do would be to take the buggy and send us walking. Obviously, they weren't going to drive it, so that would leave them just telling us to "get that thing off the road before we take you guys to jail." Without any further speculation, we took off and eventually made it to my home without further incident. At the time, we thought we had pulled off a major coup.

Roger and I broke the shift linkage one day and the only person we knew that could weld it lived in town. So, we drove "the buggy" into town, got the linkage welded, and drove away like outlaws in a cloud of dust. I told Roger that the people on the streets probably had fun saying "I saw the Beverly Hillbillies in town today!"

We drove that thing for what seemed like forever. We never put in a radiator; just stopped and gave it a drink once in a while. It was delivered to the scrap yard once it finally died.

Not long after "the buggy" died, Roger approached me again with another plan. This time, Dickey told Roger he would give him his '49 Dodge pickup truck if he would throw the boulders out of the bottom of his barn. So, Roger got me involved and we started throwing out the rocks.

About the time we got to the biggest rocks, which were in the farthest part of the barn, Roger came up with the idea of going and getting the truck and I could finish getting the rocks out of the barn. Reluctantly, I told Roger to go ahead and get the truck.

The agreement was that Dickey wasn't going to give Roger the truck until the last rock was out of the barn. So, I had to have the rocks out before Roger came back with the truck in case Dickey followed him back to the house. He made it clear that if he found out that we had lied, he wouldn't go through the deal.

Well, I got the rocks out of the barn and Roger drove the truck in. It had a new paint job, new tires, and chrome wheels; clean from front to back and top to bottom. Even the floor mat was brand new. It ran and drove perfect.

Roger wanted to go out on a date with Karen and he wanted me to go with her sister. I wanted nothing to do with the sister, but Karen would not go out with Roger unless I went and took her sister along. What could I do? I agreed to go.

Roger got the idea of driving the truck and parking it on the outskirts of town. It wasn't licensed and it had no insurance. We had no business driving it. I told Roger as soon as we got into the truck to leave, the police would catch us and impound it. He said, "No, they won't. We'll stay out late and get in the truck after the whole town has settled in and the cops are eating donuts."

At about three in the morning, the girls dropped us off and we snuck into the truck and fired it up. I told Roger to be careful because the police were probably behind a building and waiting for us to pull out. I was right. As soon as we pulled out and got on the road here came the police with flashing lights and screaming sirens. I hated being right that night. They impounded the truck and we walked home.

The next day, Roger and I went to the garage up town and there sat the truck. According to the tow driver and impound lot manager, the cops had told them that the truck could not leave unless it had plates and insurance on it. Roger was sixteen. I was fifteen and neither one of us had a driver's license. We certainly didn't have insurance and registration. So, we couldn't get the truck and no one was going to help us.

As we were walking away, I told Roger to go trade the pickup for the '64 Chevy Malibu SS that was sitting on the lot with a For Sale sign in it. He had the title for the Dodge truck that Dickey had signed off and so he went back to the guy and made a straight across trade.

The Malibu had shiny red paint, a white convertible top, stock SS hubcaps, white bucket seats, and an automatic shifter in the center console. It was beautiful and the 283 cubic inch V8 purred like a kitten. We couldn't drive the truck out, but no one said we couldn't drive away with the Malibu! So, we did.

Beat the Clock

by Ron Gadwa

My dad gave me a picture of his '40 Mercury when I turned 16. He had written on the back of the picture so I would always remember the story of his early days behind the wheel. Part of those notes, were his instructions for me to "drive slow." His advice must have worked! In my 50's now, I've been through lots of cars and motorcycles, and I'm still here. Although I didn't always "drive slow," I only managed a couple of mishaps over the years, and they never re-

ally amounted to anything too serious. My dad is 92 years young, still driving, and still a very interesting old guy.

After his early years, cars never meant much to him other than transportation, but he sure enjoys riding in my hot rod! I currently have a '36 Ford Five Window Street Rod that he gets a thrill out of being in when we go for rides. I also have a C-5 corvette that gives me a thrill when I go for rides, so I'm hoping that unlike my dad, the good vibes of being a car guy stays with me!

Back when he was young, dad really did embrace his '40 Mercury and he was well known for "ripping up the road" between Aberdeen and Montesano on Highway 12, at the base of The Olympic Peninsula in Washington State, known as The Olympic Highway.

Let me take you back... just the way he told me it happened.

There would be the usual young crowd hanging out at the local malt shop in Aberdeen and in those pre-World War II days, they didn't have a care in the world. Dad doesn't remember the exact name of the place, but it was on Wishkaw Street; the opposite end of the block from Kress's. This was very late 1940 or early 1941, because after December of 1941 most of the guys went off to war.

Of course, all of these young and happy-go-lucky guys would be talking cars and speed. Once a month or so the talk would cease and a ten-mile race to Montesano would be on. Usually, it was just the driver taking the challenge. However, Elmer Collins rode with my dad a time or two. Just over the bridge from Aberdeen, one guy at a time would start. Because it was a two lane highway and the race was so long, they were at least of sound enough minds to make them timed races and not side by side who can get to the finish line first contests.

Everyone was on the honor system and they would click a stopwatch just after the bridge out of Aberdeen. In approximately 10 miles, just after the bridge over the Wishkah River at the exit sign for the town of Montesano, you would click it again. Runs usually took 9.2 to 10 minutes, or so, on the dark and lonely highway. Downhill, speeds would reach as high as 90-95 MPH.

There was hardly any traffic back in those days. So, that wasn't really an issue for the most part, but there was a narrow old bridge on the highway and the competitors had to be very cautious with their approach. My dad says he only saw one wreck during all of those of unsanctioned time trials.

Once in a while, the following car would catch up with the lead car and the Wynooche Bridge would pinch them down a bit. Occasionally, someone would get trapped and slide off into gravel and then finally settle to a stop in a softly plowed field. It never really upset the farmer whose field they landed in and he would gladly tow them out with his tractor early the next morning before authorities discovered what had transpired... for a fee!

Of course, dad had his '40 Mercury, which he believed had a 95 horsepower flathead V8 motor, not the less powerful Ford 85 horsepower version of the flathead V8. He wasn't 100% sure on this fact, but my personal research has proven him correct. The Mercury had a bigger bore that provide 18 more cubic inches and a whopping 10 more horses. In any event, my dad's car was always among the faster cars.

There were all kinds of cars involved; some much faster than others. Norm Carlson from Aberdeen had a '39 or '40 Plymouth coupe that was extraordinarily fast for what it would have been in a stock condition, but ol' Norm never gave up his secrets to horsepower and so no one knew why he ran so fast. All the Chevrolets had six cylinders in those days that only weighed in around 78 horsepower. One night, a guy came through in a Graham that was supposed to have a super charger on it, but he didn't really fare very well and they never saw him again. Another guy named Ted, from Ocosta out on the Westport Hwy, had a '34 ford with a Mcculloch Super Charger that was a real challenger. Aside from sheer horsepower, driver's skills and road conditions are what really accounted for top speeds and lowest times.

These races were pretty informal with no spectators or officials; just guys having fun and it never turned into anything more than that. The road was one lane each way, fairly straight, fairly dark, and the runs were usually after 11pm or so at night so, cops were never seen; just an occasional stray car.

I've heard rumors of the guys in Darrington doing the same type of timed runs to Arlington in the late 60's. At almost 28 miles, that would have been nearly three times as long of a race and I have no idea of the times they clocked. Of course, none of these extended high-speed runs would be possible these days.

Dad bought his Mercury in late 1940 from the Royal Cab Company when it was a year old and he drove it until 1953. He was meticulous in its care and maintenance, and wound up trading it in on a brand new '53 Ford. I'd love to have either one of those cars today. I guess I'm a big enough old car nut for both my dad and me.

The Tin Indian

by Tom Glide

I 've loved old cars from first the moment I can remember. I bought my first car, a '48 Chevy sedan, when I was fifteen years old for $35. Mom and Dad weren't all that happy about it; in fact, they thought I'd lost my mind.

They weren't really "car people," but they watched and supported me in my folly as I poured through Hot Rod Magazines and went out to the garage and applied what I had learned to my car. They decided to follow their crazy teenager in the family car when he announced he was driving the barely completed car to the Street Rod Nationals in St. Paul, Minnesota. That may have had something to do with the fact I had just finished it and only driven it around the block a couple times.

It was a crazy idea, but it made it with only a few small hiccups along the way. Looking out over a sea of old cars there brought back enough memories for them to catch the old car bug that had infected me.

Not long after that, dad heard of a car for sale in a nearby town. It was an old Pontiac that someone wanted to get rid of, so we went to look at it.

Tucked away in an old barn under twelve years of dirt, hay bales, and silt we found a mostly complete, but not running, 1942 Pontiac Sedan Coupe that a young man had inherited from his grandmother. He had turned the wiring to spaghetti in a half-hearted attempt to get it running and then lost interest. For $300 he would be happy to get what he considered a big pile of crap out of his barn.

As Dad pushed the dirt off the car, stood back, and looked at the sleek lines, ornate dashboard and perfect original upholstery, I could see he was being magically transported from 1978 back to 1942. It was an important year for him. It was the year he met Mom. It was also the year he became a radio operator on a B-17 bomber, went to war over Germany, and wound up a POW.

Right before my eyes, the silver haired, bi-focaled man I knew as dad, started to become the cocky, muscular kid with jet black hair that I had only seen in grainy photos in old photo albums.

A deal was struck and I bought him what we referred to as the Tin Indian as a Father's Day gift. We figured because it was in pretty good condition, we'd have it going in six months, tops. By next spring, we'd be driving it.

As it goes with even the best-laid plans, a few snags began to slow us down. When we got the car home and began to wash the years of dirt off it, we noticed the body wasn't in as good of shape as we thought. It was solid, but the years in the barn weren't kind to the old girl. It appeared that literally everything under the sun had been thrown on it over the years, resulting in a huge amount of dents on every top surface of the car. The grandmother that originally owned it wasn't very good at backing out of the garage either. Creases ran down both sides of the car.

We also learned that, because of limited wartime car production, there had only been about 14,000 Pontiacs built that year. There were only 1,776 of this particular body style produced and the few parts it did need were extremely scarce. It wasn't going to be as easy to find parts for it as it was for my common Chevy.

While trying to find the trim and body parts it needed,

we shifted towards the mechanical end. I had hoped we would put a modern drive train in it, like my Chevy, but soon found Dad wouldn't have anything to do with that. This car must be ORIGINAL.

Begrudgingly, I rebuilt the old flathead six, and we got it running. Amazingly, we found a brand new dent-less hood at an antique auto parts store in Port Huron, and the project began to pick up speed. That was until Dad decided to "help" with the bodywork and began to sand the car off while I was at work. He sanded around the trim the car did have, rather than take it off, and left some scratches in the irreplaceable parts, which infuriated me. We were having enough trouble trying to find the parts that were missing and now what we had was full of damn scratches!

Work slowed as we continued the search for parts, and eventually ground to a complete halt in 1981 when we learned that Mom had cancer. Years of hospital visits, chemotherapy and suffering for Mom raged on as we helplessly watched her pass away. After she was gone, both of us forced ourselves to work on the Pontiac, but neither of us seemed interested. It was something that was for them. Something would always be missing.

In 1986 I got married, and time spent on the Tin Indian became little more than brief spurts in between long periods of time when we never seemed to have enough time to accomplish much. There were kids to support and bills to pay. Eventually, I was able to find more time to dedicate to the car, so Dad sent the bumpers out to be rechromed and I bought a new set of tires for it. The father-son project took new life once again!

As the years went on, Dad began to show signs of confusion and irritability at times. One day he'd be fine and the next he seemed distant and standoffish. He was forgetful and repeated himself often. I told my siblings, all of which lived a great distance away, what I was seeing in Dad and that I suspected it was the early stages of Alzheimer's. So began a very tumultuous time for him and my whole family.

He became less trusting, especially of me, since I was the one who suggested he had a problem. I missed Dad and our time together, working on the Pontiac, his visits to our home, or the occasional Friday night dinners at a local restaurant. I found myself on the outside looking in, trying to get him to talk to me again.

He was spending most of his time away with my sister, so I couldn't do anything with him. When he said he didn't want to see me, she honored his request. His "best interests" became a term I loathed. If I couldn't do something with him, I'd do something for him.

I talked to my family about getting the Pontiac out and finishing it, which went over like a lead balloon. Dad be-

came more upset that I was now "stealing" his car too, and the result was my brother putting a huge chain across the front of his garage to ease his mind. "Why do you have to upset Dad so much over a junk car that doesn't even run?" my brother asked.

Truth be known, I could have legally taken the car, as Dad had signed it over to me in 1985. But, I just wanted Dad back in my life and not the car, so I left it in his garage to calm the turbulent family waters.

Time passed and I continued to try to reach Dad to no avail. Eventually, he wound up in a nearby nursing home where I was able to see him as much as I wanted, but by then he had suffered a mild stroke and the Alzheimer's had greatly advanced. He was a mere shell of who he used to be and unable to communicate. I never got the chance to reach the man I once knew and honestly don't know if I reached who he had become.

Upon his passing in 2001, I was almost amused to learn I had "inherited" the car whose title had lain in my safe for years. In my mind, it had always been and always will be his, despite what the title says. The only thing that mattered was that his suffering was over and he could rest in peace. I did take great pleasure in cutting that ridiculous chain and liberating the Tin Indian though.

It had sat for years in an abandoned garage and most of the hard work Dad and I had done was for naught. The four brand new tires I had put on it were flat as pancakes and split wide open. Someone had drawn a circular target in the filth on the windshield, and practiced their marksmanship with a BB gun.

The hood yawned wide open and the radiator was punched full of holes, the screwdriver that was used to do the deed still sat on the left front fender. Old greasy starters, carburetors, and other old car parts that Dad and I had collected through the years were piled in the interior, ruining the original upholstery A lot of the original trim was found in a nearby storage shed, under some old lawnmowers and junk, bent and rusted beyond repair. Still more was never found.

As I watched my friend winch it out of the garage, it sickened me to see it pulled right out of its own tires that remained rotted to the cement floor.

I thought about getting rid of it. It was in sad shape, and I remembered how hard it was to find parts for. Then, while we secured the car to the trailer, I thought of Dad and the look on his face when we went to look at the car for the first time. I remembered long hours in the garage together, working on it to the wee hours and talking about anything and everything. I remembered how hard he laughed when we tried to start the engine for the first time and it backfired loudly and belched fire out of the carburetor, sending me running from under the hood.

I couldn't sell it. The car meant way too much to dad and he meant too much to me. The car was a member of the family.

Years of working on old cars had improved my skills and tool arsenal greatly, and the daunting task of working out all the dents was now no big deal. I also had the internet and the whole world at my fingertips to locate parts, rather than just the monthly Hemming's Motor News, that rarely had any Pontiac parts older than those for a GTO or Firebird listed in it.

It turns out all the old parts that were piled in the car were now quite valuable on eBay and selling them gave me the cash needed for the parts I lacked. The biggest advantages I now had, were an understanding lady friend, willing to put up with being a "car widow" (unlike my ex), and my friend Charlie (who helped me retrieve the car) and his body shop, Lakeshore Collision in Port Hope, Michigan. He also loves old cars, and does a lot of work on them in his shop. But, it is the collision work on modern day cars that feeds his family and takes the lion's share of his time. In exchange for doing work on some of the restoration projects he had going for customers, I was able to use his state of the art shop and tools to work on my car; an arrangement that worked out great for both of us.

Ironically, it took about six months of sometimes endless days and nights to bring the Tin Indian back to life, just not the six months Dad and I figured it would take so long ago.

The body is perfectly straight now thanks to my son Jake and I, followed by Charlie and little pieces of masking tape to mark spots needing more work. It now wears a beautiful shade of deep blue paint reminiscent of the Pacific Ocean in Hawaii, where Dad loved to go.

All of the missing and damaged pieces of trim were located on the web except for the one piece of trim that Dad had scratched those many years ago. Although it could have been buffed out using technology that has come along since then, it really didn't look all that bad, and it was his contribution to the restoration. So, the part was installed as is.

I have replaced the original drive train in the car with one from a modern car, because just like all of my previous older cars, I plan to drive the shit out of it for great distances. If something happens, I want to find parts in any auto parts store, rather than whittle them out of tree branches along the road just to get home. Somehow, I don't think Dad would mind the changes.

Amazingly enough, its first real outing since its completion was on Father's Day in a car show in the town where Dad worked, was well known and liked for years. Many people he knew stopped by, admired it, and shared stories of memories they had of dad. It wound up taking first place in the GM division that day.

People that have seen it since it was finished walk around it, stand back and admire it, and in reference to its rarity and monetary value ask, "Do you know what you could get for this car?"

I've bought and sold enough cars to rival Barrett Jackson in my lifetime. I was even able to come up with a number I could live with to watch my old Chevy drive away. With the condition the Pontiac is in now and the extremely low production numbers, I suppose I could get a fair amount of money for it. However, none of that interests me. With this car, it's not what I could get for it as much as what I get from it. With every trip, I bring back happy memories of dad and my childhood.

How do you put a value on that?

Pandora

by Chris Kimball

In Greek mythology, Pandora's box is the large jar carried by Pandora that, once opened, unleashed many terrible things on mankind: ills, toils, sickness, and worse. At the very bottom, however, when all seemed lost, there was one more thing left... Hope.

So, what does this have to do with a 1972 pre-L Pantera? Let me start at the beginning.

Back in 2006, I realized there wasn't much in life I'd always wanted to do but hadn't had the chance to experience, save that one thing I always wished for: The chance to own a DeTomaso Pantera. In December of that year, after searching hither and yon I found what I was looking for... on eBay, no less.

I flew from Washington State to New Haven, Connecticut, where I saw the car, fell in love, and drove it away. Well, actually I had it shipped to Tacoma and then drove it home.

When I drove into my driveway, my wife was waiting at the front door. She had heard me coming from a block away, and watched with amusement as I tried to extract myself from the Pantera. As I clumsily attempted to exit the car, my foot caught on the seat, and I almost landed on my keister in front of the whole neighborhood! Vicki chuckled and said, wryly, "Any cool factor you may have by owning that car will immediately be obliterated when they see you trying to get out of it!"

Anyway, as a new member of Panteras Northwest, I was relieved to have my fellow club members around to help me figure out what needed to be done to the car. Quite a bit, as it turned out.

After having the stock motor "worked on" by a local mechanic, which I did without first checking with my Pantera buddies, it proceeded to smoke like an inmate on death row.

Over the next year, after installing new axles and a host of other parts too numerous to mention, I decided I'd drive my Pantera, blue smoke and all, to the POCA Fun Rally in Las Vegas, and bring along my oldest son, David.

We made it as far as Medford, Oregon before I realized that it might not be wise to attempt crossing a desert in the car, which burned a quart of oil every hundred miles. I left it at the home of an understanding, fellow Pantera owner, Paul Rimov, and David and I drove the balance of the trip in a rented econo-box.

After returning from Reno, I determined I would do whatever it took to get to the 2009 Fun Rally in my car.

In January of 2009, I decided the only logical choice was for me to buy an entirely new motor. I enlisted help from members of Panteras Northwest and all the great people who populate the Pantera email forum.

I'm not very motor savvy. So naturally, I asked advice about what parts I should use, how I should have the motor built and so on. In retrospect, what I now realize is that the guys were all telling me what they would do if they were me, except it was my money being spent! Nonetheless, I was using a well-known, local engine-builder who was happy to oblige, and the final decision was to use a sonic tested Cleveland block bored and stroked to 408 cubic inches. The modifications and price went up from there...

At this point, I reasoned that with the new motor's additional torque, I might need to have the frame checked. The last thing I wanted was to end up with a Pretzel-shaped DeTomaso.

I was referred to a gentleman named Larry Rebsamen who was known for expert frame work, so Panteras Northwest club members Mike Thomas, Doug Braun and I took the car to his shop (a large metal building bursting at the seams with tools, parts, and a half-dozen cars in various stages of restoration).

Before taking the car to Larry, I had noticed the inner edges of the car's back tires were significantly worn. One look at the situation, and Larry announced that the frame was in such bad shape the shock towers were collapsing into the engine bay!

The next thing he did was get underneath the car with a large screwdriver and began whacking various locations on the frame. The alternating sounds of "thunk" and "shloop" were mirrored by his murmurings of "that's OK" and "Oh, that's bad." The final result was that the rear portion of the frame would have to be rebuilt and the shock towers replaced entirely.

It was then that Doug and Mike decided since every car needs a name, my Pantera should be named "Pandora" due to the fact it seemed there was an unending parade of issues to address. At the same time the frame was being repaired (March of 2009), the new motor was being built.

Here's where things get interesting, and this is the part of the story that demonstrates exactly why "Pandora" is the perfect name for #3846.

In late March, the new engine was complete. I took my

family's SUV, and using a borrowed engine cradle, brought home my prize. In a repeat of what they had done for me less than two years earlier, the local club members showed up on a Saturday to help me install the new 408.

We installed it, and once started it, sounded fantastic. I was excited, because I had at least two months before the POCA Fun Rally to work out any bugs that might develop. Unfortunately, it wasn't long until said bug did develop in the form of a rear main seal oil leak.

In a brief moment of brilliance, I had asked the engine builder if he backed his engines with a warranty. He assured me he did, so when I called him about the oil leak he said he'd take care of it. His shop was designed only to build engines, not to install them, but he told me he had a good friend who was a mechanic with a shop close by who would extract and replace the engine once fixed. I said that sounded good, though it turned out to be a big mistake!

I dropped the car off at the engine builder's shop and he told me the engine should be out of the car, repaired and replaced within a week or so. Later that day my cell phone rang. It was the engine builder, who said the mechanic had arrived, but was unable to open the rear deck, and now the key was jammed in the lock. I explained that the lock had never worked, and all that was required to open the deck was to apply slight downward pressure while pushing in the button. Too late. The lock was jammed for good. He said that at his expense he'd have a locksmith repair the damage.

A week later, I returned from a trip and called the engine builder to check on the progress. I was surprised when he told me he hadn't yet received the engine from the mechanic. He said to check back in a day or two; he would contact the mechanic to see how things were going.

I checked in a few days later and was told that, unbeknownst to the engine builder, the mechanic had moved his shop with no forwarding address. I asked for the mechanic's phone number, but when I called, it went to voice mail. I left a message asking to be contacted. No contact occurred.

At this point, I was getting nervous because the Fun Rally was quickly approaching, and I had no Pantera. In fact, I had no idea where it was. At the end of May, the engine builder said he had reached what appeared to be the mechanic's girlfriend. He told her to have the mechanic call him ASAP.

Days went by, no response.

Meanwhile, I'd been trying to reach the mechanic several times per day with no luck and was now getting a stupid "voice mailbox is full" message every time I called. A day or two later, however, I was able to leave a voice mail, which I did, imploring the mechanic to call me back. I left another message the next night, and another the next morning. The engine builder also left a message letting the mechanic know that I was talking with my insurance company, Hagerty Insurance, about filing a lost vehicle report. We figured if he heard that he'd respond for sure.

Still nothing, so I told the nice folks at Hagerty to get to work on finding my car. They promised to start trying to track down the mechanic. At this point, I was pretty much (sadly) resigned to the fact I'd be driving the Magnum to Reno. For 2009, I had promised my younger son, Donny, he could attend. After a year of preparation, to be denied the experience of a lifetime for Donny and I because of some mechanic's incompetence was very difficult to swallow.

The way I figured it, there were several possibilities for what was going on.

1) The mechanic was completely lackadaisical and hardly ever checked his voice mail,

2) The mechanic had screwed up the car so badly he didn't want to face the engine builder or me until he figured out how to fix what he'd ruined (which might be impossible if he didn't have a clue about Panteras), or

3) The mechanic was a charlatan who was selling my car piece by piece on Craig's list.

I figured it was probably a combination of #1 and #2.

It was now June 3, and I began getting very worried. I put the word to the Pantera forum that if anyone saw anything on E-Bay or Craig's list that looked suspicious (including a great deal on a dark green '72 Pantera with a new engine), to please let me know. I also asked that if anyone knew the whereabouts of the mechanic's shop to let me know immediately.

On June 8, I filed a police report. It turned out they had a residence address for the errant mechanic. They agreed to deliver a note to him asking him to call me, and suggested that if no response was forthcoming, I should hire a litigation lawyer and pursue it as a civil matter.

That seemed like a big hassle, of course, but the saddest part was I wouldn't be driving my Pantera to Reno. I was bummed out.

By the third week of June, there still had been no contact with the mechanic or my car, so I again called the police. This time, (against regulation, but as a favor to me) they gave me the mechanic's address. I plugged it into the GPS and set out on a 35-minute drive to his house.

As I drove up, whom should I see just leaving but the man himself. I flagged him down, he got out of his truck, and I introduced myself. Strangely, he seemed to be expecting me, since he said, "I figured it was you."

I was cordial, as was he, and we engaged in a long conversation about cars, engines and such. Finally, I asked him where my car was. He gave me the address (only a few blocks away) and apologized for taking so long. He said he had a friend's truck in the shop blocking access to the Pantera, but as soon as he was done with the truck, he'd finish my car. He claimed it would be done by that Wednesday. "Sure it will," I thought.

By the way, before I left he mentioned he still had the lock rolling around on the floor of his pickup because he hadn't had a chance to get it to the locksmith yet. Hmm, almost two months and he hadn't had a chance to get to the locksmith. Right!

He also said that since he was so large, he couldn't fit into the car, so to unhook everything at the front of the motor, he was forced to hang towels over the window edges and lean through the windows for access. Well, he was large, and even with towels draped over the doors, I knew that metal was thin and would dent very easily; especially when straining to support a 400-pound mechanic!

After talking with him, I was really, really nervous about what state the car would be when (and if) I finally got it back. I then drove to his nearby "shop" (which turned out to be nothing but a large garage he was renting from the owner of the nearby house).

I peered through the window and sure enough, hiding in the back of the garage, barely visible through the window, was Pandora. Ironically, even if I were to have arrived with a flatbed, there would have been no way to retrieve the Pantera, since it was trapped behind the partially disassembled tow truck he was repairing (and I use the word "repairing" loosely).

To give you just one example of why I was so terrified; while discussing my car he said, "Man, there sure were a lot of washers in that car. I've never seen so many washers. I'll try to put them all back in."

And the nightmare wasn't over.

On June 29, I called the engine builder one final time and told him I had met with his mechanic friend. I told him I was not confident in the mechanic's abilities, let alone timeliness and I wanted the car back by Thursday. He apologized profusely about the situation and said he wished he'd never used his friend the mechanic.

Here's where it turned ugly.

He said he would try calling the mechanic, but when I pressed that I wanted my car delivered to me by Thursday, either together or in pieces, he said he had no way to get it. He sounded irritated that I would expect him to do anything more than try calling the mechanic, especially when I told him I thought he should just do what I had to do; namely, physically drive out to the mechanic's house (since the mechanic, as you'll remember, had a penchant for ignoring phone calls).

I got the impression he now thought it was my problem and not his. I gave him the mechanic's home address and suggested he hire a flatbed to get my car back. I then decided to speak with an attorney for some advice.

It was now July, and I told the engine builder I wanted the car delivered to my house the next day. I didn't care what condition it was in, I just wanted my car back. He became indignant and said he had no way to get it. I told him to rent a truck.

Knowing the chances of him taking action were slim to none, I contacted a good friend named Vince. He had known the engine builder personally for years and offered to talk with him. Long story short, Vince called back and said the engine builder was working to get the mechanic to finish the car that night.

The good news was it seemed there was a light at the end of the tunnel. The bad news was that a mechanic who thought Panteras had too many washers was the one putting it together.

Vince and his truck-owning friend agreed to help me retrieve the pieces of my car. The Auburn Police Department said they could easily do a "civil standby" whereby they dispatch an officer to monitor the proceedings.

Before the embarking on the "repossession" of my car, I thought it wise to revisit the car's location and contact the owner of the house whose garage the mechanic was renting. I needed to be sure she would be home to let us in when we arrived with the flatbed, in case the mechanic was a no-show (d'ya think?)

I tried to call the mechanic, but of course, he didn't answer and his voice mail was again, you guessed it... full. When I went back to the "shop," the owner wasn't there. The neighbors saw me looking forlornly through the shop window and asked what I was doing. I told them the whole, sad story assuming they'd sympathize.

I guess they didn't, because soon after, the mechanic called. He was furious, and said his neighbors told him I was planning to come to his shop with the police (which I was). To say the least, this didn't sit well with him. After a barrage of profanity he said he'd been working on the car for the last three days, and was trying to get it done. He claimed he had tried to call me back several times, but was forwarded to my office. I explained that's what happens when my cell is off; it forwards to the office. Why he didn't leave a message is beyond me. He said he was irritated that I had tried to call him so much. Why he didn't return my calls was also beyond me.

He claimed he was going to try and fire it up that day, but didn't think he could get the rear deck on by himself, so he might just leave it off (bad sign). I told him I'd be glad to help him put on the rear deck, or better yet, take the entire project off his hands. He went off about how he would get it done and he wasn't the fastest mechanic, but he'd been doing this for 37 years. He again complained about the small size of the car, and said how nothing ever goes together as quickly as it should, and here's the bad part; he had never worked on a Pantera before!

He told me not to bother him again and to only talk to the engine builder. He said he thought we had a good conversation when I visited him at his house the week before, but that the talk he heard of me getting the police involved... Well, he told me, and I quote, "I don't need that #*&$%#!" Apparently, he had other issues going on with the police.

I gently reminded him that when we had talked he assured me he'd have it ready by Wednesday or Thursday, which elicited another burst of expletives. He made it painfully clear he resented having to work on the car over the weekend, which really wasn't my problem, of course.

As far as I was concerned, this guy was a loose cannon. The smart thing for me to do, I thought, was to try my best to keep him calm, and then have him deliver it to the engine builder's shop so I could retrieve it as expeditiously as possible. What a nightmare!

On July 9, I got a call from the mechanic. He said he was finally "done" with my car. But "done" didn't mean the car was actually finished. It meant he simply wasn't going to work on it anymore and he wanted me to come and get it.

He said the motor was in, he had run it for a couple of hours, didn't see any leaks and was confident I could drive it home.

However...

1) He couldn't get the rear deck aligned and had chipped the paint.

2) He couldn't get the rear deck shocks to mount correctly, so they were laying in a box with a bunch of other parts.

3) The rear deck lock was still messed up and not even installed. For the trip home the rear deck would have to be held down with bungee cords.

I didn't how many other things he might have screwed up, but I told him I'd come and get it the next day. I realized I might need someone to help me and also be a witness; someone with a good camera. I remember thinking, "I'll be talking to the lawyer again."

The next day, Vince, his friend Don and I took Don's truck to the shop and met the mechanic (miraculously, he actually showed up). I could tell he was sweating even more than usual. After all, there were three of us and only one of him.

he good news was the Pantera drove on to the trailer under its own power. The bad news was it looked as though somehow the mechanic had dropped the rear deck under a moving locomotive, and then jammed it down on something, bending its top edge (where it meets the roof). This tweaked the hinges and chipped the paint all along the leading edge of the deck and the corresponding roofline. There was a little rippling on the roof, too, where the deck lid had been forced against it.

In addition to the deck hinges being out of alignment, the license plate light was sitting in the passenger foot-well along with the frozen rear deck lid lock and other miscellaneous nuts, bolts, and more of those "pesky" washers. The rear deck lid shocks were laying in the engine bay, unconnected to the deck lid, the shifter needed adjusting, the air filter and cover were sitting next to the other parts on the floor, and there were numerous paint chips along the back of the car just above the "Pantera" script. I was fearful of what else I might find upon closer inspection.

The nervous mechanic said he had talked to the engine builder about the situation, and that things would be "taken care of." He said he already had a body shop owner friend of his come by and give him an estimate of what he thought it would cost to repair the damage, although, he said he figured "I'd probably want to use someone I knew." Was that even a question? I was afraid to think of what the difference would be between reality and what his friend thought the repairs would cost.

I don't think anyone had any idea of the actual repair cost. The following morning I gingerly drove the wounded Pantera to a nearby body shop, which I had used before. They are really good... not cheap, but really good. They were horrified at how badly the car had been defiled, and at once began calculating a repair estimate.

The final bill was approximately $4,000.00. I called Hagerty Insurance, they contacted the body shop, and within a week, the check arrived to cover the damage. (Note: I have had two claims with Hagerty and in my 36 years of driving have never had such incredible service from an insurance company).

It took some time, but I finally got the call from the body shop. My car was done!

I immediately went to the shop and reclaimed Pandora. The paintwork was absolutely beautiful and the car seemed to run great, although the trip from the body shop to my home wasn't long enough to confirm everything was truly OK. I was determined to give it a longer run, just to be sure. I drove it for a couple of weeks and discovered another oil leak.

This time I decided to use Panteras Northwest resources, for obvious reasons. It appears when the engine builder replaced the motor he munched the edge of the oil pan, where seepage ensued. To fix the problem, I tightened the oil pan bolts, especially the ones around the damaged area.

Things might be turning around for Pandora. In 2010, I was contacted by Micro-  soft, and they came to Ta- coma, took 500 digital pictures, and are now us- ing my Pantera in their new "Forza Motorsports III; Drive the Dream" vid- eo game. I consider that a good omen.

I also successfully drove the Pantera to the 2010 Fun Rally. I guess third time's a charm! I'm planning to do the same this year.

Will I make it? Well, when it comes to Pandora, there's always hope.

She's been featured in a couple of magazines, and I now have twenty trophies won at various car shows held around the Pacific Northwest.

I love the way she looks and drives... and she sure goes fast!

A Ride to Remember

by Jim Muckenfuhs

In 1978, I got a job at Busam Datsun, in Cincinnati, Ohio, a year after I graduated high school and started as a mechanic, doing pre delivery preparation and inspections, undercoating, and whatever else I was asked to do; all for a whopping $4.50 per hour. The owner's son, John Busam, ran the place. John was what I called a PHD (Papa Has Dealership) and a bit of a horse's ass. I got along OK with him, but for the most part, he was a pain to deal with and always acted as if he was above those around him.

A year after I started, I moved up in the shop, got a minor raise, and purchased a '69 Camaro. It was a true SS 396 four-speed car. It wasn't real pretty, but it sure could run. John thought it was a piece of crap and reminded me almost daily. "It's all noise" he used to say. He had formed his attitude based on its well-worn appearance. What he didn't recognize was the simple raw power that was expelled through the exhaust. All he heard was noise.

In 1980, Datsun installed a turbo on the 280ZX. The in-line six-cylinder engines suddenly became much more powerful and John thought these cars were the fastest things around. I have to admit, they were fast, and fun to drive, but it was apparent that John hadn't been for a ride in a real fast car. He had never taken a ride in my car.

One day, John decided to take some shoe polish out back and put a note on my window that read, "$99 Special - Today Only." He took a Polaroid picture of it and gave it

168

to me, laughing as he walked away. Sadly, this is the only picture I have of this car. I was pissed off at first, but now I'm glad I have it. A couple of weeks later, he came back to the shop whistling to himself, and said "Hey, when are you gonna take me for a ride in the "special?" I was eager

to get him in my passenger seat and said, "Let's go before you change your mind."

We got in the car and off we went. Leaving the parking lot, I turned right into heavy traffic on E. Kemper Rd., a major arterial, and not a place for high jinx. But, a quick 100 feet or so and another right put us on Lippleman Rd, a small two lane street. I drove nice and easy; following the 35 mph speed limit until the road came to a stop about 3/4 of a mile away. Turning right again, I made a quick left into a circular driveway of a large old house. We always used this turnaround for short test drives. Exiting the drive, a quick right, then a quick left and we were heading back the way we came.

A quick note here... the 396 wasn't stock. It had a big cam, three-inch headers, and three inch straight exhaust all the way to the back bumper. This is why John always said, "It's all noise." Just as I was about ready to rock his world, he half yelled, "SEE, I TOLD YOU..."

I put my foot to the floor and unleashed its full explosive power. It kicked the car into a hard fishtail to the right, which is exactly what I wanted. I held my foot to the floor while looking out the right side of the windshield and I could kind of hear my passenger screaming something, but didn't care.

When I slammed it into second gear, the force caused

the rubber dash pad that covered the entire length of the dash to fly off into John's lap. (Damn, I kept forgetting to replace those clips). The pad had also fallen into the steering wheel, but I was too focused to stop now. Fishtailing to the left now, the screaming was getting much louder, but I still couldn't make it out clearly.

I slammed it into third, revving between gears enough to go sideways one more time before shifting to fourth, and coasting.

This all happened in a matter of seconds, but it must have given John time for his life to flash before his eyes. The scream had turned to a mild whimper as I reached over with my right hand and lifted the dash panel back into place. As you can imagine, we returned to the dealership rather quickly. Pulling back into the lot I started to mock John, saying "Yep… it's all just noise right?"

John didn't hear a word of it. He had jumped out of the car while it was still moving, rolled quickly and got back up; all in a nice suit and tie mind you. He ran into the showroom and didn't talk to me for two days. After that day, the man never got in a car with me again. I've not talked to John in over 25 years, but I know Busam Nissan is still there and I guarantee he still remembers that ride.

If I Could Turn Back Time

by Rich Tringali

Like many young guys growing up in the mid '70s, I was sixteen years old when I got my driver's license and, of course, I immediately wanted a car so bad I could taste it. One night, after an inspirational viewing of American Graffiti, my father and I went out in search of the perfect car for me. Being a real car guy with a penchant for building and fabricating, he figured we should get something that would allow me to get my hands greasy and learn how to build my own hot rod.

A chopped '37 Ford coupe turned out to be just the thing we were looking for. It was a body on a frame with no running gear. We bought it and because we didn't have a garage, had it dropped in the middle of our back yard. Thus began an every night father and son adventure that turned into one of the coolest hot rods in the area.

We started by taking the body off the frame and my dad showed me how to install a 12 bolt posi rear end. Next, using his cutting and welding skills, Dad split the wishbone to accommodate a small block Chevy motor and tranny mounts.

The real fun began as we went to the local auto body supply-house and got everything we would need to get the frame grinded, filled, sanded, and painted. As we lived on a major road, people started watching the progress and soon a few brave souls stopped to have work done. So, by the time I was seventeen years old, I wound up with a little business I could call my own. I was learning how to do things that many people never learn and it was all pretty exciting.

Before long, the frame was done and we added the body and finished the chop job. As I finished the body on the '37, I added stock rear fenders, a '32 grill shell, little hot-rod fenders, then primed it and added smoked glass. I was also working on my brother's custom '55 Chevy.

We were really getting into this hot rod lifestyle and started going to all of the cruise nights like Capt. Fowlers', the Pizza Tower, and Jolly George's. Never the shy ones, we made our presence known and many soon recognized us as the Tringali Brothers.

My dad rebuilt an old 327ci Chevy motor that he had and put tri-power on it. We installed that and the tranny into the waiting hot rod, which had been begging for a heart, and the first day it was running we went out for a shakedown run. We hadn't install exhaust yet and sure enough, the man who lived across the street was a MDC cop. He ran out of his house in pajamas and flagged me over for running open headers. I got lots of tickets in those early years, but the first one was by a guy in his sleepwear!

There were a few more weeks before winter set in and we did as much as we could before finally having to leave it sit with a tarp over it. To my surprise, but because I had been building a reputation as an up and comer, I got invited to the Mass Street Rods Car Club Christmas party. I really felt like I was becoming a full time "gear head."

We had no garage and I had to wait until spring, but once the weather allowed, I painted my car in the open-air right there in our backyard. I had chosen Canary Yellow with Flames. Over the long winter, I had kept the trunk lid in my basement. I learned to use an airbrush and duplicated the album cover to American Graffiti on it. It was a major accom plishment and wound up being praised by

many as a work of art. So, with the paint done and the trunk lid installed, the car was done.

My brother, Donny, and I then hit the local cruise night and unveiled our finished cars. It was a family affair. I took my dad in my '37 and my mom went in my brothers '55. It was a night to remember. The local club members would point and say, "There's the Tringali Brothers." We had become really well known by then and it felt great!

About the time I had started a car club known as The Sinners, a local nightclub known for their '50s era music had Bill Haley's Original Comets featured one night and I went to go see them while I was out with my '37 Ford. One of the members of the band noticed my car outside and asked if they could take a group shot with it. I said "Hell yea!" and to my surprise, someone had told them that I played guitar and they asked me to "sit in." I played lead guitar as the crowd danced to Rock Around The Clock. It was an event that I will never forget and I knew from that night on that Hot Rods and Rock and Roll would always be a part of who I am.

The next year I made a custom flip nose for the '37. I added '59 VW glass headlights, '59 Caddy taillights, a four speed, and primed it old school brown.

After my dad passed away, I sold my car to the owner of Fonzie's Auto. I drove it over to his place and said a fond farewell. It hurt like hell, but it had to be done. We sold most of our family belongings and moved our mom to Florida. Once she passed, I moved back to Massachusetts and to my knowledge Fonzie's Auto had closed and moved, so I never expected to see the old '37 again.

Decades passed and one day I saw my '37 on Craigslist. It was for sale and looked just the way it did when I sold it to him. The ad read, "Built by a father and son team" and I nearly cried. He had kept the car in his private collection and wanted $28,500. I had sold the car for $4500. I called

him and told him who I was and he said it was the same as the day he bought it except he had sold the tri-power off it and added a cake box hood scoop.

Like many old hot rodders, I didn't have the money to step up and buy what I used to have when I was younger and I'd have given my soul if I could have turned back time and still have it. It was full of memories of great times with my dad and the learning experiences he gave me.

Today, I own Righteous Rods and have built many clones of the famous '32 Ford driven by the character John Milner in American Graffiti. I am close friends with many of the cast, including Bo Hopkins, Candy Clark, Paul Lemat, and Cindy Williams and they have used my personal car for many shows. Street Rodder and George Barris even did a DVD about me.

Put a fork in me... I will live, sleep, breathe, eat, and die a True Hot Rodder!

Telltale Skirts

by Domenic Tringali

At twelve years old, I started buying every hot rod or custom magazine I could get my hands on. I was destined to grow up being a motor head. My father was one and my older brother was falling right in step, as well. Again, it was my destiny. I would have felt the same way regardless of family, though. I just always loved cars!

My brother started building hot rods at age 15 in our back yard and we have both made a lifetime of building and playing with old iron. It was in the old man's DNA and he passed those strong genes to us. He was also in the plumbing business and by the age of sixteen I was working in his shop, so I have always had the mindset of how to make things fit and work.

All of my friends were car guys, too, and so I was always around cars and people were always bringing me cars. One such car is the theme of this story. It started out with a blaring horn coming through my bedroom window one morning from the driveway, waking me from a deep slumber and dreams of bare metal, welders, paint, and upholstery. Isn't that what everyone dreams about?

The horn was coming from a '55 Chevrolet that had been given to a friend by his brother's widow. They had driven for two days from Texas to New England and needed money more than they needed the car. He offered it to me for $500. The car was in bad shape. There was no interior, other than the driver's seat and the only paint on the car was a gray primer. The three speed floor shifter needed bushings, but the 265cid V8 purred like a kitten. It ran like a brand new car. I gave him cash.

My brother, Rich, and I got right to it and by the end of two months, we had the car as straight as an arrow and painted a rich light blue. The interior was completely custom with custom seats and both the headliner and rug done in a rich blue fur. The Moon steering wheel and chrome record player completed the interior.

Designed to be a period piece, we had installed '59 Caddy taillights, a tube grill, and wide whites accentuated with spinner hubcaps. The door handles were shaved and the hood emblem and all side chrome were gone. It was lowered in the rear and the crowning touch was the addi-

tion of '55 Ford fender skirts. There was certainly none other like it. It was a one of a kind car.

I would have kept it forever, but when our dad wanted to put a deck on his house shortly after it was completed the con-

tractor said he didn't want money, which dad didn't have anyway, he wanted the '55. I hated to get rid of it so soon after it was finished. It was just the way I wanted it and my brother and I had both put our hearts and souls into it, but at the moment, we decided it was just a car and dad needed a deck. So, we said OK. In reality, he got the better of the deal. The deck bid was $5,000 and the car was worth at least $8,000. Oh well, we'd rather build cars than decks so we said good-bye to the Chev, thinking we'd never see it again. It broke my heart and I missed it more as every day passed.

As it turned out the contractor moved next door, but the car was nowhere to be seen. He had sold it a guy named Sonny, whom we found out, had sold it to someone else. The car wound up in New Jersey and then sold again to a guy in New York. She was being passed around like a cheap whore. My poor baby! I lost track of her after that and once again, believed I'd seen the last of her.

As time went by that car kept tugging at my heart-strings, but I kept pushing her to the back of my mind. I really had resolved to quit thinking of her when in 2002, my brother and I were at the New England Summer Nationals walking and watching all of the cars go by when a very familiar baby blue '55 Chevy rolls up. I about fell over. I stepped in front of the car, forcing the driver to stop. I went to the window and told the guy that it was my car. We had built it "back in the day" and it was exactly as we had done it.

The guy was insistent that I was wrong. The car had been built back in the '60s and I would have just been a little kid. He was going on and on with a story that someone had fabricated and he had embraced as reality. I told him he was either lying or very misinformed, but I could prove him wrong right then and there. He thought I was full of shit and took my challenge, adding that he'd give me $100 if I could prove him wrong and convince him I was right.

When we built the car, the only way we could get the '55 Ford fender skirts to fit was to weld two 5/16" brass closet bolts to the inside of each skirt. Then we drilled holes in the body and secured the skirts with wing nuts on the inside. So, that was going to be my proof. I told him in detail what we had done and let him know what I was going to do. He was hesitant, but agreed. So, I reached under the car and removed the skirt, showing him the bolt, wing nuts, and holes in the fender. I told him that because we had built it to be a period piece; I considered his insistence that it had been built in the 60s a huge compliment.

He invited me to drive the car and to come over to his house for dinner so I could spend some time with her. After dinner, my brother and I spent about an hour talking with him, reminiscing about old times. I suspected that her owner was not only being gracious, but had ulterior motives, as well. He figured he had a big fish on the line and wound up asking me if I'd like to have the car back. Well, of course, I would. But, what was the price? He casually threw out the $40,000 price tag and I about choked, knowing that I would never get her back in my lifetime. That was way too steep for my blood.

Resigning myself to saying goodbye, I bent and gave her a final kiss on the hood and walked away. I was so upset that I even forgot to take any pictures. Walking away, I didn't look back and I've never seen her again, but I keep going back to the New England Summer Nationals every year.

Good Job, Kid

by Tom Glide

When I was a kid, I used to ride my bike to a junkyard three miles out of town where the local Chevy dealer dumped the wrecked or worn out cars they couldn't sell. My mission was to visit a '48 Chevy that had captured my heart.

It had been painted black... with a brush. Parts of old screen doors were riveted over rust holes and the wheels had been spray painted silver, the paint covering half of the tires, as well. It looked as if someone had tried (operative word) to dress it up to sell, which had never happened. Now, it had been relegated to sit, forlorn and abandoned under an old oak tree in the back corner.

I'd slide behind the huge steering wheel, peering out the tiny windows, and dream that I was driving it. Of course, in my dreams it was pristine rather than the rusting hulk sitting in the briars on two flat tires that it really was. "Someday, I'm gonna have one of these," I'd tell myself.

When I was thirteen, I got up the nerve to ask the owner, Paul Geyer, or P.G. as everyone called him, about buying it. He let out a huge belly laugh and told me "Ga-home kid." But, I kept after him, hoping someday he'd take me seriously.

The day before my fifteenth birthday, I had just finished mowing a lawn when I noticed him standing in front of his dealership across the street. He was wearing his usual bright yellow plaid pants, shiny patent leather white shoes, bright green suit coat, and white straw hat with a rainbow colored band. He was puffing on a fat cigar, looking over some new Chevy's that had just been delivered.

I hopped on my bike and rode over. As I neared him, I noticed an oh-here-comes-that-damn-kid-again look on his face.

"Still interested in that '48, if ya figgered out how much" I said, which had become my standard line for breaking the ice over the past couple of years.

"Ya don't want that heap, kid," he said.

I was shocked. It wasn't his standard "ga-home kid" response and there was no belly laugh either.

"What'cha need is one-a 'dose," he went on, taking the cigar out of his mouth long enough to point it at a gleaming, brand new '74 Z-28 Camaro that was dark green with white stripes. "Come back when ya got money, kid, and we'll put ya in one," he said, turning to go back inside.

"I do have money… and I'm not interested in that! Well, I guess I am interested. It's a nice car and all, but it's not what I want (or could afford). So, just tell me, how much for the '48 in the bone yard?"

You just ain't gonna let up on that, are ya kid?" he asked.

"Nope."

"Ya say ya got money, too?"

"Yep."

"How much ya got?"

I thought of the five bucks I had in my pocket and began to tally how much I knew I'd stashed in my piggy bank back home. I figured I had a little over 100 bucks.

"Thirty five bucks" I muttered sheepishly. I fully expected to hear his laugh echo between the dealership and Jerry Toole's General Store across the street.

"I'll be damned!" he snorted. "That's exactly how much

I figgered it was worth! Looks like ya got yer-self a car, son," he said, holding out his hand.

I stared in disbelief and shook his hand. I had my first car! I didn't have a license yet, no idea if it even ran, and no real income to fix it. But, I finally had it.

Oh yeah, there was one more small detail. I still hadn't brought it up to mom and dad. I thought I'd tell them about my plans that night and we'd figure out a way to get it home from there. I went home and paced back and forth in the living room, practicing my speech over and over, coming up with answers to everything I thought they could throw at me.

A short time later, I heard a truck pulling up the hill leading to our home. When I looked out, I saw Rick Lautner, the mechanic at the dealership, backing an old Chevy wrecker into our driveway with the '48 hanging off the back.

"What'cha gonna do with this pile a shit?" he asked as he lowered it to the ground.

"I'm gonna fix it and it's gonna be my first car."

"Yeah," he snorted "Good luck with that!"

"Hey! It ain't that bad!" I lied.

"Kid, you and all the money in the world ain't gonna fix this dog turd,"

Rick always was an arrogant S.O.B. that I didn't care for, but deep down inside I wondered if he was right. I had never touched the inner workings of a car, but I knew I loved the looks of the older cars like this one.

"Besides, you're just a kid. What do you know about cars? With any luck, you'll screw it up so damn bad, it'll never see the road" he sneered, climbing back in the tow truck. That cemented what I thought of him, and my resolve to someday, somehow drive this car.

When he left, I looked at the car with briars and tall

weeds hanging off it and listened to the tires losing air. Well, so much for gently breaking the news to mom and dad about what I was planning to buy.

Two of the rotten tires had gone flat again by the time mom got home and pulled into the driveway with a bewildered look on her face. When dad got home the shit hit the fan. Obviously, I had lost my mind. Had I thought of how I was going to fix it? Moreover, what was I going to use for money? Did I have any idea how hard it was to find parts for old cars and how expensive they were?

I stammered through some half assed, half thought out answers to each of his questions, none of which were ones  I planned for until he announced he was going up to Geyers to give him a piece of his mind.

I pleaded with him. I'd do anything he asked if he'd just let me keep it. Besides, it was only thirty-five bucks and it was my money, right? I could be spending it on a lot worse stuff than this.

It worked! That, and the fact one of the first cars mom and dad had was a '48 Chevy.

I subscribed to every car magazine out there and poured through how-to's in each issue. I hung on every word Gray Baskerville and Pat Ganahl wrote about iconic builders like Lil John Buttera, Pete Chapouris, Jim Jacobs, "Magoo" Dick Megourac, and Barry Lobeck and studied the pictures of their latest works to learn how to do it myself.

The car was the first of many cars I've owned, but it technically didn't make it as my first car as it was nowhere near drivable by the time I was sixteen.

That honor fell to my dad's hand me down '69 Camaro.

It would be four long years before I drove that '48 under its own power, but it was worth every skinned knuckle, bloodied hand, shed tear, and hard earned dollar that went into it.

Why would all that work be worth so much to me?

Well, it was mostly because I did it myself, with no formal training. The only thing that wasn't done by me was the chrome on the bumpers and the upholstery. Mom did the upholstery, once I took the seat covers apart for patterns so she could make new ones. A family friend's son who owned a chrome shop for a bargain out the back door price did the bumpers.

Was it a showstopper? Not hardly. It wore a coat of rattle can hot rod red primer. It had a set of used chrome reverse wheels, slightly pitted, that I bought at a swap meet for ten bucks and looked decent enough. To those wheels, I added just the right size bigs and littles (tires) and it had that same "stance" I'd seen in the magazines. I did the bodywork over and over until it was straight and didn't look like a fifteen year old kid did it.

One thing it did have going for it was a nasty sounding 327 Chevy V8 that made all the right sounds. It was a mis-match of parts that really didn't complement each other very well, all of which I picked up for free or next to nothing... which was my budget at the time. It could barely  wheeze out of its own way on takeoff, but it had a lumpy cam gave it that hot rod sound. To me, that was good enough.

It also gave me the proudest moment in my life and one I cherish to this day. My best friend Don and I took it to Columbus, Ohio to the NSRA Street Rod Nationals. The night before the show, we were looking at all the cars in a hotel parking lot, many of which we had seen in magazines. All of them made my car look like a pile of crap.

As we made our way through the sea of cars, I almost literally ran into none other than Gray Baskerville, who was standing there talking with Buttera and Chapouris. We introduced ourselves, told them we were their biggest fans and I mentioned my car, albeit not worthy of sharing the same ground as theirs.

Gray seemed intrigued. "Ya mean that primered Chevy ridin' around is yours?" he asked.

I shook my head yes, not knowing why he asked and hoping I wasn't the butt of an inside joke. "Man, that car sounds bitchin'! Good job kid."

He could have said nothing. He could have berated it for the amateurish heap it was in comparison to everything there. He could have blown us both off and gone back to his conversation with two legends in the car world. Instead, THE absolute car guy (in my humble opinion) found something good to say about my car.

Its first tank of gas was a glorious moment, too. What's so great about a tank of gas you ask? I got it at Geyer Chevrolet, which offered full service. I actually paid more for the gas there, because it was full service. Why?

Because the mechanic, my nemesis, Rick Lautner, would have to drop whatever he was doing and give me polite and courteous service.

He never said a word to me while he pumped my gas, but I couldn't resist. When I paid him for the gas, I looked him straight in the eye and said, "Guess I didn't screw it up so bad, huh?"

That car started the addiction to cars I still have to this day.

Why I Love White Cars

by Larry D. Brooks

You know how sometimes you just seem to click with somebody or something that just seems so natural for you. I have felt this many times in my life.

I have had a love affair with cars since I first knew what they were. I did not play or care at all for sports. As a kid, I saved my allowance and spent every penny of it on auto-related items and bought Hot Rod and Car Craft magazines religiously. I bought model cars and built them. When I could force myself to save my money long enough, I would purchase a factory promotional model.

Later in life, as I began purchasing real cars, I noticed a trend developing in my preferences, mostly in the color. It was not intentional by any means. It just occurred on its own. Or so I thought. That color was white and after I bought my first white car, I noticed I just enjoyed sitting and looking at that car.

I did this much more than with the other cars I had owned and finally realized it was because of the color. I noticed the lines of the car seemed to look better when finished with white paint and when the car was clean, well, it REALLY looked clean! I felt that the chrome accents and chrome wheels on the car truly stood out on a background of white paint. I noticed this more and more as I bought more white cars. It was becoming an obsession!

I have owned probably twenty or more white cars in my time. Relatives, friends, and co-workers alike have all asked me, at one time or another, why I like white cars so much. I'd always tell them the reasons stated above, but I knew in the back of my mind that there was more to it than that. However, for many years, I just could not put my finger on it.

Then, one day I had an epiphany. If you do not know the definition of this word, look it up as it has a strong bearing on the outcome of this story.

In 1957, when I was five years old and already a huge car lover, my father decided to purchase a new family vehicle. He left home one day to search out his dream car.

Apparently impressed by the success the Pontiacs were having in NASCAR racing that year, he came home later that day with a '57 Pontiac Star Chief two-door hardtop. It was the complete opposite of the car he had driven to the dealership, a '51 Buick Special two-door sedan that was dark green with gray interior and black wall tires. It was a drab and frumpy car even in my five year old mind.

However, this '57 Star Chief was as beautiful a car as I had EVER seen in my short life. It had wide whitewall tires, spinner hubcaps, fender skirts, rear antenna, and a funny looking triangular sort of emblem on the front fenders. I asked my dad what that was and he said it stood for the Tri-Power engine in the car. I remember his lifting the hood, telling me to look under the huge air cleaner at the three carburetors. I did look, but I did not understand what tri-power was or did. He told me that was what made the Pontiacs so fast!

The car was truly modern looking compared to the old Buick he had and it was WHITE. It had a dark red spear down the side and the leather interior was dark red and white. I had never had a car affect me like that one did. Then we rode around in it and I genuinely felt special. I remember what a brilliantly sunny day it was in Atlanta, Georgia on that afternoon. The weather was warm and we had all four windows down. I absolutely loved it and was excited that it was about to be ours. After my dad, mom, sister and I arrived back home in it, my dad told my mother he was going to go back and try to make a deal with them on this car. My mother gave her approval and off he went.

He came back home a couple of hours later in a new '57 Pontiac... but it wasn't that Star Chief. It was a Chieftain two-door hardtop with wide whitewalls and small hub-caps. Its main color was aqua with the white side spear; and it did not have the Tri-Power. I remember the huge let-down I experienced even at that age. He said he could not afford the Star Chief so he had to go to the Chieftain line. It was really a bummer! That white Star Chief had been burned in my mind and obviously still is to this day.

The next big experience for me was in 1959. By then, we had moved to Mobile, Alabama. My dad was the manager of an insurance agency there and one evening after supper, one of his agents came by our house to show us his new car. It was a '59 Chevrolet Impala two-door hardtop with wide whitewall tires, spinner hubcaps, fender skirts, dual rear antennas, and a pair of crossed flags above a chrome V emblem on the hood. The agent asked my dad if he knew what the crossed flags indicated and he said he did not. Neither did I.

So, he opened the hood and I saw massive orange valve covers with a huge black air cleaner above them. The man told us to look under the air cleaner and I noticed this car had three carburetors, too. Wow! Suddenly, all the memories of that '57 Star Chief came flooding back into my young, but impressionable mind. Guess what color that '59 Impala was. Yep, you guessed it. It was white. It had a bright turquoise interior and he had all four windows down. This car was even more beautiful than that Star Chief was.

Being a proud new owner, he asked if we would like to take a ride in it and I remember saying, "Well, yeah!" They both laughed at that and in the car we got. Then more magic happened. He started the engine and the exhaust reverberated through the whole body of the car. As we proceeded down the street, it roared. My dad inquired about the smooth rumble and the guy told us he had taken it to an exhaust shop as soon as he bought it and had them install new glass-pack mufflers. I really was in heaven; proud to just be seen in this car and it became emblazoned in my tender, young mind. I remember asking my dad sometime after that if we could get a car like that and he gave me a stern "NO!"

I honestly believe this is the reason I love white cars so much now and have for so many years. I own six cars and four of them are white. I can find no other reason for my absolute obsession for this wonderful hue for an automobile than the imprint that was left on my young and impressionable mind.

When the time comes that I am done obsessing with cars, it will be because my soul has passed from this earth; and I hope when that time comes, I will be carried to my final destination in a white funeral coach.

Dad, I've Got to Have a Car

by Hank Callaham

I was a gear head from the time I was about 11 years old. During junior high school, I'd stare out of the windows, watching all of the young guys cruisin' by in their hot rods with the loud pipes and pretty girls sitting beside them. That was who I wanted to be and I never lost that dream.

Going through high school, I was always ready to buy my first car. I'd put a down payment on a car and bring it home and have my dad take a look to see if I could buy it and he'd say "No, it's got too much horsepower or didn't have any horsepower… something like that. There was always a good reason in his mind. He did this every time. I kept trying, though.

Once, I found a two tone green '57 Chevy with a 409cid motor and brought it home. It was a cool car and I wanted it bad. He said "Absolutely not! Take it back!" I expected no less, but still, I kept trying. Then there was a '49 Merc that was in primer that ran real good and I took it home to see if he'd accept that. Same deal; I had to take it back.

At this point, he just laid down the law and said "No! You're not going to have a car until you get out of high school!"

I said, "Dad, I've got to have a car. I've got football practice and this and that kind of practice and besides, Mom doesn't drive, so I've got to be able to go do things."

In reality, I wasn't completely without a car. Because my mother didn't drive, but still needed to go places, I was delegated quite often to be her driver. That meant that on Saturdays we would drop Dad off at his shoe store and I would take Mother to see her brothers and sisters. While she was visiting, I'd pretty much have free run of town in my dad's '57 Chevrolet. It was a 210 four door with a 283cid V8 and the three speed transmission with over-drive. I wasn't too concerned with the Overdrive part, but I did enjoy the power that it produced in first and second gear. I guess I wasn't any different from any other teen-ager in that respect and I raced it every chance I could get!

I kept bugging him about being able to buy my own car, however. This was never met with positive results. Fi-nally, he said to me, "You can buy your uncle's car two months before you graduate."

Oh boy! It was a '47 Chrysler Windsor four door with Fluid Drive. It was a huge executive model car that most guys my age considered a boat! I said to him, "You really know how to build a guy's ego!" But, I dealt with it as best I could. At least I had something to drive.

Once I graduated from high school, he actually sold me his '57 Chev. That surprised me, because he knew I had been running the wheels off of it every time I got a chance.

One night at dinner months earlier, the subject of tires came up with his casual comment of "I can't figure out why the back tires on the car are wearing out before the fronts. It's the fronts that get the most wear." I choked a bit and said, "You mean the fronts are supposed to wear out first?" He looked straight at me and firmly said, "Yes, sir, they are!" Dinner got real quiet for a while until he calmly interjected "I think I know the solution to the tire issue." And then he looked at me and with his voice a few deci-bels higher yelled, "You're buying the next set of tires!"

Well, I learned about cars and tires pretty quickly. In the remaining time I borrowed his car, I quit racing it. Well, sort of. At least I quit tearing up the tires.

Today, I'm retired and playing with my '62 Impala, a beautiful car that I love to show and drive any chance I get.

Victoria: Class of Thirty Two

by Dale Moreau

In the fall of 1931, Henry Ford was preparing to end the successful run of the Model A. Under extreme technical difficulties and very late in the model year, he introduced the V-8 to lighter pockets than had been available before.

The last engine of the Ford Tri-Motor airplane roared to life as Burt Richardson "tied" his self in, all the while acting as if he wasn't scared. Burt was one of the salesmen that had been to Detroit previously for the Model A roll out in '28, but they took buses that trip. It was a short flight from Buffalo, but the butterflies were enjoying the flight more than he was. "This better be one great car Henry has to show us," he muttered under his breath. Actually, the plane was very comfortable, and popular to the newly burgeoning commercial flyer. Burt had been lulled to sleep during the flight, but awakened during the decent into the Motor City. While he was more relaxed than usual, he white knuckled just the same, remembering he had to go home in this thing. Lake Erie isn't the Atlantic, but Burt wasn't Charlie Lindbergh either.

The unveiling of the '32 model line for Ford dealers wasn't as glamorous as one might think. The dealers and some of their salespeople arrived from all over the country and herded into buses for the short trip to Ford heaven. Today, manufacturers call this kind of place the "skunk works"; a place where they design and build the prototypes. At that time, Ford's was a series of long wooden buildings with skylight windows and planked floors. Security was fairly tight by the standard of the day, almost making Burt feel uneasy as they passed through the gates entering a large courtyard with high solid fences topped with curly wire. Even with the Model A roll-out fresh in his memory, Burt wasn't prepared for the '32 Ford.

"Katie bar the door!" thought Burt, as he gazed upon the three-window coupe, the Phaeton, and all the other great bodies. He couldn't wait for his test ride. They rolled the various models out onto a banked test track to try out the suspension and steering, which combined with the hot new V-8 was a real performance machine and head turner. When Burt got his hands on a load of these babies, he wouldn't have to sell any of them. People would be begging him to take their money.

Several months later, the first shipments arrived at the Ford dealership on Locust Street in Lockport, New York. A gorgeous Victoria caught Burt's eye and he knew exactly whom he was going to show it to; a pretty little nurse that loved to drive named Mary Margaret Sullivan.

My mom started working as a nurse in 1926 at age 17. At that time, a person didn't need a driver's license and mom hit the road young. She kept going with a succession of automobiles until she was 85. In all those years, she never was ticketed and only had two accidents, neither of them her fault, she said.

By 1932, the year of "the" Ford, she had driven a Dodge phaeton, a Ford Model A roadster and an Oakland coupe. Being a young single female in those times, it wasn't easy to find places to live. So, many of the nurses at the TB sanitarium where she worked lived in dormitory style housing provided by the institution. It was in these surroundings that my mom met Mary Margaret Sullivan.

Mary Margaret was a very independent woman, especially for 1932, and the confines of these living conditions really bugged her. It was during the start of their friendship that they met Burt Richardson and started a trend that would last over thirty years. You see, Burt was a car salesman, but not the stereotype one might imagine. He loved cars, he cared about his customers, and he was very quiet.

It's not clear just how he came into the girls lives at this point, but for their sakes, it was a very good thing. You see, Burt took care of his customers before, during, and all the way to the next sale. Burt never stopped caring. Every year or two he'd just show up with doughnuts and asking if the coffee was on, and an "Oh, by the way, I've got a car outside you might like." Burt never had a car the girls didn't like until many years later, but in 1958 the tail fins were stacked against him.

Late in 1932, Ford put on its biggest roll out since 1928 and the introduction of the Model A. The first Ford V-8 was touted to be quiet and fast! Burt had found a car he could love and sell, and when Mary Margaret saw the car that he brought out to the "San" to show the girls, she was in love, too. Truth be known, Burt liked the car and the girls so well he just brought it out to show them as an excuse to drive it. Shortly after Mary Margaret saw it, he never got to drive it again. In reality, Burt closed sales long before he ever realized it half the time and he was really just an innocent bystander in this love affair. The Vicky stole Mary Margaret's heart.

September and October in western New York State are a sight to behold. The colors along the Niagara River are second to none, but it doesn't last long and one day the thrill is gone and winter is there big time. Mary Margaret's Victoria was not going to sit outside in winter… ever. They salted the roads in New York State and she couldn't stand the thought of the fenders falling off her '32 Ford, so she rented the upstairs of a house down the road from work. It was perfect, because the genteel lady owner had an empty garage that would allow the '32 to repose during the long winter months.

From November 1932 until the spring of 1951, the Vicky spent every winter in the same garage. For nineteen years, she took the bus to work in the winter even though she had a car in the garage. A '32 Ford had upstaged poor Burt and he wasn't alone. The '32 Ford is still having the same effect 75 years later. However, he had my mom and in 1933 showed up at her doorstep with a maroon 1933 Ford Tudor and best of all, it was faster than her Oakland by a bunch. She loved it and Burt had to walk home again!

The list of cars got longer over the years, only slowed by WWII. My mom kept her 1940 Pontiac for eight years. She had a lot of Pontiacs because the Ford dealer moved and Burt stayed. So, he sold Pontiacs. He didn't have to walk home so often.

In 1955, mom bought the first Pontiac V-8. It had a three-speed stick shift on the column. She kept it for six years, which was long enough for me to become a teenager and learn how to drive and eventually drag the local cruise spots. Teaching me to drive consisted of sitting in the passenger seat, reading the newspaper while I bumped and jerked the clutch, barely getting to second gear by the time I ran out of driveway. This was the just beginning of my own fascination with cars!

Later, when we had moved to a new place, her best friend Naomi would arrive in her beautiful '53 Ford Victoria. I'd jump into that car as soon as she got there and after making a few dozen trips around the circular drive, she would have just enough gas to get home to Middleport. I had a rich buddy around the corner. He and I used to run up and down his long driveway in his mom's '53 Buick Skylark convertible, a beautiful car and definitely a step up from the Pontiac three speed I was used to!

Up until 1951, my mother's friend Mary Margaret had filled her life with her precious '32 Vicky and the sick kids she cared for every day. At thirty-nine years old, she had spent her energies, talent, and time on her career. Then Chick Daily showed up. He was forty-five, had lost his wife during the war, and didn't expect to fall in love ever again. Using her life savings, Mary Margaret had bought a house in 1940 after the owner had died. Eleven years had passed and the house needed some work. Chick was the first contractor she called and the rest, as they say, is history.

By this time, I had been to Mary Margaret's house many times as a little shaver. I'd sit behind the wheel of the '32 in her driveway and dream of rolling down the road, even though I couldn't see over the wheel. I distinctly remember the smell of the car, the feel of the mohair matted over, and the big long shifter and foot pedals I couldn't reach. I loved that car as much as Mary Margaret did!

Chick had a nice house in Carlisle Gardens on the west end of Lockport that he had built when the area was just

growing and, once they had cemented their relationship, he and Mary Margaret set to living there in 1951. She rented her house out to a young doctor and his wife and the Vicki was moved to the new garage. Chick had a Buick and a Ford pickup, so Mary Margaret's beloved Vicki was retired; put up on blocks and covered with a tarp.

In the late '70's, I would go out there with my kids and

Mary Margaret Sullivan Daily would tell me "Dale, get out there and show your son the Vicki!" So, Jay would sit in the seat I had sat in so many years before as I watched him wonder at the long shifter and the funny upholstery, making "vroom vroom vroom" sounds like he was driving!

Life goes on. I moved to the west coast and my son grew up. We've had lots of hot rods and bikes and I'm fully into a motorhead mentality. My work, automotive photography, takes me around the country every once in a while and so over the years I have visited my mom and home town several times a year all along the way.

Chick passed away in 1983 and Mary Margaret Sullivan Daily carried on with her life. When I was in town, I'd go out to the Gardens and visit her. If she had ever found that I had been home and didn't come out for pie, cookies, or sweet cherries from her trees, she would have been wounded. The last few years, I took her to Gasport for ice cream and to some local car events at Olcott Beach to see the "old cars." She resented the terminology, because to her they never grow old. She still had the Vicki and in her mind, it was still a new car.

As Mary Margaret found herself nearing 90, she decided she had to do some planning. She called and inquired as to when I would be home again, telling me she had some things to discuss. I gave her my schedule and she was very glad to hear I'd be there in a week. She asked me to come to the house on Sunday for dinner. Who could pass that up?

I went over late in the morning, after spending some time with my mom. As usual, I visited the old Ford out there in the garage underneath the same tarp that Chick had put over it nearly 40 years before. That tarp had seen much better days, now quite full of holes and barely able to do its job. I gently pulled the tarp away, climbed in and sat on the mohair. I could reach the pedals now and the

197

shifter had shrunk, but sitting there made me feel like a little kid again.

Well, I was in for quite an eventful afternoon. Another guest had arrived for dinner. His name was Seaward Elwyn Sand and he was Mary Margaret Sullivan Daily's lawyer. He had been her lawyer since the 1960s and obviously cared a great deal for her. They spent a lot of time explaining the plans for her estate and for me. She told me the story of her friendship with my mom, the saga of the car, and of having cared for me since I was little. She also expressed her belief that I loved that '32 Ford Victoria as much as she did and then told me something that absolutely rocked my world. She was turning the Vicky over to me right then and there with the hope that I would restore it in her garage.

I was overwhelmed. I never imagined that this would happen and nearly broke down in tears. I thanked her and assured her that her trust was well placed. I would cherish the Vicky just as she had for all those years.

I immediately laid out a rough outline of bringing the Vicky back to life. During the next few years, I spent a lot of time in the garage cleaning and repairing the car while my mom and Mary Margaret would go to lunch with the girls from their nursing days or just kibitz on the back

porch about former times. They had a lot to remember. These ladies went to church in buggies and had seen a bunch of changes over the years.

After many visits and some major surgery on the Vicky, it came to life again. For forty-four years, it had waited to hit the streets of Lockport again with new life and just a little more horsepower. Mary Margaret thinks both the color and the new motor are just a little too loud and questions why the front tires are smaller than the rear, but she enjoys the air conditioning and the Big Band sounds on the stereo radio. We take rides to Niagara Falls and out to the ice cream place on the way to Gasport. However, what Mary Margaret Sullivan Daily still can't figure out is why everyone is smiling at her and waving. She's forgotten that she's had that same smile since 1932.

The Foolishness of Youth

by Dave Alvar

In 1964, I was seventeen and dating a girl, Sue. She had two older brothers that worked on tugboats going to Alaska. One had a new Mustang coupe and the other had a new red Falcon Sprint convertible with the 260 and a 4 speed. When the brothers were gone, they left their keys with little sister. I was driving a '57 Ford at the time.

When we went out, we usually had a choice of taking my Ford, the Mustang, or the Sprint. Well, a red convertible, V8, four speed made it a no brainer! One day I was driving up Whidbey Island in the Falcon Sprint, top down, Sue riding shotgun, sun shining... Life was good. Up ahead, I saw a blue Falcon four door. He was doing the speed limit, and I was doing about twice that, so I quickly overtook him. I pulled out to pass and as I went by, I realized that Sue's dad was driving the Falcon. I didn't have a clue what to do, so I waved and kept on going. That was probably a bad choice, because the next thing I knew, I was banned from ever driving any of their family cars.

About a week later, the battery on my Ford gave up the ghost and being totally broke, I was afoot. I and another guy, Steve, walked over to visit Sue, who lived about a mile or so up the beach. The dad was still pretty pissed at me and quickly tired of my company. After a short while, he suggested to his daughter that she drive us home. He specified that we go in his car, not the convertible, and also reminded her that she was to do the driving, not either of us.

On the way home, Sue mentioned that she might know the whereabouts of an unsupervised battery. About a mile south of my home, a new residential community was being built and the hillside was still shaped, having only a steep road just cut into the face of a cliff. Sue said that she had seen the battery at the bottom of the cliff. I never thought to ask her how she had gotten down there in the first place.

Now, I need to paint a picture here. It is after dark and it has started raining heavily. The "road" in question runs flat from the main road, toward the beach. It then takes a 90-degree turn and starts down sharply. Next, there comes a 180-degree switchback with a large boulder on the inside of the corner. Then there's a long, slender, steep, straight section cut into the cliff face and finally, another 90-degree turn onto the flats at beach level. At this point, it is all mud.

With Sue driving, we made it safely to the bottom, only to discover that the battery was long gone. Sue announced that she was absolutely not going to attempt the drive back up. That left me in the driver's seat.

We made it around the first corner and most of the way up the straight section before the six-cylinder, automatic Falcon bogged down and came to a stop.

There was no getting going again, as the tires spun on the slick, muddy clay. I instructed Steve and Sue to go sit on the trunk, hoping that the added weight would afford some traction. It didn't work. Finally, Steve and Sue got off the trunk and slogged around to the passenger window. As we were discussing what to do next, I suddenly realized that they were moving away from me. However, they weren't moving. I was. The brakes were locked, but the car was sliding down the hill and toward the edge of the cliff. I peered out the side window and saw that I was looking straight down, probably 150 feet, to the bottom. Another few seconds, and I would be down there and if I lived through it, Sue's dad would kill me for sure.

I did the only thing I could think of. I released the brakes and let the car roll down the hill, slowly steering it away from the edge as it picked up speed. When I hit the bottom, I slid the car backwards around the corner and brought it to a stop. My heart was beating about a hundred miles an hour.

Finally, I stopped shaking, and decided to try the up-hill run one more time. I took the bottom corner as fast as I dared and did everything I could to maintain my momentum as I fishtailed ever higher. When I got to the switch-back, the car slid sideways and just missed the boulder. But, it kept going, all the way to the level area at the top.

We drove slowly back to my home, and spent quite a while hosing the mud from the Falcon and then Sue went home. I don't remember what she told her dad about why it took so long to take us home, but it must have been a good story, because I'm sure he would have mentioned it to me, otherwise.

The moral of the story…

I never did figure that part out, but I do keep good batteries in my cars these days and stay out of four door Falcons that don't belong to me.

Diamond T Boat-Tail Roadster

by Steve Walker

L ike most of my cars, the Diamond T Boat-tail Roadster was designed by a confluence of napkin sketch dreams and parts at hand. The dream part involved an ongoing fantasy of transcontinental races utilizing the highways and truck routes built during the Second World War. I imagined a variety of classes ranging from 500cc up to Unlimited in much the same manner of hydroplane racing. I envisioned courses that would have included the Trans-Siberia, the Alaskan Highway, Pan-America, or I-5 border to border.

The smaller classes would be dominated by three-wheelers or lightweight single-seaters resembling Formula Junior racers. The Unlimiteds would be giant truck-like vehicles crewed by drivers, navigators, and mechanics and powered by massive super-charged or turbo-charged V 12 engines. For this class, there might be a maximum weight to preserve the roads and maximum dimensions to clear underpasses and allow them to pass each other on highways.

Unlimited hydroplanes were something I grew up with; a sport that would be impossible to create now, but whose thunderous spectacle of scale, noise, and danger are grandfathered in. Conversely, city-to-city car racing succumbed to safety concerns early in the twentieth century. But, imagine if it had not.

Imagine races that are thousands of miles long with pit stations strategically located along the route and corporate sponsorships splashed across the billboards of immense

 bodies. Starts would be staggered in reverse order with the heaviest and fastest classes last so the entrants would converge upon the finish. Highways are closed sequentially as the race progresses.

Towns along the course would erect grandstands to view the passing cars. Camera crews for all the major media would be staked out at challenging corners and mountain passes. Aircraft would pursue the leaders and broadcast reports of their progress. The 3.0 liters, 1500s, and especially the featherweight 500s would excel in the twisty bits through the mountains, adding to the advantage of their earlier start. But, once the race descends to the long straights that stretch away into the horizon, the monstrous Unlimiteds truly come into their own, eating up the miles in great gulps of speed, sucking the smaller cars along in the waft of their passing.

The events never happened and they never will, but I built the cars anyway. One of them is my Diamond T GPT (Grand Prix Truck). The other is the Diamond T Boat-tail Roadster.

The parts-at-hand consisted of a pair of Diamond T trucks slowly returning to the earth on a farm north of Kirkland. Charles Van Ness, who had abandoned hope of restoring them and believed I might create something from them, gifted them to me. The two flatbed trucks, a '44 and a '48, had suffered severely from rust and vandalism, but the remains of the magnificent art deco grills were sufficiently inspiring to me to begin yet another custom car. I was between studios and had to persuade my friend Lynn Taylor that his back yard would look better with a car project. I left him to persuade his wife that this was true. He built her a greenhouse and for that, she allowed us 12 months. Her agreement came with an assortment of conditions about messiness and working hours, all of which we violated, but we did complete the yellow roadster within 11 months and in the end, Roxanne was referring to the project as "her roadster."

Early on, I contributed my three-ton '62 Chevy work van for the platform. I had intended to power the beast with a 350 Chevy. Lynn acquired instead a 350 Olds thinking it was the same thing, but it would not mate up with the "rock crusher" gearbox in the Chevy frame. So we installed the Olds along with its automatic transmission, telling ourselves we would replace it with a Chevy as soon as we blew up the Olds. Thus far the Olds has persisted, despite our best efforts.

We moved the radiator well back to expose the front axle, chopped off the front bumper mounts, and located the Diamond T bucket headlights on the frame channels between the front wheels. The Diamond T front fenders were moved to the rear where they proved to be large enough to enclose the dual rear wheels. The engine louvers came from an old oil furnace. A sub frame of ½ inch square tubing was shaped to support the new body panels and the boat tail... well, that was just slow labor.

The woodwork and narrow twin cockpits are, to me, reminiscent of the coachwork on early touring cars and recalls in particular the famous rosewood Hispano Suiza.

Paul Cooper sprayed it with One Shot Chrome Yellow; one of my favorite colors.

The Boat-tail Roadster won First in Class in the very

first car show we took it to and it trophied at almost every car show the first summer. We learned to step away from it and listen to the spectators. We got our ears filled with "My dad had one of those!" "Diamond T only built six of these!" and "I watched 'em race as a kid!"

At an Anacortes, WA show, the roadster was featured on the show poster, a wonderful piece of art done by Bill Mitchell. The posters had been distributed throughout the area and on the ferries. As Lynn and I approached town in the roadster two small boys by the side of the road were jumping up and down and gleefully screaming "It's here! It's here!"

On the second day of the show, James Fitch introduced himself. Chief engineer for the Diamond T Motor Company during the last sixteen years of the company's existence, he had retired to Anacortes. Mr. Fitch was delighted to discover that someone had built a Diamond T hot rod. He gave us an autographed copy of his book "The Motor Truck Engineering Handbook" as well as an assortment of Diamond T memorabilia, including Diamond T cuff links and a Diamond T string tie clasp that I cherish.

"Salmagundi," the Diamond T Club newsletter published photos of the car. "Monster Garage" filmed it for their program and the committee building a statue of J. P. Patches and Gertrude in the north end of Seattle asked me to chauffeur the famous TV clowns to the ceremony.

One day, my daughter, Leila, was talking on the phone to a high school girlfriend who suddenly exclaimed "Holy shit! The coolest car in the world is going by outside! It's huge and it's yellow!" "Does it have a wooden butt?" asked Leila. "Yeah" said her friend. "That's my Dad's car!" said Leila.

Lynn had a black, checked leather holster he had picked up at a yard sale. It looked like something a policeman would wear. We mounted it on the firewall even though we don't have a gun for it. It's not visible unless you lean into the cockpit. I had occasionally experienced individuals taking the liberty of climbing uninvited into the open cars I have built, trying them out, testing the pedals and steering. I'd like to give them the benefit of the doubt, thinking that their enthusiasm for the car has momentarily overcome their manners. The empty holster stopped all that. Once they spot it on the firewall, they stop climbing in, step back, straighten up, and glance about looking for the owner. We call it our security system.

The painter, John Moilanen modified a series of photos of the roadster, creating backgrounds to locate the road-ster at races or rallies in Monaco, Berlin, Morocco, Indianapolis, and Alaska, illustrating its fictitious racing career.

There may never be races like the ones I've imagined, but for now my contestants not only draw a lot of attention and admiration, they could inspire others to build the cars that infiltrate their dreams.

Diamond T Grand Prix Truck

by Steve Walker

I keep doing drawings of cars. A lot of them featured Diamond T grills, because after building the first Diamond T Boat-tail Roadster, I still had one more grill to use. One design in particular caught the eye of Colin Case, an architect, art collector and yachtsman in San Francisco. "We need to build this," he said.

He wrote a generous check to initiate the project. Furthering the history of Diamond T racing, this would be the model succeeding the Boat Tail. It would be mid-engine, like the pre-war Auto Union Grand Prix racing cars and  would have four-wheel independent suspension. It would retain the distinctive, identifying grill and the long rear body would be crested with a large graceful tail. The straight sides would rest on fat side pods, given the car visual gravity. Overall, it would be at least as big as the big yellow Diamond T Boat-tail Roadster.

Like Lynn and I, Colin was a big guy. So, I was not going to repeat the small cockpit. This would seat two huge guys with a cooler between them. There would be plenty of legroom and lots of storage compartments, as well. I wanted to sit high, with a good view of traffic.

208

I drew up a space frame with '60s formula car suspension, scaled up to truck size.

I sent Colin, who lived in San Francisco, drawings of the frame and body designs. He wasn't quite satisfied with the fin and insisted the engine needed to be a V-12. "You get it and I'll put it in," I told him. But in the meantime, to prove the engine bay could accommodate the length, I installed a six-cylinder 250cid Chevy truck engine. The engine and suspension arms bolt to aluminum plates. I had seen this technique on formula cars in the early '70s. It would also expedite the engine and transmission swap when Colin came up with his preferred engine.

As usual, I sawed up my work van for parts: straight six engine, front hub carriers, master cylinder, and such.

I launched into the most laborious parts first, hand cutting and welding the frame, selecting hundreds of lattice boards and planking the body. Most important was to get the shape right, and I knew I could do that in wood. Later it could be the fiberglass form, if needed.

I created elaborate scissor action hinges for the engine bay doors by the time-honored method of trial and error. Some salvaged Diamond T latch handles provided the appropriate detail on the doors.

Colin went to work selecting the color.

He sent a color chip, which in reality was an exquisite English made die-cast model of the "Chapman Special," second place finisher at the '55 Indianapolis 500. It was a lovely turquoise blue and as color chips go, it was a knockout. But, when Colin later visited Seattle, he spotted the model on my desk. "Is that the one I sent you?" Yes it is. "No, that's not the color. It looked better in the photo." I think he meant the blue of the Blue Crown specials of '47 and '48.

Sadly, Colin died, an unexpected and abrupt death, before the car was done. He was a classy guy and devoted friend that I will sorely miss. At his wake, I shared pictures of our last, unfinished project.

Colin's death took the fun out of it for me. The car languished for some time under a tarp in a corner of my shop until I finally resolved that it deserved completion. So, in the summer of 2010, I stripped it back to the frame and dove in with renewed determination to see our car on the road.

My goal was the Tacoma Hot Rod a Rama; my favorite local car show.

I worked twelve and fourteen hour days as the show approached. Friends would drift in, get "Tom Sawyered" into the project, and work to exhaustion helping me out.

For wheels, Trail Ready custom machined American cast billets to my specs.

The wood, I sprayed with four coats of varnish, adding just a tint of "Blue Crown Special" blue to the third coat, which I feathered in along the fin, tail, and edges.

I designed the upholstery and had Mobetta Shows stitch it together. Endless trips back and forth to hardware and automotive stores were made to find fittings and adapters to tie together all the disparate parts. Seat belts from the black Chevy van were installed, along with tail lights from Bent Bike, Harley rear view mirrors and, of course, Diamond T headlights. The headlights, on testing, worked just fine for about six seconds and then went dark. Of course! What a bozo move!

In 1948, they would have operated on a 6-volt system. I replaced them with modern 12-volt sealed beams and they are perfect.

I hired a sign painter, Sergio Nicoli, to paint number "523" on both sides (my wedding anniversary... "Look honey, I built it for us!") as well as the classic Mobile red Pegasus.

I also had Sergio paint a prominent logo for "Colin Case Racing" on both sides of the fin and he produced "Close Enough Engineering" decals for the doors and "Diamond T" emblems for the cowling. He reported that when he looked up Diamond T on the internet, the first thing that appeared was a picture of the fictitious Boat-tailed Roadster, now more famous than the venerable truck company was.

The night before the Tacoma Show, I struggled with leaking brake lines and power steering fittings. I replaced all and then maddeningly, the Chevy 10 brakes were frozen. In the shop, I scrounged a set of Chevy 20 brake calipers and ground them to fit. At 10 o'clock on the morning of the show, with the car just hours from completion, I conceded defeat and drove

my Alfa instead. Later, bitter at having missed the show, my friend Greg Nowak put it in perspective for me. "Steve" he said, "when the biggest problem we have is which car we're driving to the car show, we're really not that bad off."

It was to be the last Tacoma Hot Rod a Rama.

The first show I actually got the GPT to was my new favorite, the Rat Bastards Infestation car show at the XXX Root Beer stand in Issaquah, WA. Jennifer rode with me.

I made up a "history" of the car and the Grand Prix Truck Races that I framed and perched on the seat. Almost immediately, a fan began telling me that their great uncle had competed in the Grand Prix Truck Races.

The car was a hit at the show and garnered its first of many trophies.

Following is the history I have printed up and display in the vehicle at car show:

1948 Diamond T GPT

Commissioned by Privateer Colin Case for the 1948 season of Grand Prix Truck racing.

Long distance Grand Prix Truck racing started up after the Second World War. Races were held on demanding transcontinental roads built to move men and material during the war such as the Alaskan Highway, Burma Road, Trans Siberia and Trans Sahara.

Sportsman – entrepreneur Colin Case, (an avid yacht racer who also sponsored formula and sports car racing teams, gravity racers, bicycle racing teams and a hockey club), decided to enter the wildly popular new sport of Grand Prix Trucks.

Colin selected Diamond T to fabricate his GPT racer. The premier truck manufacturer in the world from1911 to 1966, founder C. A. Tilt started out building racecars and established a reputation for innovation and reliability.

Colin commissioned an entirely new design inspired by the forward thinking pre-war Auto Union Grand Prix cars. His mid-engine vehicle features a welded tube space frame, independent suspension, power steering and a straight six engine.

After many seasons of hard campaigning followed by long neglect, this vehicle was in sad shape when abandoned in the Close Enough Engineering parking lot by the last owner, Charles Van Ness.

The ongoing restoration has stretched over years due largely to the shifty character and slack work habits of the occasionally paid personnel of Close Enough Engineering.

Hot Car

by Chris Kimball

For several years, I had been eagerly awaiting the opening of the LeMay Car Museum in Tacoma. During the first weekend in June, it finally happened. To demonstrate our ongoing support of the facility, I'm a "Gold Key" member of the museum, and my family has a commemorative tile located in the entryway. In the tile, in addition to the names of my family and me, I also included "Panteras Northwest" since Panteras Northwest is a "club level" member of the museum.

Our club is fortunate that one of our members, Warren Lubow, is highly involved with America's Car Museum, as it's called, and he was able to arrange spaces for PNW members on the museum's front lawn during the grand opening. Not only that, he was kind enough to also find spots for my sons, David, with his 1981 Camaro, and Donald, with his 1990 Rover Mini. I must say, it was truly a dream-come-true to have my sons there with me--each showing our own, classic car. I can't help but think their cool car choices resulted from the trips David and Don each took with me to Pantera Owners' Club of America Fun Rallys during their formative years.

A month or so prior to the event, I decided it was time to add the "Pantera" rocker-panel decals to Pandora (the name bestowed upon my '72 pre-L by Mike Thomas and Doug Braun for reasons too numerous to list), so I attempted to apply the decals in my driveway. After applying the

Driver's side stripes and lettering, I wasn't satisfied. There were several bubbles and a small tear, which bugged me, so I ordered another set of decals from Asa Jay. When they arrived, I took my car to a local detail shop, and they did a marvelous job of applying both sides for $120.00.

Now I was ready for the big show!

The appointed day arrived, and David's Camaro, Don's Mini, and Pandora had never looked better. We left early Sunday morning (and when I say "early" I mean about 8:30 AM--that's early for me) and our three-car parade made it to the museum with nary a hiccup.

As I drove on to the show field, followed by David and Don, I slowed and rolled down the window to receive my goodie bag. As I burbled past one of the vendor booths, a gentleman commented on how great my car sounded. "Thanks!" I beamed, forgetting the old adage about pride going before a fall.

Not thirty seconds later I heard someone yell "Fire!"

"Oh no," I thought, "I hope it isn't a bad fire. I'd hate to see a beautiful car get damaged."

It was then I glanced in my rear-view mirror and saw the flames and thick, black smoke. I had a pretty good view of the inferno; it was about two inches from my head, erupting from my very own engine compartment!

As people scurried about in search of a fire extinguisher, I grabbed the one I keep readily accessible between the seats, jumped out of the car, opened the deck lid, and sprayed into the engine compartment between the engine cover and the fiberglass trunk. Fortunately, the fire was quenched almost immediately, although the adrenaline lived on.

Once we knew it was safe, a group of LeMay volunteers and other drivers helped push Pandora (and her now sheepish owner) to the assigned spot on the field. After David and Don got their cars in position next to mine, which is what I had hoped for, thanks to Warren, I emptied the trunk, pulled out the tub, and braced myself for the carnage I expected to see.

Imagine my surprise when I saw virtually no damage whatsoever.

Years ago, I mounted a couple of auxiliary gauges on the right side of the engine cover, viewable from the driver's seat by looking over my right shoulder. They monitor water temperature and oil pressure. The small, plastic tube running from the back of the block to the oil-pressure gauge was the problem. The tube had somehow vibrated and fallen onto the passenger-side header. Of course, as soon as that occurred the plastic tube melted in half and began squirting hot oil on the header, which, along with the plastic tube, created the Dante-esque result. It's odd that scenario never happened before; sometime during the recent past someone must have knocked the plastic tube out of place.

With such a short distance between the flames and the gas tank, I was extremely thankful my entire car didn't end up the subject of a song by Deep Purple, The Crazy World of Arthur Brown, The Doors, The Ohio Players, Bruce Springsteen, Johnny Cash, or Jerry Lee Lewis. Having one's car burn to the ground can really dampen the mood at a car museum's grand opening I shudder to think what might have happened if the fire had started while I was on the freeway heading to the event, or stopped at a busy intersection.

Since the LeMay Museum doors didn't officially open until 10 AM, I had time to clean the fire extinguisher's residue from the engine bay. With a little sweat and a lot of Speed Shine, by the time the first visitors arrived my car looked great. Of course, I had to hide the charred ends of the plastic tube.

During the show, Warren took me into the bowels of the museum to search for parts that might allow Pandora to get home under her own power, but we could not find the correct size of brass plug I needed to screw into the hole in the engine block. At this point, I was doubly glad my sons were there. Don took me in his Mini to a local O'Reilly's Auto Parts store where I purchased the correct-sized plug. A few minutes after arriving back at the LeMay show field, Pandora was back to running condition.

Following a great day of car gazing, both on the show field and in the museum, my sons and I made an uneventful trip home. A few days later, I bought a new oil-pressure hose and fittings and now things are just as they were, except now the plastic tube is encased in a much thicker rubber hose and routed in such a way that it can never get close to the header.

If you have a chance, you must visit Tacoma and take a tour of America's Car Museum. It is spectacular, and even if Pandora's not there, you'll see a lot of hot cars.

New Lady to the Old Car World

by Sue Nader

I always had a little interest in cars. I grew up with two younger brothers who love cars and my best friend is a car fanatic, so I was accustomed to the idea of classic cars. I was not accustomed to the world of car shows, car meets, cruise in's and some of the other events I have been exposed to lately.

I would see these really cool cars parked in parking lots of the Wendy's or the A&W and admire them from a distance, noting which ones I thought looked nice and which I didn't care for esthetically. That's as far as I ever got before a year ago.

I met Tim, my significant other, a year ago and he is a car fanatic. He owns and runs his own Custom Hot Rod Garage and he has slowly started introducing me into his world. At first, I have to admit, I was dragging my heels when it came time to go to shows or cruise in's or the track. I would say to him "No honey, it's OK; you go on your own. I'm going to go out with the girls" or "I'm going shopping with my mom."

I couldn't understand the point of spending an entire day in a parking lot looking at these old cars. The idea of it baffled me, but I did it because it meant a lot to him that I come and I wanted to express a sincere interest in "his world."

So, that's what I did. I took a "suck it up pill" and I went to the track and I went to a couple car shows. Then the season ended and I took a sigh of relief and thought, "Great, now I don't have to go to any more of these shows!"

Little did I know...

The year went on and all of a sudden, the weather started to change for the better. The days got longer, it was lighter out longer into the evening, and we all know what comes with the new weather... Car Season!

All of a sudden, he had every weekend planned for us with car shows! That didn't register to well with this woman at first. But again, because it meant the world to him, I went to these shows. Surprisingly, during the first show we went to, I found myself starting to like being there.

I actually enjoyed looking at the cars a little more closely and admiring the work that people put into these cars, some of them rolling works of art. I started to change my outlook on the car shows and the car world in general. I was really seeing Tim in his element while talking to car owners and guys who have had their cars in his shop or talking to guys who  have been to some of the bigger events, like the races at the Bonneville Salt Flats. I started to see and feel his passion and love for this whole other world and I was starting to be fascinated, as well. We now joke that the winter is to what I want to do and the summer is his time. Lately, I'm getting the best of both worlds.

We recently went to the Good Guys show in Seattle, WA and I found myself submersed in the old car world again, except this time I wanted to be there. I was really enjoying myself. We were there to photograph the show and while I am not a photographer by any means, I started to play around with the camera, taking pictures of the cars and the people. By mid-day, I was having a blast!

I think I almost gave my other half a heart attack, because I wanted to talk about cars, different angles to take pictures, and what kinds of pictures would be cool to get. I couldn't believe how much fun I was really having.

We got home that night and I thought, "Wow, I didn't think the day would ever come where I would actually enjoy being at a car show!" Now, I am looking forward to the next show, partially because I get my own camera to play with this time, but mostly because I enjoyed the last show so much.

I like the atmosphere and the energy, seeing people's proud faces as they display the cars they have busted their hind ends creating, detailing; some driving from long distances to attend. Most of all, I like the feeling of it being a family event because I am a big family person. I can picture myself bringing our kids to these shows and pulling them around in their own mini hot rod or classic car one day, listening to their dad talk to them about cars.

If I could offer one piece of advice to the women or men out there who are dreading going to these shows (I know you're out there!), it would be this…

"Give it a chance. Give it a fair shot because you may just end up liking it. Find a way to make it enjoyable for you, as well. Whether it be checking out the clothes (love the shirts by the way!) or taking pictures… have fun! This is quality time that you get with your partner or family that you can't get in any other way. It's quality time without the TV, the computers, or gaming systems. Enjoy it!"

Aurora Speedway

by Steve Walker

On weekends, Dad would pack mom, my older brother Bill Jr. and myself into the Ford and drive us all to the Aurora Speedway to watch the Midgets races. Just to the north was Playland Amusement Park with carousel and roller coaster rides that Bill and I might have enjoyed, but we never knew it was there. Dad was careful about that. There wasn't going to be any debate about where we were going.

The racing was spectacular. We sat on sagging splinter infested speedway bleachers and ate salted peanuts; cracking the shells open, and letting the remains fall through the bleachers. The air filled with the cackling and snarling sounds of the furious Offenhauser engines and the intoxicating aroma of burnt fuel and hot oil. The roaring cars would slide into the turns in thick clusters, belching flames and  bunching together before squirting out of the turns, separating briefly in the short straights and then bunching together again in the next turn.

Lap after lap they stormed around the track whipping up a great whirlwind of dust and wrappers that buffeted the crowd in the stands. The racing was close and the drivers impossibly brave. They would tangle wheels and tumble or push each other through the plywood fence. The yellow or red flags would come out while the debris was sorted and cleared from the track, wailing ambulances sped away, and then the race would go on until, at last, there was a victor.

At the conclusion of the races, we would cross the track and wander through the greasy infield pit. The lushly painted cars, still boiling hot, emitted clicks and drips as they cooled. A rainbow of color tinted the gleaming chrome exhaust pipes, testifying to the heat they had endured.

Dad knew some of the racers. We would stop and visit, seeing their perfect gem-like cars proudly nestled in the only clear space in the middle of a tiny garage packed with tool-cluttered workbenches and shelving.

I learned how exhausts were tuned in the '50s. An engine would be run up to temperature and the pipes marked for cutting where they stopped changing color; or how welds were checked on a frame; hanging it from a rope and striking it with a mallet. If it rang true like a bell, the welds were good. Small secrets were revealed. If square gear keys separated under the enormous torque, they could be replaced with lathe tool-bits. An aluminum cigar tube with a nut for ballast could become a hydrometer, scribed to indicate mixture density when floated in a soup-can of fuel.

Dad was hooked. He wanted to go racing. But, mom would have none of it. She had seen too many crashes and too many ambulances carrying drivers away from the track. With two small boys to raise, Dad was not going to be allowed to do anything so dangerous.

So, he bought a set of plans from Ted Jones and we built a 7 Liter hydroplane instead.

The Tikimobile

by Steve Puvogel

In 1968, I was thirteen years old when I met my first love. It was a car.

During a family camping trip to Rainbow Falls State Park, in Washington State, my life was forever changed. A vehicular vision of chrome and fiberglass appeared before my young impressionable eyes that fateful weekend. I had never seen anything like it.

Near the campground, there was a gathering of various hot rods and old cars and something I had never seen before; a fiberglass 1923 Ford Model T C-Cab panel truck. I knew about old cars and hot rods, but this was something totally different and I immediately fell in love with it. It was a custom vehicle that was driven on the road and I told myself, "Someday, I am going to own one of these."

By 1977, I was married to wife version 1.0 and had a new baby. At the local swap meet, there was a fiberglass 1923 Ford C-Cab pickup cab for sale for $125. It wasn't a panel body, but it was a C-Cab and that was close enough for me. I bought it, got it home, and decided I would mount the cab on a VW bug chassis and running gear. I then found an old VW Bug for $100 and the project was underway. Being a young newlywed and having a new baby, money was very tight. Alas, the C-Cab had to be sold and I was heartbroken. Wife 1.0 said to me, as it was being hauled away, "Don't worry, someday you are going to own another one of those."

By 2006, I had upgraded to Wife 2.0. Life was better and money was not as tight so, I was fully entrenched in the old car hobby. We were coming back from a T-Bird Club cruise and had stopped at an antique store when Wife 2.0 said, "Oh look, there are some old trucks here." Of course, I had to check them out.

I walked around the corner to see the exact same C-Cab body I had sold 30 years earlier, sitting right there in the driveway. It was in the same condition as when I sold it, including the crooked transmission tunnel cut. My first words were, "I'm going to buy it!" Wife 2.0 was very confused. "What are you going to buy?" she asked. I explained the story of the C-Cab to her and told her "Everything's for sale." She was still a little bit confused, but said "OK." You just gotta love upgrades.

The owner of the C-Cab, realizing that he had too many cars anyway, sold me the C-Cab body for $250. I would  have paid a thousand dollars, if I had to. Now, I needed to find another VW bug and resume the project. I watched Craigslist for several months with no luck. I was always too late. There was a VW based dune buggy, with a plywood body, that had been listed for eight months. I figured that I didn't need the body anyway and if it ran well, I would just tear the plywood off and scrap it. Now, this vehicle looked like a one and a half scale King Midget and it was ugly, too, but I paid the guy $800 and drove it home.

I had no problems driving it home and it was time to start ripping that body off it. I had the front bumper off and was just about to start tearing the plywood off when Wife 2.0 comes out to the garage and says, "Stop! Don't tear it apart, it's too cute!"

"What do you propose I do with it?" I asked.

She said, "You'll figure out something." I then told her that this would just be another vehicle and I still wanted to do the C-Cab project. Wife 2.0 said that was OK, but she liked the little beast and we could have both projects. In my mind, that translated to... I had to figure out what to do with the VW sitting there covered in wood.

So, one evening I spent about three hours in the garage, staring at every angle of the wood clad dune buggy. I had to do something to cover the sides of it, because it had some real weird angles. Then it hit me, "Surfboards, I need surf-

boards!" I would put one on each side, and they would cover a lot of the body.

Apparently, it decided to take the form of a "surfers rig" and I began my quest for surfer type accessories.

I found a couple of old surfboards, laid them on the fenders, and got ready for another "stare at the car" session. The solution was to make a flatbed type setup, for the back of the car. That way the back of the car would be one width, all the way back. I found a couple of bunk bed safety rails to make up the bedsides and function as surfboard mounts. It was still pretty ugly, but getting better.

I found a couple of Tiki Masks on eBay and put lights in the eyes and mouth to function as turn signals. The Tikis were mounted on either side of the "grille" and a fake shrunken head was installed as a hood ornament. It was starting to come together in my mind and I liked what was happening.

The body remained completely wood, including all of my modifications. I still needed to upgrade the rear lights and my choice was '59 Cadillac taillights. I thought I wanted to countersink them into the plywood body, so I went looking for something that would work and found that kitchen sink drain baskets were a perfect fit. However, instead of countersinking the lights, I used kitchen drainpipes, mounting them so that they came out of the back of

the bed like insect antennas. Since the lights were taller than the boards, they could easily be seen. Perfect.

I have since filled the flatbed with vintage luggage, a guitar case, and other surfer accessories. Deciding that the VW needed to have a name, it became the "Tikimobile." We have driven the "Tikimobile" around for a few years and I have had more fun in it than any other vehicle I have ever owned.

But, now it's time for me to get back to my first love, the C-Cab, and build it. Plans no longer call for VW power. It will also be Tiki themed, but will be built on a Toyota motorhome chassis. In today's vernacular, it will be a Rat Rod Tiki Bar when finished. There will be severe modifications to the motorhome section in order to match up to the C-Cab body, but that story is yet to be written.

Yeah, I guess I am an "Old Car Nut"!

Biohazard in Blue

by Edward Munday Jr.

My father, Edward Munday, Sr., owned and operated Munday's Auto Trim Shop in Hickory NC, now Moore's Trim Shop, from the time I was born until 1998, when he passed away.

He would sometimes buy "old cars" to restore; redoing mostly the interiors and convertible tops or vinyl tops. With a family and a shop to support, he did everything he could to make ends meet. The extra money from the occasional car passing through his hands went a long way towards getting by.

Originally, he had a shop in the town of Granite Falls, right where there is now a red light in front of the Granite Falls Wal-Mart on US Hwy 321. Back then, 321 was a two lane road. The shop was also located in Hudson N.C. at one time and even in Florida once. He opened up in his last location in Hickory, N.C. on Hwy 70 West, where he put in long hours and a lot of work.

Dad didn't live too far from the shop, so if he had a car finished, or someone wanted to drop one off, he was always willing to go and open up for them. One time that he opened up was to let a tow truck drop off a car that someone wanted to give him.

If you restore old cars, the information in this story might be of value to you and give you food for thought. My Dad's story goes to prove that some of the articles you read in magazines are more important than you might expect. Such was an article that was read and set aside many years ago.

In August of '98, Dad called me to say he had a very bad backache and wanted me to make an appointment with a doctor for him. So, I did. I had told him time and time again to get a family doctor, but he would just say that he didn't need one because he never got sick. Obviously, he was very old school.

The doctor I set him up with told him he thought he had a kidney stone and gave him a prescription to pass the stone. The next day dad called the doctor and said he thought the meds were making the pain worse. So, we went to a kidney specialist who took X-rays. The X-rays showed that he only had a very small stone and the doctor said that it shouldn't be causing that much pain. Appointments were made to get more tests.

Dad felt he would not be able to afford all of this treatment and there was not a coalition for small businesses to have health insurance and so, dad always paid cash for everything. The prospect of a long string of doctor's visits worried him. He didn't have to worry for very long.

Five days after the pain had started, we ended up in the Catawba Medical Hospital emergency room. They took X-rays of his chest first thing. The doctor came out of the office, put the X-rays up on the screen and then he just dropped his head. He turned and said "Mr. Munday, you have stage four lung cancer." My wife and I, and my dad, were all absolutely stunned.

We all asked what we should do next and the doctor said there was nothing that could be done. We needed to make final arrangements. Dad was ready for hospice right away. He died one month to the day of having the initial back pain. The death certificate read "Lung cancer of unknown origin."

Years before, when I worked at the shop there was an auto trim and restyling magazine, which pictured and told of a car you didn't want to work on without proper precautions. The car was a blue '63 Dodge and it reportedly had asbestos behind the headliner and under the carpet for insulation purposes.

I had shown the photo and the story to Dad a long time ago, but it was set aside and not much thought about it after that initial look. The magazine worked its way to the bottom of a stack like so many others that arrived in the mail before it.

When I went to close up the shop while the hospice team and a family member were caring for Dad at home, I noticed a car that was almost finished. The car was a '63 Dodge and it was even blue. The seats were finished, the carpet installed, and about half of the headliner was installed. I later found out that an older lady had the car hauled off from her home because it no longer ran and she couldn't afford to have it fixed.

She had seen on TV where companies would haul old cars off for free. Her daughter knew of my Dad and his shop and she got the Dodge back from the junk yard and gave it to him.

She didn't know that the car was a biohazard and Dad was just going about his business, fixing up another old car to make a profit. Neither realized how the story would end.

It's difficult to say that this one car could have affected him so quickly, but over a period of time, he had probably encountered other cars with similar materials. How many cars out there have passed through the hands of restorers that had similar secrets?

In the end, there were no lawsuits or big insurance payouts... just a great auto trimmer that went home to be with Jesus.

Old Cars Keep You Young at Heart

by Chuck Holmes

When I was 15 years old, I got bit by the desire to have my own car. It didn't matter that I didn't have a license. I wanted to get a car to fix up and call my own. My Dad told me that if I wanted a car, I would have to go and get a job and buy it with my own money. He didn't have a problem with me getting a car; he just wasn't going to fund it. Back then, it took a while to save up enough money for a car, but I finally had $50.00 burning a hole in my pocket and my Dad and I went to a wrecking yard in South Seattle.

We wandered up and down the aisles looking at the hulks of old iron that still vaguely represented what had once been functioning and drivable cars. About the time, I was certain that we wouldn't find anything suitable for me, we rounded an aisle, and there it was… a 1940 Chevy Business Coupe. I was amazed and in awe. It was nothing like the junk we had been looking at so far. It sat there proudly displaying shiny light green paint on a pretty straight body. A peek inside revealed an interior that was in good shape, as well. We inspected it up one side and down the other and decided that if the price was right, the car was right. The owner of the yard told us that it was towed in with a bad motor and if I wanted it, I could have it for $50.00. Bingo! We had a winner.

Things are sure different on today's roads, but in 1957, my Dad towed it home with his 1955 Chevrolet two door BelAir. We got it down to our back yard and I began my adventure. Without a driver's license, all I could do was work on the car and work on it I did. This car planted the seed for a lifetime interest in rebuilding and restoring cars and I went through a couple of parts cars getting it ready for my senior year at Highline High School in Burien.

The first one was a real score. One of my good friends and I were walking in a semi-rural area when we spotted a 1937 Chevy Sedan sitting in the middle of a chicken coup. That seemed an odd place for a car and it raised our curiosity. I could certainly find a better use for the car than the current owner had! We found him standing on the back porch, eyeing us with great interest. We approached him and asked why the car was sitting there acting as a shelter for his poultry and he told us to follow him. We did and he took us into the coup and opened the door of the car.

It was in pretty fair condition other than the fact that it had no seats in it. The owner went on to explain that he had been a smoker and one night when he tossed a cigarette out the window it flew back into the car without him realizing it. Before he knew it, the interior of the car had caught on fire. So, not wanting to spend the money to fix it, he parked it and took seats out of it so chickens could live in it!

He must have figured that the chickens weren't that attached to it and told me if I could get it started I could have it! Upon closer inspection, I discovered that the car had only 37,000 miles on it. My buddy and I ran home, dragged back a battery, and to my surprise, it started right up and purred like a kitten. A little air in the tires and an apple crate to sit on and I got it home, driving down the back roads to avoid the local authorities. It ran great and while

I could have made this car whole and called it my own, I saw it more as an engine for my '40. It was a 216 cubic inch 6 cylinder, just like the one in the '40. So, being the inquisitive sort that I was and still am, I tore the engine apart.

My Dad had a friend, Mr. Griffin, who owned an auto parts store in Burien on 1st Ave South. Knowing what I was up to, he said if I were willing to work it off in labor, he would give me a 235 cubic inch short block to build. He saw this as a great learning experience for me and as a way to share his knowledge with a young motor head in the making. I thought it would be pretty cool to have a new engine that I could soup up and so, I agreed and repaid him by cleaning up around the shop, mowing his yard and such. He inspired me and helped me with my many questions. Mr. Griffin was a great mentor and I spent that whole summer, when not doing things for him, working on the car. He gave me some great ideas and really took an interest in my project. I remember him fondly and could never have repaid him for all he taught me. When I was done with the engine part of my mission, I had installed twin Stromberg carbs and a split manifold with dual exhaust. It was going to run strong and sound smooth!

By the time it was completed, I had spent two complete summers in the back yard getting my '40 ready for my senior year in high school. The engine, and the rest of the running gear was tightened, freshened, or replaced and the paint polished and interior detailed. My car was ready for the road and its debut at school. My first stop was to pick up my girlfriend and then a couple of close buddies. Of course, a business coupe only had a front seat and it was a narrow car to begin with, so we were all jammed in like sardines, but we didn't care. This was a regular thing and on Friday and Saturday nights. We would cruise Lou's

Drive-In on 152nd Street and 1st Avenue South in Burien and then over to the White Center Lou's. From there, we'd head on over to West Seattle and check out the action at Dick's Burgers, which is still a growing chain of old style burger joints where young and old alike still hang out. Lou's is not there anymore, but the memories of fries and tartar sauce still linger.

The girls from West Seattle liked to jump into the car and ask us to head back to Lou's, so their local guys would pursue them. It was all in good fun and there weren't really any altercations. As time has gone on, I've run into several of them and swapped stories of the good old days.

Another cool thing about the business coupe was the huge trunk. I could get five people in the trunk to sneak into the Valley Drive-In Theater. This went on for countless weekends until one night when we got caught!

On that particular night, there was an extra guy that wanted to tag along. That made six guys in the trunk and just that much more crowded. By the time we got to the entrance and started to approach the ticket booth, they had all had too much time impersonating a package of hot dogs and they were banging on the trunk lid to get me to stop the car. I jumped out and popped the trunk and  they all started piling out. Needless to say, the ticket booth guy was on to our ongoing scheme, saying he recognized the car and wasn't going to let the car in. After some batting of her eyelashes and pleading by my girlfriend, he let her and me in with the car. But, that left the boys from the trunk on foot. I was sorry it turned out that way, but did my best to enjoy the movie and the time alone with my girl.

I've been through a lot of cars since that first Chevy and I have a 1940 Chev Special Deluxe Custom Coupe today that takes my mind back to that first one every time I get in it. That's the thing about old cars; they keep you young at heart!

A Way of Life

by David Dickinson as told by Bud Worley

My name is Bud Worley and I'm an Old Car Nut! It all started in 1955. By the time I was fifteen years old, I had already been bitten by the car bug and was seriously infected. At this point, I'm sure it's a terminal disease. I've had many cars over my life and my '56 Chevrolet Nomad is probably my last car. In my mind, you have to ask yourself, where are you going to go after a Nomad? But, that's just my thinking.

At that unwitting young age of fifteen, when many young guys are thinking about sports and girls, I was already focused on cars. I had $100 and used it to buy a '46 Ford Tudor with a stock six cylinder motor and a beautiful black and rust paint job. Today, it would be considered a highly prized patina. Back then, it was just old paint and new rust.

I couldn't get my driver's license until I was sixteen but that didn't seem to be much of an issue for me, because I went ahead and drove the old Ford on the sly. Man, was I slick, right up to the point where the Bremerton police chased me down and questioned my good judgment. By the time I got done with the judge, I was restricted from getting a driver's license until the ripe old age of sixteen and a half. Of course, at fifteen, it seemed like forever and the worst possible penalty one could be subjected to.

Fast forward to the day I did get a driver's license. Now, it was time to start cruising for chicks! I fell in line with all the other cruisers and played my role in what has become a favorite American pastime.

My intentions have always been good and I was not overly mischievous as I was growing up, but I was a red-blooded American male and taking a little risk was part of the game of life. The driver's side glass on my '46 was cracked and I knew where there was another old Ford with the right glass sitting in a field, apparently considered junk.

I had two friends that did nothing to discourage me from going and taking the glass. Instead, they encouraged me, and escorted me to the field to procure it. The owner of the junked car didn't appreciate the liberties we were taking and called the cops. Caught again! This was getting old and I discovered a penalty worse than not getting a license. I got to spend time in "Juvie" and it was a well learned lesson. I made the decision to buy any parts I needed from then on out.

I developed a love for what are called the shoebox Fords. From '49 to '51, Ford really got it right and I went through about four of them. I didn't customize them or hot rod them. I just loved and drove them. First came the '50 convertible and with the top down and the wind blowing through my hair, I was riding on clouds. A couple of '49 Tudors filled the gap between the convertible and the '51 business coupe with its short passenger compartment and deep trunk. It's hard to say which one I liked the best, because I loved them all.

In about 1960, I found a new passion in the form my first '55 Chevrolet Bel Air two-door hardtop. It was a great car, as it was, but I wanted to make this one more personalized. It came with the stock 265cid V8 and a Powerglide automatic. I had several changes in mind and so I pulled the car into a one car, dirt floor garage, set about converting the running gear to something with a little more power, and added a manual transmission. The motor was a 283cid bored out to 292cid with a four-barrel carb. The automatic shifter on the column was converted to manual and I got pretty good at banging gears.

Under the supervision of my uncle, who did interiors for a living, I reupholstered the Bel Air in stock fabric to match the light turquoise solid body paint job. It was a great looking and running car and it earned me lots of attention from the girls and motor-head guys, as well.

As an active member of the Handlers Car Club in Bremerton, I was part of sponsoring the drag races at Bremerton Raceways, did a little racing for fun, and got that bug out of my system.

What I really liked to do back then was cruise for chicks and was always ready to make the regular cruising route with everyone else. We'd go up and down the main streets, stopping at the XXX Drive In and another spot called Grahams. Both places were set up so that when you pulled into a parking spot, you'd flash your lights and a pretty girl would come out and take your order. While cruising is still popular, there aren't many places you can go these days where a comely young carhop comes out to take your burger order.

I bought two new cars in my life. The first was a '65 Impala SS that I acquired for a little less than $3,000. While not a lot of money now, as an apprentice meat cutter at Safeway, it was more than I had and so, it was also the first car I bought on time. That Super Sport had a 327cid V8 and a four-speed transmission. It was a fun car to drive and with the Sequoia Green paint, black vinyl roof, and black bucket seat interior, I thought it was as gorgeous as it was fun. The '65 Super sports have gained popularity in recent years and I think it's because more people are realizing what I knew way back then. They're cool!

I had entered what I refer to as "the three year mentality" when it came to buying cars. At the end of the three years, I had paid the '65 SS off and traded it in for a '68 Impala SS that came with a new roofline for Chevrolet. Instead of the fastback roofline, my new Super Sport came in what they called a sports coupe. With a squared off roofline, the car had a distinct appearance. It was a nice car, but I have to admit that I liked the '65 much better than the '68.

Like a lot of young hot rodders chasing chicks, I actually caught one. Once married and starting a family, I had to leave the classic car lifestyle behind me. However, as many know, I was not done. In the mid '80s, a friend invited me to go down to Hot August Nights. I was overwhelmed with all of the cars and came home, infected once again, with the classic car bug.

I found a '48 Chevrolet four door sedan that had been gone through and was an absolute beauty. Normally, a four door would not be in the cards, but it was a great second car for the family. This was not your mother's four-door sedan. It had been lowered and it sported Fiesta hubcaps. The motor featured Fenton headers and it sounded real sweet driving down the road. It had a gorgeous blue paint job and the interior had been restored to new. It was a fun driver and I was hooked on classics once again.

In about 1989, I went to a car show called "Return to Renton" with a friend that was looking for a car to buy. A guy at the show told him about a '56 Chev Nomad that was for sale in South Seattle and so, we went to look at it. It was in fairly good condition, with a new red and white paint job, but needed a lot of work to make it a road worthy driver. My friend said, "It's cool, but I'm not interested. It's more than I want to do!"

I looked at it with a completely different view. I saw it as a diamond in the rough, sitting in its garage with a rebuilt 265cid V8 and no transmission, waiting for SOMEONE to do SOMETHING to it! I guess you could say it spoke to me. I had to have it.

The owner wanted $10,000 for it and I negotiated him down to $9,500 because he didn't have a transmission for it. Finding one wouldn't be a problem and I had time to scout one out. I felt I had really made a score. There was just one hitch in my git-along. I didn't have $9,500. I gave the seller a $500 deposit with the understanding that I would sell my '48 as quickly as possible and finish the transaction. He was amiable and so I advertised my sedan in Cruisin' Magazine and started telling everyone I knew that the car was for sale. Too much time went by and I had no buyer for the '48 and started to panic.

I went by the seller's place a couple of times when I had some extra cash to give him and finally expressed my fear, saying that I hoped he would not sell the car out from under me. He chuckled a bit and told me that he wouldn't do that. "We shook hands!" he said and put my fears to rest. Years ago, there was an article in Nomad Post Magazine called "Nomad on a Handshake" that recalled this very transaction.

Well, I still hadn't sold the four door Chev and so I dropped the price and kept giving the Nomad owner more money as available funds allowed. I thought I'd told everyone I knew that the car was for sale, but one day a co-worker, upon finding out I needed to sell, said to me "I know this car. My neighbor built it. I'll buy it!" I immediately had visions of getting the Nomad home when he interjected that he'd have to check with his wife. I figured that was the end of that and went back to wondering when this drawn out car business would come to an end. Well, she gave her "permission" and the guy has the car to this day.

That was over thirteen years ago and I still have the Nomad, as well. It has become a car that everyone in the local car scene recognizes and knows is mine and while it is always a loyal and worthy driver, I continue making upgrades each year. It still wears the same paint job from back then with minor cosmetic repairs to panels along the way. I've always been fascinated with Nomads and I will always own this one. It is my last classic car.

I will forever be involved with the classic car scene and I am a proud member of The Washington State Hot Rod Hall of Fame, having been inducted in 2008 with some of the finest people I know. Besides the Hall of Fame, I currently am a member of seven car clubs, including the NW Chevy Club, Rainier Classic Chevy Club, the Chevrolet Nomad Association, Goodguys, the Rogues Car Club, the  Baloney Car Club, the Handlers Car Club, and the Steeds Car Club.

The Chevrolet Nomad Association is a worldwide organization that meets annually and in July, we will be heading for Sacramento in the '56 for this year's gathering. The Rogues Car Club dates back to the '60s and the Handlers Car Club, formed in 1956, has been promoting drag racing events at Bremerton Raceways, one of oldest facilities in the United States, for over half a century. The Baloney Car Club got its unusual name when an announcer at a car show called Joe Bellotti "Baloney" by mistake. It stuck. I just recently joined the Steeds Car Cub, formed in 1962.

When I gather with my car friends, I am in my element. Very rarely do you find someone in my social circles that are not examples of how we should all be. Supportive, caring, gracious, and giving are words that come to mind. I love old cars and old car people. For me, and many others, it's a way of life.

The Tale of Dalton and the 'Vette

by Keith Nichols

The bright blue 'Vette rolled up next to us and the guy in the car revved his engine, then did a very impressive smoke show, lighting up the rear tires in a massive display of power.

I looked over at Dalton, who was driving a Challenger at the time, and said, "Man, that guy just won't give up for nothing."

Dalton laughed and revved the small block Dodge motor up and held the brake, dropping the clutch in first gear at 3500 rpm, lighting up the tires. The blue smoke filled the interior and we both choked.

After the smoke cleared a bit, I looked outside the window and the 'Vette was still sitting there, the tinted windows rolled up. "Dalton, I think this joker wants to drag," I said, chuckling to myself and taking a drink from my soda.

"Well, I'm down with that, man" Dalton retorted, adjusting his shades. The light was still red. We were at the intersection of 224th St and the Old Mountain Highway. It was eight o'clock at night on a warm summer evening in 1993.

The Dodge Challenger was Dalton's baby. He had gone over every square inch of the car, carefully detailing the engine compartment and getting the engine tuned just right. We had raced several people in the car and the tires always broke loose on the green light. It would never go in a straight line when Dalton ran it hard, but from the looks of the 'Vette, we would have to run it as hard as we could. The light changed green rather quickly and the 'Vette roared off the line, the rear tires squealing and smoke trailing from the rear of the car. Dalton grabbed the gear shifter, a short throw B&M specially modified to fit the four speed in the 1970 Challenger, lit the engine up to 2000 rpm, and slipped the clutch.

Maybe it was the heat. Maybe it was because of the smoke show that we had done. Maybe it was fate.

The Challenger apparently decided, at that very moment, to "hook up." The tires dug into the blacktop, not slipping a bit, and the whole 3000 pound car lifted into the air like some strangled beast clawing for the heavens.

Inside the car, in the passenger seat, I saw only bright blue sky through the windshield. Dalton didn't even flinch. He slammed the clutch back in, and the car came down hard on the blacktop. Then he grabbed second and lit that small block back up again.

The windshield cracked from end to end as the car lifted its nose skyward again. I remember clearly watching the crack slowly spread across the window. At this point, I was certain we were going to die.

Dalton, meanwhile, had a race to win. I didn't know if we were still accelerating or if we had already destroyed the drive train. He nailed the clutch again, screamed "Fly you bitch! Fly!" and grabbed third gear.

The Challenger again went airborne. This time all four wheels left the ground; a standing hop, I think we called it later. When Dalton stabbed the gas pedal down as far as he could, something came loose.

The whole works crashed back down to the road, now bent and twisted somehow on the front end, the wheels making terrible sounds and even worse noises coming from under the hood. Smoking and defeated by sheer power, we rolled to the side of the road and drifted gently to a stop, all sound seeming to have ceased.

We sat there for a few moments, listening to the ticking of the cooling components. Dalton fumbled for a smoke and lit it with a shaking hand. "Holy shit man." he muttered. "Holy shit…"

I lit a smoke of my own. "I don't think the gear shifter is supposed to look that way," I said, pointing at the B&M shifter, which now lay at a forty-five degree angle.

Dalton pulled on the interior door handle and had to push on the door pretty hard to get it to pop open. When it did slowly open, it did so with a loud and grating squeal it had never made before. "That can't be good," he said, as he maneuvered his large body out of the seat and stood up.

I followed him and stood by the car. Smoke and steam were issuing from under the hood. The windshield had cracked in three great streaming lines and the chrome trim was completely gone. The passenger side tire was at a crooked angle and the fender seemed to sit higher than the one on the driver's side, where Dalton was surveying damage, as well. "This isn't good, man," I said to Dalton.

He tossed his smoke off into the road and walked over to the hood. "It's not good," he said, as he began trying to get the hood to pop open. It was stuck and he finally had to use a chunk of re-bar he found along the road and managed to pry it open.

The hood popped up. He glanced inside and slammed it shut again.

I remember asking him, "What's wrong man?"

He looked at me a bit pale. "It's sideways," he said. "It's broken and just sitting in there sideways."

I lit another smoke and dug around in the car for my soda. Then I sat on the side of the road and Dalton hiked over to the pay phone to call for B.J. to come with the truck and drag our happy asses' home.

We never saw the 'Vette again and I think he left the line so fast he had no idea what happened behind him.

The Feel of the Wheel Makes the Deal

by David Dickinson

The title of this story is from an old car salesman notion that you need to get a buyer to drive a car before they will take mental ownership. As an old car salesman, I have always believed that to be very true. However, I got a taste of that psychology early in life.

When I was eleven years old, I used to hang out with the neighbor, who was a few years older than I was. He was a great guy and had patience with me, just a young punk, and not even a teenager, like him. When he wasn't around, I'd spend time visiting with his parents, Carl and Ruby, and developed great friendships with both of them. If I wasn't sitting at the kitchen table listening to Ruby tell stories about her youth in the Deep South and her Bible thumpin' Baptist upbringing, I would visit with Carl out on the front porch, in the yard, or that most sacred place, the garage.

One day, I was just hangin' out on the front porch with old Carl, who was about 60 years old, close to Methuselah, as far as I was concerned. He reached his arms to the sky to stretch and casually said, "Well, we'd better pull the old Chevy around back to the garage." This was a common occurrence, because during the day the car would sit out front. It was much easier to navigate the front street during comings and goings than the pot riddled, narrow chasm called "our alley."

What wasn't common was when Carl said, "You want to drive?"

I could hardly believe my ears. As I was trying to conceive that I had heard him right, notions of the guy on TV handing out vast sums of money to lucky and deserving individuals flashed through my head. The show was called "The Millionaire" and if that guy had walked up to me right then to hand me a check, I'd have pushed him aside and told him not to bother me; I was about to drive a car.

Before I came out of my mental wonderland, Carl slapped me on the arm and said, "Well, you want to or not?"

Startled, but beginning to believe that all of my dreams were about to come true. I ran to the car, pulled open the driver's door and jumped in. I can still remember the smell of the interior and the shine off the hood in the late afternoon sun... at least the part of the hood that I could see over the behemoth steering wheel I held in my hands.

So, Carl came around and calmly sat down in the passenger seat, with me wondering how he can be so calm at a moment like this. Didn't he realize I was about to take his personal vehicle on a magical mystery tour? I'm sure I must have thought he was crazy to take such a risk.

In any event, he was calm, and took his time with detailed instructions. As he reviewed all of the functions of the shift lever on the column, the gas pedal, brake and clutch pedals, I squirmed and twisted the wheel, intently listening, but wanting to get to the part about the ignition key. Of course, there was more to it than just a key. First, you had to turn the key and then push the button over on the other side of the dash. Finally, he finished his dissertation on how to make all of the stuff work and get the car to move and said, "Go ahead and turn the key on!"

Man, oh man, we were about to really do this. It wasn't just a cruel joke designed to alienate me and keep me from coming over and bugging him. He was really going to let me drive his car. Honest and for real!

I gently reached down and turned the key to the right, fearing that somehow I might make a mistake in the simple, yet critical move. Click... it moved effortlessly and I saw the needles around the speedometer jump with the current that gave them life. This was going to be great!

"OK, be sure and press the clutch all the way to the floor," said my driving mentor. "Next, you need to push the starter button. Don't hold it too long, just long enough."

Somehow, I instinctively knew how long to hold it in. Of course, I was no dummy. I'd been watching people do this for years. I was a completely experienced passenger. This wasn't my first trip around the block.

But, wait! It was my first trip around the block behind the steering wheel of a car. This thing was about to roll under my personal direction. I was in control and could make it go anywhere I wanted it to go.

Actually, I was about to make it go exactly where Carl said to make it go. I didn't want to blow this once in a lifetime opportunity. I remember thinking that I would drive lots of times, but I only got one shot at doing it the first time. I wanted to make this perfect!

The engine roared to life with the simple push of my finger and I swear I had never heard a more satisfying sound.

The Blue Flame Special in that 1949 Chevrolet purred and we were one step closer to movement.

"Alright, David, the next thing is kinda tricky and it may take you a few tries. But, that's OK. Put your foot on the clutch, push it all the way to the floor, and hold it there. Keep it all the way down. You're going to put the transmission in first gear. Remember where that is?"

I knew exactly where it was. I really had been paying attention. Besides, my dad had a car just like this one or at least pretty close. I pulled back on the stick and then down confidently. The grinding noise I heard nearly scared me to death. Oh, man. I'd blown it now. What was Carl going to say?

Of course, being the gentle soul that he was, he explained that I needed to slow down and listen. He went on to explain about synchros and such. The bottom line was that I should have put it in second or third gear, which was straight up or straight down and then go to first. How could I have been such a fool? I had watched my dad do that move all the time.

So, I got the shifter into first gear. I looked over to Carl and said, "What about the emergency brake?" He smiled and nodded. I reached down and released the brake. We were about to roll.

"Got your foot on the brake?" Carl asked, as the big old Chevy started to roll. Holy smokes! I jammed my foot down hard on the brake and the much larger now than a moment ago behemoth jarred to a stop.

"That's OK," the old boy said and chuckled aloud. "You have to keep a car under control at all times, boy," he drawled with his soft Midwestern accent. "Alright then, you need to lift your left foot slowly off of the clutch and let your foot off of the brake. Once she starts rolling let your foot all the way off the clutch and push on the gas like there's an egg under the pedal. We're gonna go slow, OK?"

I executed the maneuver just right except for the jumping and bucking right before the screeching halt. Carl, once again amused, said, "That's to be expected. It'll take a few times to get it right, but you almost had it. Let's go back to the starter button and try again. Foot on the brake and push the clutch in."

After a couple more tries and to my delight, we were rolling forward slowly and I WAS DRIVING! Yee Ha! We gradually made our way down to the end of the block and turned left. I did it perfect, but I was working hard to get that big old steering wheel cranked around enough to execute the turn. He told me to relax my grip on the wheel and let it come back to where the car was going straight and it did just that. No had no more than straightened out and I had to turn again into the alley. Another left turn and we were bumping down the alley, finding every pothole known to man. I think someone must have imported extras just for my benefit. The alley was narrow and I fought the wheel hard to keep it straight. We must have been going at least ten miles an hour. We were flying! In reality, I had never shifted out of first gear.

I have to admit, I never realized how long our block was. We lived on the corner, so I drove all the way down to the next street and then all the way back up the alley to Carl's garage. It was quite a trip. I stopped in front of the garage, turned the key off, and took a deep breath.

Well, I was hooked on cars from that moment on and at the ripe young age of eleven, I became an Old Car Nut! What the old car salesmen say is true. "The feel of the wheel makes the deal!"

Woodville Hill: A Test of Courage and Speed

by Gary M. Hughes

The road between Butte and Helena Montana is now Interstate 15. In the 1960's it was simply a two-lane highway then known as US91. Leaving the A&W Root Beer Drive In and heading toward Helena on US91 you encountered a hill known as "Woodville Hill" that climbed to the Continental Divide. It was straight and fourteen miles long with a considerable elevation increase.

A teen ager in the '60's could prove himself by taking his ride to the top of Woodville hill, turning it around and timing how long it would take to get back to the A&W. Most speedometers at that time had a maximum of 100 MPH, so the only method of determining the speed was by timing the trip. Any time less than 9 or 10 minutes was very respectable and earned bragging rights. Bobby always had the fastest time. He was an older kid and no one could ever top his time. I didn't like or hang out with Bobby because he was "crazy bad," a little arrogant and usually in trouble with the cops. Later, the fool changed his name to Evel and gained some notoriety crashing motorcycles.

Several years later, I ended up in Seattle and met the perfect woman. She was gorgeous, drove a candy apple red '66 Mustang with a 289 V8 stick shift, and always had a cold beer for me in her refrigerator. Our first date was at a racetrack. It just doesn't get any better than that! It was easy for this "car guy" from Montana to fall in love with her. One day in 1970, we stopped at Bel-Kirk Motors, and for the first time saw the most desirable sports car to come about in decades, the Datsun 240Z. What a car! I can't say enough about the styling, handling characteristics, and power of this car. It is absolutely the most pleasurable driving experience I have ever encountered. Colette and I had decided to make our relationship permanent, so we placed our name on the eight month waiting list for a Z car. Yes, it took that long to get one! The color we chose was British racing green with black interior. We took delivery in the summer of 1971 and used that beautiful Mustang as a trade. Hey, you can't keep them all.

The following year, we drove out to visit some relatives in Minnesota and eastern Montana. Returning home to Seattle, we arrived at the top of Woodville Hill late in the evening. Interstate 15 was just completed and was now a beautiful, newly paved four lane interstate. I looked over at my bride and she was sound asleep in the passenger seat. Memories of my youth overwhelmed me and I mentally regressed to an earlier time. Once again, I was sixteen years old at the top of Woodville Hill. The difference this time was I was driving a beautiful aerodynamic machine that conquers hills like this. The speedometer in the 240Z has a maximum of 160 MPH. I had never driven a car 160 MPH. Although I would have no one to brag to because the A&W was probably closed at this hour, it still seemed like the perfect opportunity to beat Bob's time at last.

I saw the sign marking the curve in the road for the new bypass when the car was achieving 130 MPH. In an instant, I aged from sixteen to adulthood and said to myself, "HOLY CRAP, THIS ROAD IS NO LONGER STRAIGHT"! I gained a lot more respect for the braking and suspension of that automobile while I was navigating the curve sideways in the road with all four wheels locked up. There was a screeching sound coming from the tires and another screeching sound coming from my mouth. I learned the perfect woman gets very grumpy when awakened suddenly. For the rest of the trip, she wouldn't let me drive anymore and didn't like me much. The good news is she stayed married to me and we've tested that 240Z to speeds of up to 130 MPH.

Some cars you can keep. It still has a place in our garage and in our hearts.

eBay Racer

by Dave Alvar

A few years back, I was browsing through the eBay auctions, looking for a rod project, when I came across a '28 Ford that really caught my attention. It was an old, single-seat racecar, with a narrowed frame and a hand-formed aluminum body and belly pan. The polished radiator shell was from a tractor and bore a plaque that read "Earthmaster Farm Equipment." Behind that grill were louvers in the upper and lower areas of the cutout aluminum hood.

16″ wire wheels with knock-off centers married it to the ground and it had a great stance. It even had a clear Washington State title. We were talking love at first sight and there was a "Buy It Now" price of $3,500, so I jumped in  and bought it on the spot. I talked my brother-in-law into helping me haul the car home from Tacoma on his old trailer. It was so cool that once I got it home I spent hours just looking at it.

The engine was an original Model A four-banger with an Alcoa aluminum head and aluminum side cover with a Thomas aluminum intake manifold that sported twin carbs with aluminum scoops. The vintage Mallory distributor got its spark from a coil that looked like a cross between a canteen and a hand grenade and the exhaust header ran down the right side of the car. It looked just right!

Behind the engine were a three-speed transmission, a shortened drive shaft, and a rear end with a quick-change cover. I never did find out if it was a real quick-change, or just for looks. Either way, it was very cool!

Inside were a bomber seat and a beautiful old steering wheel that operated the steering box, which poked out on the left side by the firewall. On the dash were a vintage Stewart-Warner speedometer and a weathered "Rusetta" timing plaque, which proclaimed that one Adan England had driven the car to 101.12 MPH at Mirage on 10/19/58.

Aft of the abbreviated body, there was a funny-looking gas tank and a single tail light with the word "Stop" displayed on it. Attached to the license plate was an original Gilmore lion frame.

At that point, I had to ponder... What am I actually going to do with this masterpiece? Well, it collected dust in my garage for a year and a half before I finally admitted to myself that I wasn't going to do anything with it. It needed to go. I listed it on eBay and quickly scored a $2,000 profit.

The fellow who purchased the car claimed that he knew the history behind it. He stated that it was the "father" to a car called the "Cat Pizz Special," built by Neil Brislawn. I can't vouch for his story, but I know that he wrote it up nicely, took some great photographs, and made another $2,000 profit when he turned around and re-sold the car... on eBay, of course.

My Greatest Car Regret

by Lloyd (Bud) Norton

In the early 1970's we started looking for another muscle car to replace the '66 Olds 442 that we traded in on a very cool '72 Chevy C-10 "Eagle by Chevy" pick up.

We looked at a green '68 Dodge Charger R/T; but we couldn't agree on a price. Then we checked out an orange '70 Ford Torino GT Cobra Jet at a local dealership, but their price wasn't even close. Finally, we found a '68 Dodge Coronet R/T. It was red with a black vinyl top and black interior. It was gorgeous!

This was a rare 'stripe delete' model, although it had the standard R/T 440ci, 375hp motor with the 727 auto transmission. It was very fast. We didn't do much to it except add Sonic Maxima 60's tires on Ansen Sprint II dish mags. This was a pretty wide set up and we had clearance problems in the front wheel wells when turning. We had to jack up the torsion bar suspension so that the tires cleared the wheel well. Then, we measured the height of the front end at the center of each wheel well to make sure that we were level from side to side and installed three-inch shackles at the back of the rear leaf springs to level the car from front to back. That R/T had a very cool, aggressive look.

There came a time a couple of years later that we decided that we needed a more economical family car. At the time, we were living in Minot, ND while I was working for Boeing, modifying the Minute Man Missile silos. A short time later a young man, who worked for a local service station, answered my For Sale ad in the newspaper.

I wouldn't let him drive it, but I took him for a test ride. When I got the car on Highway 2, I thought that I would show him what it could do. When we were travelling at about 65mph, I punched the throttle. In about 3 seconds we were going over 100mph. I turned my head in his direction and calmly stated that, "It has a little wheel hop at 105mph.

I noticed that he kept grabbing at his backside. Apparently, he couldn't get to his wallet fast enough and he kept missing his pocket. Well, I sold the car for the $1,000 we paid for it and felt that was a good sale… at the time. Of course, the car would be worth about $40,000 to $60,000 now.

To my great shame and regret, I replaced our beautiful, fast muscle car with a little Pinto wagon. My only excuse is that I was a family man with three kids and a long commute. Of course, that was no better excuse then than it is today. Isn't hindsight grand?

In Memory

Automotive Treasures

by Bill Walker

I have been a certified old car nut for most of my 65 years. It started when my older brother would teach me the names and the years of the passing vehicles while we rode in the back seat of our parent's car on road trips and vacations.

My brother, Larry, was eight years older than I was, but we were close just the same. I looked up to him like a hero. When he turned sixteen and bought his first car, it was almost like having a car of my own because he would let me hang out with him and his buddies sometimes.

Larry and some of his friends had Model A's with flatheads. I remember a lot of the cars in the group, like a purple and pink primered '37 Ford, a '40 Ford Sedan delivery, a '47 Ford coupe, a variety of Hudsons, and a stunning light blue, lowered '53 Ford hardtop. There were others, as well, and to a little kid it seemed that everyone had a car but me. The majority of these cars were finished with rattle can and vacuum cleaner paint jobs.

This was the early to mid-fifties, so by the time I turned eight I was listening to Elvis, Pat Boone, and the Big Bopper! Most important, I got to ride shotgun with my brother when he'd take me. He couldn't always take me.

Larry somehow managed to convince our Dad that he could make money junking out cars in our front yard. So, as this enterprise increased, more and more old iron such as Buicks, Pontiacs, Fords, Chevys and more came along and got junked. Today, they'd take parts off of them to sell, but back then Larry would buy a car for ten dollars, bash it down as flat as they could to stack it and then scrap it for twenty-five dollars. It was great profit, but I cringe when I think of the great parts that were lost in that venture.

Before the sledgehammers started beating down the cars, I was able to sit in the front seats and look at the art deco gauges in total wonder. I could shift the gears and imagine myself racing and beating a make-believe opponent or just cruising down the highway with my arm hanging out the window. I fell in love with every one of those cars and had to go hide when it came time for their demise. Each destroyed car was like losing an old friend.

The years leading up to the time I could get my own car were a blur. I was so enamored with the cars and having my own, that I was single minded; always looking forward to the day I could get my own special ride.

Like a lot of kids my age, I delivered newspapers to make money to buy my first car at fifteen. It was a '50 Oldsmobile with the 303 OHV V8 and a 135 HP. It was a "many door" (four doors), but it was mine. It had faded blue paint and bald tires. Perfect! I got tires, cleaned it up, and did some repairs it needed and then ran the wheels off of it.

Eventually, the Olds morphed into a beige '50 Mercury through the magic of "horse trading." There was a lot of car trading going on back then. It seems we were always going from one car to another.

At one point, I was working in a gas station and making some money, so when my friend Jon and I could get the time we would cruise the back roads of Federal Way and Puyallup looking for hot rod material.

On one of those fanciful excursions, we saw the nose of an old car sticking out of a barn. We stopped in and talked to an old gentleman about the car, asking if he would consider selling it. After looking the car over, we found that it was complete with the exception of not having any front seats. We started into our high-level negotiations to get the car, a 1934 Chevrolet two door sedan. It had a title, but the last time it had ran or been moved was in 1952.

After about five minutes of haggling, the owner agreed to sell the car for the astronomical sum of ten dollars. But, there was a catch. We couldn't have the car until he made sure that he had removed all of his chickens and any eggs that might still be residing in this cherry "chicken coop."

We paid him the ten dollars, at which time he signed and handed over the title. Jon told him that we would be back after it in about an hour or so and we jumped into my '50 Mercury and took off to get a chain to tow our rare and exotic barn find to its new home. At that time and age, most of my friends and I didn't know what a trailer or a tow bar was. We had chains.

We took a good old hand tire pump and borrowed a tire off my Dads utility trailer that had the same bolt pattern as the old '34 Chevy. It seemed a good idea to have a tire that we knew held air just in case there was a minor problem. We stopped at my buddy's house where he picked up an apple crate, so he had something to sit on as he drove the car. It was my tow car, so I got to tow the Chevy rather than steer it.

As an afterthought, Jon brought along his raincoat complete with a hood. We ended up back at this old farmer's house in about two hours. He had managed to collect his valuables and use his tractor to pull it out of the shed it had been partially sitting in. After getting the old tube tires blown up and holding air for most part, we thanked him and told him of all of the good things we were going to do to his old Chevy to make it a cool cruiser. We then hooked up the long chain to the '34 and to my '50 Merc. I started the Merc, racked the single glass pack a time or two to let the world know that we were towing a future hotrod, and began the slow trip home.

We didn't have too difficult of a time getting down the road and safely home. Well, at least I didn't! Jon definitely showed inspiration by bringing the raincoat. Every time we would hit a bump, it seemed that a plethora of chicken mites, spiders and other creatures of many legs, and unusually disgusting demeanors, would fall down his neck or wind up in his lap. Of course, the old tin was reinforced with an entirely rotten wood framing. I believe the luxurious green moss helped to strengthen the body from shifting around to the point of total collapse. Each time we hit a bump it would not only bounce high, but resembled an old Conestoga wagon with the body swaying to the movements of the ruts in the highway.

We succeeded in getting it into the back yard where only a few of the neighbors could see it. It got washed down with soap, Comet, and a stiff wire brush. After some hesitation, my Mom even let us use her good vacuum to suck out what bugs Jon did not take home inside his clothing.

I never did get that Chevy to start or even fire and I wound up trading it to someone for a Vespa scooter that didn't run. In retrospect, if I had simply checked the timing chain, that was probably the problem. Of course, I have a lot more experience to draw on at sixty-five than I did at fifteen.

This early adventure in car recovery was the beginning of a series of '50s Mercs, '40s Fords; a huge variety of years, makes, and models of "automotive treasures" that comprise the approximately seventy or so cars and trucks I've owned over the years.

For the time being, I now have a '34 Ford and a '41 Olds that I consider a hotrod and a street rod and we drive them a lot, in good weather and bad. If we have to, we drive my black Colorado or the red Jeep, but only if it is really bad.

Still lost in the 50's and 60's and loving it, I will never lose my fascination for the American Automobile and its performance and style.

Sadly, Bill passed away a month after sending me this story. He was a friend and fellow Steeds Car Club member that will be missed. -David Dickinson, Creator and Editor of The Old Car Nut Book.

Flames and Backfires

by Jim Moreno

Like many old car guys, my interest in cars started early on when my brother used to bring different cars home. My cousin, Bob Biehler, and I used to mess around with our bikes to keep busy before our own cars came into the picture.

During my teen years, my mom owned a bar and she would run bar tabs for the regulars. Cars were so cheap they would occasionally pay off their tabs by turning over their cars. I would get the car fixed up and my mom would sell them. So, at 14 years old, I was the detail staff and junior mechanic doing oil changes and tune-ups, getting the cars ready for her to sell. When I look back at that time, I had some pretty nice cars go through my hands, including

a '48 Ford, '50 Ford, '48 Olds two door and many more.

When I got old enough to drive I ended up with a '48 Chevy four-door sedan with the vacuum shift. It was green with mohair interior. One day my cousin and I were sitting around looking at the beast and got the infamous "wild hair" to put flames on it. So, we went down to the cellar of our house, where my mother stored paint, to see what we could put to good use. Well, we found all kinds of oil paints and some small brushes, so we went to town flaming the beast. We got done in a couple of hours and it looked damn good to us.

Needless to say, it did not impress my mom and my cousin's mom just shook her head. This probably would not have been too bad but the reality of it all was that this was my mom's "spare" car and when her "real" car broke down she and my aunt had to drive it. So much for that cool idea!

She didn't like the flames and insisted that we get rid of what we considered some fine custom work. So, I had to get the car painted and I thought a dark purple would be really cool. My brother knew someone that would paint it for $30. That was great, but when we went to pick it up, the paint was more of a light purple. Really, it was more of a dark pink than anything. It all worked out, because the guy didn't charge me and somehow over the next 6 months the paint faded to a very acceptable light beige tone and was a great paint job.

Around that same time, my cousin got a '48 Chevy Fleetline Aero Sedan. It was straight, but needed paint and so we figured there was no better crew to paint it than the dynamic duo of Jim and Bob. Standard Brands Paint had cans of black spray paint for about 39 cents a can and so we stepped up and got about twenty cans and put together another custom paint job. We thought we were pretty good at this and took great pride in our newly finished paint job.

The '48 Chevy four door that my mom made us take the flames off got traded for a '35 Ford 4 door. This was my car! Wanting something with a little more spunk, I put together a string of trades and wound up with a real powerhouse. It went like this... I traded the original flathead engine for a Browning Shotgun, and then traded the shot gun for a full race flathead engine with aluminum heads, 3 deuce intake cam and a magneto ignition. That motor ran great once it was started, but it needed an 8-volt battery to turn it over. When you are a kid, that kind of upgrade is expensive, so we pushed it or rolled it down hill to start it.

Luckily, our house was on a hill. So, I could park it up on the hill and let it run down the hill and pop the clutch to start it. That was a simple enough solution and we didn't mind pushing.

One Sunday, my buddy and I decided to go for a drive. The car wouldn't start when we rolled down the hill so we pushed it down to the next hill, which ran down in front of the Catholic Church and school. The Priest and nuns were not too happy with the noise the car made as it backfired, snorted, and howled when we popped the clutch to get it started. This happened more than once and we would get disapproving looks upon each event.

On this particular Sunday, as we were going down the hill, I popped the clutch and the car backfired through the carbs and caught on fire. Church was just letting out so we just made a U-turn, smiled, and waved at the good people. We didn't hear the end of that one for a while and the Priest would bring it up in conversation with my mom and aunt at any given opportunity.

I usually only drove the car to school and back, as those were the rules my mother laid down. All totaled, that amounted to about a hundred miles and I pushed it twice that much and so I got great miles per gallon.

I ended up putting an Olds V8, automatic transmission and rear end in it; all with ¼" Drill, hacksaw and what wrenches and screw drivers I could beg, borrow or, well, you get it… all the best tools. My Mother sold it for $125.00 because it was in her name and I was only 17 at the time. Why did she sell it? Well, I wasn't always on my best behavior and she felt like teaching me a lesson, so she sold it out from underneath me.

Those were my early days of playing with cars and I have had a lot of different cars since. I found a '56 Ford at a local used car lot. It had flames on it, but they were fading; along with the rest of the paint job. Back then, you could get your car painted by Earl Scheib for $39.95, so I had it painted black. I went to pick it up and it was an excellent job, but you could still see the outline of the old flames under the new black paint. I figured that was what you get for that price, but everyone else asking how the paint job was done and telling me how cool it looked. I decided I got a custom paint job for a bargain price. What was a mistake at the time is what they call ghost flames now. I still laugh!

Like I said, I've had lots of different cars, including a '59 Impala with a 348cid V8 and 4sp. I really enjoyed that car, but I sold it when I discovered a '63 Fuel Injected Split Window Corvette for $2500 from a Corvette shop in San Diego. The Corvette was a theft recovery and it had everything but the injection. I found a solid replacement for sale for $125, installed it and kept the car for 6 years. In about 1972, I traded the '63 Split Window for a '71 Corvette hardtop (oops!) and kept it for 25 years. This is one of those times when after you think about it, you want to kick yourself for getting rid of a '63 Corvette, but that's life and I'm not the only one that has that type of mistake in their past.

My wife and I bought a '56 Ford F100 in around 1991, while we were in San Diego and started working on it in our spare time. We decided to move to Olympia Washington in 1994 and had our vehicles moved up here on a trailer. On that trailer, we had a '71 Corvette, '56 Ford and an '84 Chevy Blazer.

Over the years, we sold the Corvette and the Blazer but we kept the '56 Ford. My cousin, Bob, and his wife, Tanya and their two kids had moved to Washington State years before, so we were able to reconnect with them. Bob had a portable welding rig and started Mr. Weld Hot Rods. After  a year or so of driving the '56 F100 around Washington, carrying a grease gun to keep the stock steering system greased, Bob put a Chevelle front clip in for us with power steering and power disk brakes. It drives like a modern car now and we love it. Thanks, Bob!

Over the years, many other upgrades and improvements have been made to the pickup. I widened the rear metal fenders two inches, swapped the old motor and tranny for a ZZ4 short block with a Turbo 400 transmission and painted it Taxi Cab Chrome Yellow. About four years back, Bob laid out some flames on it and I did the interior on their 32 Roadster in repayment.

Now, we have my Chevy Pickup and wife's El Dorado (second one, I wrecked the first one) as daily drivers and our 56 F100 for car shows and Sunday drives. A couple of  years ago, we bought a 35 Chevy four door sedan that had been sitting in a garage for the last 20 years. Supposedly, the engine was completely rebuilt before parking it for 20 years. The car was repainted to original colors and new brakes were added. To this day, the engine has not been started since being parked it all those years ago, but it was turned over every day by hand crank. We haven't done anything with it to this point and it needs a new starter before we can start and drive it, but we'll have to see what the future holds.

My cousin, Bob, passed away suddenly in April 2012 and I have lost interest in this car stuff for now. He was a very gifted man and a big part of my car world.

Things will get back to normal someday.

Southern California Dreamer

by David Dickinson as told by Tanya Biehler
in memory of Bob Biehler 1942-2012

This is part of a series of stories to commemorate the life of Bob Biehler, who passed away on April 13, 2012.

Roland "Bern" Biehler was a "Jack of all trades" and his son, Bob, was proof that "The apple doesn't fall far from the tree." Bern had fifty-four jobs in his lifetime and seemed able to do just about anything. If there was something that he wanted to accomplish and didn't know how, he'd run down to the library and read, absorbing knowledge like a sponge. He would then go and apply his new-found knowledge and become an expert. Similarly, his son Bob seemed able to do anything he set his mind to. Things came even easier to him, as was proven over a lifetime of

designing and constructing equipment, cars, art, or anything else that was creative and required concentration and dedication.

As he progressed through his life, Bob Biehler gained many admirers and fans; people simply in awe of what he could create in his mind, plan out and then construct, sometimes using the most common materials laying around that others would throw out or send to Goodwill. Maybe the best example was the custom air cleaner he fabbed up for a famous car he built called "The Defibrillator." That little unit that so many people admire was made out of a Chinese wok. There's more to that story and it wasn't just an air cleaner. Let's just say that Bob became a world-class hot rod builder with lots of tricks hiding up his sleeves; and under his ever present do rag.

Bob bought his first car when he was fourteen years old. While he couldn't drive it, he could spend hours of tinkering, repairing, and personalizing his new baby so it was just right when he got his license. That car was a 1948 Chevrolet Fleetline and it was the just the first of many automobiles that tugged at his heart strings. This was a fun car to play with, but Bob wanted to  build hot rods. He had dreams of fast cars, with no tops; cars that were fun to drive and would catch the eye of everyone going down the road; especially the girls. Girls liked cars.

Long before Bob's dream of building a car happened, his parents had to deal with the prospect of keeping the family covered and secure. The roof over their heads came in the form of a two-bedroom tract house. Affordability, like today, was an issue and the move was made in spite of the fact that the family already consisted of Bob, his parents and a sister. So, two bedrooms didn't work for too long. As Bob and his sister grew, the need for separate bedrooms became more of a necessity than a luxury.

An addition to the rear of the house became a master bedroom and the two original bedrooms were perfect for the growing brother and sister. Time and love have a way of changing things and so the Biehler family grew a little more. With a baby on the way, they needed to make more room in the small, yet growing house. The solution came in the form of the small single car garage.

The garage door remained, but a dividing wall was constructed to create a room that was accessible from the inside of the house. That room became Bob's bedroom and needless to say, Bob was thrilled. He got to live in the garage, a natural environment for a young car nut in the making. In that bedroom, Bob dreamed his dreams, made his plans, and with a sharpened pencil and a fresh notebook began creating designs that would inspire for a lifetime.

By the time Bob was sixteen, he was ready to build a hotrod. Like many young men in those days, whose cars were literally built in the back yard or the driveway, Bob covered his first hot rod with a tarp to protect it from the elements when it was not being worked on, but it was still exposed to unsavory elements of the public in the dark of night. Many young car builders in those days dealt with the lack of security that a canvas tarp provided.

That lack of security reared its ugly head one night when Bob's new transmission went missing. Unlike many crimes, this one was easy to solve. Bob and another guy had been negotiating for the same tranny and Bob, in the other guy's mind, had bought it out from under him. That didn't sit well with the other guy and he still wanted the transmission. So, in the dead of night, he snuck up to the house and stole it out from under the tarp, where it sat waiting for its imminent install. The next morning, Bob went over to the guy's house, walked right into the garage, and spotted the tranny on the floor.

While many have known Bob to be pretty easy going and understanding of others, this really pissed him off and fired up his temper. He picked the tranny up off the ground, went over, and threw it into the rear window of the car that the thief was getting ready to install it in and then hauled the tranny back home to its rightful recipient, his 1923 Model T roadster.

The solution to security was found in more construction. Actually, demolition would be more accurate. To get the car under cover, the dividing wall in the garage was cut out in the shape of the car and the car pulled in. Bob was now truly in his element and this was the beginning of a long and successful life of recycling old steel.

By the time the car was finished and on the road, a new decade had started. The 60's became a time of discovery and excitement for young people and Bob and his best friend and eventual brother in law, Chuck, were no exception. They had cars, time, and the spirit of adventure.

The 1960 National Motor and Sports Show at Balboa Park in San Diego was a big deal to the boys. It drew cars from all over and Bob and Chuck got to put their cars in the show. Bob's '23 T and Chuck's '32 Ford five-window coupe were on the floor with some of the nicest cars in the area that represented some of the finest craftsmanship in

SoCal. These boys were in Hot Rod Heaven and they displayed their hot rods with the same pride as those craftsmen whose work they so admired.

Once the cars were parked in their assigned spots and display ropes were up, the angel hair was laid neatly in place and the boys were ready for the show. The next day was going to be a big one. This had just been the set up for the show and as they wandered around the building now full of old cars made new, they were in awe. As the displays were completed and the old guys were leaving, the boys asked the security guard if they could spend the night and sleep in their hot rods. This was highly unusual, but the boys pleaded their case. They had no way home and back. What else could they do? Well, the guard, an understanding lover of old cars relented, providing they would behave themselves.

At first, the boys sat and played cards in the aisle beside their cars, watching the guard come and go. After watching the guard and checking their watches, they determined that it took exactly eleven minutes for the guard to make his rounds. This seemed plenty of time over the course of the night to truly inspect each car up close and personal. These were custom cars and hot rods that they had read about in magazines and had coveted from afar.

They felt privileged to sit in cars that were famous in their day; Norm Grabowski's "Kookie" car from 77 Sunset Strip, Elliot Ness' car from The Untouchables, a highly modified Olds Toronado called The Californian and one of the main attractions, Barris' Beatnik Bandit. There were the custom Mercury lead sleds that have always been popular, the tri-five Chevys that were popular to redesign, the always-coveted '32 Fords and much more. Each car was unique and a work of art by someone.

Here, in the privacy of the huge room full of cars that was Bob's bedroom for the night, they took the opportunity to sit in each and every car, careful to not disturb the displays or leave fingerprints on the highly polished works of automotive art. Some cars they would sit in together "cruising" and others they'd find their way into alone, only to yell across an aisle to each other about how cool the cars were.

That evening was the equivalent of turning two five year old boys loose in a candy store and they ate their fill every ten minutes before rushing back to their cars, seemingly behaving themselves each time the guard came by. The guard would wave or stop and chat for a moment, but always had a knowing smile for the two.

This was the first of many shows over the years for Bob Biehler and he never tired of looking at the old cars or admiring the creative art and craftsmanship of their builders. A career that started out with a Soapbox Derby car closed as world-class hot rod builder. Always looking for new ideas and sharing his experience and ideas with others, Bob Biehler was a car man's car man.

Gone to the Ages

by David Dickinson as told by Tanya Biehler
in memory of Bob Biehler 1942-2012

This is part a series of stories to commemorate the life of Bob Biehler, who passed away on April 13, 2012.

Shortly after their wedding in 1963, Bob and Tanya Biehler moved into their first home. It was a cozy little duplex in Albuquerque, New Mexico where Bob was stationed in the USAF and where Tanya had grown up.

The little home was short on space but long on charm. It was perfect. The real bonus came in the form of a small

garage. It was just what a young hot rodder and his bride needed to build a car in, so they could go out and be a part of the community that they were most comfortable with; young people in old cars.

Upon getting settled and realizing there just wasn't much money available to a young Airman on active duty making a pittance of pay and benefits that you couldn't eat or buy parts with, Bob and Tanya immediately went out and bought a car and got pregnant.

The car was a 1931 Chevrolet roadster and it had more

potential than substance when Bob Biehler first got a hold of it. But, they got the car home and in the garage and despite not having much in the way of money, they had plenty of elbow grease, tenacity and a trait that would serve Bob Biehler well over the years; the ability to make something out of nothing.

The challenge of money was not a unique one to Bob and Tanya. In the early 60s, many a young hot rodder had more desire than dollars and Bob's ability to make good trades made a big difference. The availability of the latest Air Force technology was something that Bob appreciated and took advantage

of, as well. It is important to note that Bob never stole one aluminum fitting or braided hose (not generally available to the general public at this point in time) and those that he borrowed he would have gladly returned had the USAF only asked.

Pure raw power in the light and low-slung roadster was provided by a 1956 Packard 352cid V8 with dual Rochester four-barrel carbs. It was a real powerhouse for its day as a stock motor with 275 horsepower, but after Bob was done tweaking it; it was about as powerful as anything on the street.

During the time that the car was being built, Tanya continued to grow with their first child. When she was seven months along, her grandmother came to visit and was not at all pleased to find her granddaughter under an old car, rolling around on a dirty floor, with her belly hanging out. She voiced her opinion in no uncertain terms that a woman in Tanya's condition had no business working on old cars. After the chaos subsided, they had a pleasant visit and once grandma was gone, Tanya got back under the car and went back to work.

One day after trying to get the cut just right on a radiator so it would fit in the chopped Chevy radiator shell, and having no success, Bob got so frustrated that he picked up the radiator and impaled it on a stake. This completely destroyed the radiator, so when Tanya found out, she simply told him that he would need to figure out different ways to vent his frustration and cool the engine, because there wasn't money for another radiator. A clever trade produced a serviceable radiator and Bob devised a way to mount the new radiator in the trunk.

Another day that caused Bob a bit of frustration was simply getting the radio for the car to work. What should have been a simple issue for him had turned into a seemingly monumental problem. For the life of him, he could not get the radio to work. It powered up, but he couldn't even get it to make a buzz, much less play any rock and roll. Before he could hurl the radio across the garage, Tanya took a look and asked quite innocently, "Where are the speakers, babe?" thus saving the radio a fate similar to that of the now forgotten radiator.

As the car continued to come together and near completion, Bob's sergeant stopped by one day. It was no secret, that Bob was covertly testing aircraft parts in the car, but the sergeant made the comment "If this car had any more aircraft parts in it… it would fly!" They had a good laugh and a few beers and that was the only thing said.

Bob and Tanya built this car in a couple of versions over

the eight years they had it. In Albuquerque, it was done in red with full fenders and running boards and it drew lots of attention with the throaty Packard V8.

One night, while cruisin' the '31 out of the local Bob's Big Boy and headed to the next gathering spot, a Corvette with a particularly eager driver pulled up beside Bob and Tanya at a light and proceeded to rev his engine repeatedly, trying to entice Bob into a race. Bob didn't bite and slowly pulled away as the light changed. This went on for several lights, the Corvette driver unrelenting in his demand to prove himself.

With his patience worn and his right foot starting to itch, Bob quietly told Tanya to "Hang on!" While looking over to the Corvette, Bob signaled that he was ready with a nod of his head. The race was on. As the revving peaked to a thunderous display of power, the light changed and off went the two cars, with smoke and rubber pouring from the wheel wells. In the end, the Corvette learned a quick and simple, yet valuable lesson. Don't mess with Bob Biehler. Others noticed and felt they could best the old Chev, so there was never a lack of challengers, but the old Packard V8 with the dual quads proved to be a winner each time, leaving the wannabes in a cloud of dust and wondering what happened.

By 1965, with Bob's enlistment drawing to a close, they knew they would be moving to San Diego, where Bob had grown up. The first part of that move was to get the old Chevy over to California and so, Bob and Tanya loaded it up as full as they could and their friend, Bud Billings, hooked it up behind his '58 Impala and towed it over to San Diego, with Bob and Tanya following. Bob was released from active duty in early 1966 and they left Albuquerque for San Diego in a blizzard with a sixteen-month-old baby. California beaches and hot rods were waiting for him.

After a few years in San Diego, Bob decided to redo the Chev and make it look completely different. The fenders and running boards were removed and the color was changed from red to dark metallic green. It looked great and had many admirers.

By 1972, it was time to make a change and so, Bob traded the '31 roadster that had been so much fun, and had bested so many, for cash and a Norton 500cc motorcycle which he drove back and forth to work. As time would prove, Bob enjoyed riding on two wheels as much as he did on four.

The '31 disappeared and wound up in storage for 30 years when Bob spotted it for sale in 1999 in a Rod and Custom magazine. The car was at the Bakersfield Swap Meet and Bob and Tanya wanted to buy it back. As luck would have it, the car had been sold before they could get an inquiry off and an answer back. The new owner only wanted the body and so the old Packard V8 went to a Packard museum, the dual four barrel carbs to a guy in Kansas, and the slicks to a racing museum. The old '31 was "gone to the ages," relegated to fond memories by Bob and Tanya.

Bonneville Bob

by Ron Shincke
Photos by Peter Vincent

The Bonneville Salt Flats held a place of reverence for Bob Biehler. It always has for anyone deeply interested in anything with wheels that go fast. Bob and I would talk for hours about Bonneville and the famous people and machines that we had seen in "Hot Rod" and "Rod and Custom" magazines as kids growing up. You see, Bonneville is more than just a place. It is a place of worship.

Our personal adventures at Bonneville began at Bob's 60th birthday get together. Talking about how fast the years pass and things we have always wanted to do and not taken the time the time to do, Bob says "You know, we really need to go to Bonneville" and I immediately agreed. With a few moments of thought and because he was a car guy, he said, "I'll take a car!" Me, being a motorcycle guy, said, "I'll take a bike!" So the dye was cast.

I bought a new Buell XB9 in 2003 and with the help of Latus Motors Harley Davidson, prepped it for the salt flats. Bob was unable to go with me so I went without my buddy. This was for "Speed Week" in August. I learned a lot and had fun. I didn't break any records, but I still had fun. In the meantime, Bob is working on gathering up parts for a car for Bonneville and trying to take care of business, as well.

In October, "World Finals" are held and Bob was able to go. As we were driving to the event, Bob was very animated and excited to be going. Before entering the town of Wendover, which is where everyone stays during events on the salt flats, the highway passes through rolling dessert country. There is a side road I had found by accident while "lost on my first time there." Suddenly, from the on top of a hill, The Bonneville Salt Flats is there endlessly before you. I wanted Bob to see this as I had for his first time there, so I didn't say anything. I just drove to it.

He was awe struck, to say the least, and didn't speak for a few minutes, just taking it all in. This was an extremely "special" moment for us both and a memory I will carry with me forever.

So, once we got settled in on the salt, Bob experienced going through technical inspection and all the things needed to do to participate in in the actual event. We had a great time, no records but a great time.

I had decided to build another bike for the salt flats and discussed it with Bob. He agreed it was a good idea and would help. We decided to build a 500c.c. purpose built bike and go after the A/PG record, which at the time was about 114 M.P.H. So, all that next year we worked on the new bike. We started out with a single cylinder Buell Blast motor. Basically, it's half a Harley motor. I gathered parts and Bob did 99% of the fabrication. He was building this bike for me. He still wanted to run a car.

Bob did a wonderful job, as always, building the bike. I had taken that 500c.c. bike to Latus Harley Davidson for some dyno work. We planned to pick it up on our way to

Speed Week. So, we load up the 1000c.c. Buell bike I had been running and headed for Portland to get the 500c.c. bike on our way. Well, there was a glitch and the bike was not ready. It was too late to change plans, so we took the new bike with us to Bonneville, even though it wasn't ready to run.

We put the new 500c.c. bike in the back of the pickup, so people could admire it, left the 1000c.c. bike in the trailer, unloading for each pass. Well, you should have seen all the people looking at Bob's creation. The interest was unbelievable. There were literally hundreds of questions asked and pictures taken. The design was all Bob's and nothing like anything seen there before. Bob was becoming even more famous.

That following year, the Bonneville blogs were full of questions about the bike. Who owned it? Who built it? It was becoming a celebrity and taking on a life of its own.

So, now we are into the third year. We are preparing both the 1000 and the 500 bikes for Bonneville. Bob still wants to build a car, but is short time for such a massive undertaking with work and all. Anyway, the time is closing in on us for Speed week. The motel room is reserved and paid for, both bikes are entered, and we are ready to go.

About two weeks before we are ready to leave, my Mom has a heart attack and is very ill. So, of course I can't go. I wanted to, but it wouldn't be right. So, I talked Bob and Clint into taking the 500c.c. bike that Bob had built and going to Speed Week. It took some convincing, but he finally agreed.

Bonneville's heat and altitude has an extreme effect on how motors run. One loses 25% horsepower due to these conditions and the salt is slick. It is very difficult to make things run and perform like they do at sea level. Well, the bike performed perfect on the salt due to Bob's wonderful chassis build. They had a great time. Again, no records, but they had lots of fun.

When they returned, Bob was stoked and ready to have a bike of his own to run on the salt. So, what else could a friend do? I said, "Bob, the bike is yours. You have it!" "No, I can't do that" he said. "Yes, you can," I replied. "It's yours."

Well, after some time he agreed. And, why not? He built it! Knowing Bob, of course, he wouldn't just take it. So he says, "I'll build you another one." He did just that, with my help, and there were times when we would start at 5 o'clock in the morning and work until dark on the new bike for me. He wanted to get it completed for the following year. He had to do his own work as well.

One time, we lay down on the concrete floor and took a nap; we were so tired of working on the new bike. It takes a lot of time and effort to build a bike from scratch. There were times when I hated the new bike and would get pissy, but Bob would continue with the build. He felt he owed me

and this is how he got started at Bonneville.

He went on to break the record in his class twice and made many friends and gained many admirers of his craftsmanship. He wound up being bit by the Bonneville bug. He also became known as "Bonneville Bob." There are tons of pictures of him on the internet. One of my favorites is where a photographer at Bonneville took a picture of three photographers taking a picture of Bob on "his" bike.

We had a saying that we were going to paint on our trailers. "Caution: This trailer contains an incurable disease. Motorcycles!"

Bob Biehler passed suddenly on the morning of April 13, 2012. God I miss him!

About David Dickinson
Creator and Editor
The Old Car Nut Book

It seems my life has always revolved around cars. As a child, I would lay around the living room, playing with my Lincoln logs, designing homes and landscape designs that would include lots of parking spaces for all of the cars I planned to own. As a teenager, I bought my first '56 Chevrolet BelAir with the money I had saved from working on farms, in restaurants, delivering newspapers... anything that would pay me so I could get a car when I turned 16. From then on, it was all about keeping the car running to its peak performance and cruising around showing the world my great little ride!

Like everyone else, I had to grow up. Well, kind of. I guess I never got away from cars. As the years roll by, like the odometer on an old car, I keep checking off the miles... and the cars in my past. I always seem to be looking for my next pride and joy. I've had countless cars and there are stories for every one of them. I still change cars as often as possible, but wish I could keep every one of them.

I started out by writing my own stories and I am including a few of them in this book, but I have more stories to share and so do the rest of the old car nuts in America.

The Old Car Nut Book is my way of sharing the dream with other Old Car Nuts. It is also my way of reaching out to younger car nuts beginning their journeys and fulfilling their dreams.

As this first book gains popularity, stories will continue to be gathered and more editions put into print. The response from current contributors, potential contributors and others, anxious to read these stories, has been tremendous.

I plan to release 3-4 volumes of The Old Car Nut Book and you can be in an upcoming edition by sending your story in now. Go to www.OldCarNutBook.com and click "How To Submit" in the menu for details.

Made in the USA
Lexington, KY
29 November 2014